For Brook

Mary Jane

MILK COW KITCHEN

"cow" girl romance
cheese recipes
farmstyle recipes
backyard cow keeping

by MARYJANE BUTTERS

" The friendly
cow, all red
and white,
I love with
all my heart;
She gives me
cream with all
her might,
to eat with
apple-tart."

– Robert Louis Stevenson

MILK COW KITCHEN

"cow" girl romance
cheese recipes
farmstyle recipes
backyard cow keeping

by MARYJANE BUTTERS

GIBBS SMITH
TO ENRICH AND INSPIRE HUMANKIND

First Edition
18 17 16 15 14   5 4 3 2 1

Published by
Gibbs Smith
P.O. Box 667
Layton, Utah 84041

1.800.835.4993 orders
Gibbs-Smith.com

Art Direction by MaryJane Butters
Book Design and Artwork by Karina Overfelt
Editing by Megan Butters Rae
Copy Editing by Carol Hill and Priscilla Wegars

Printed and bound in China.

Gibbs Smith books are printed on either recycled, 100% post-consumer waste; FSC-certified papers; or on paper produced from sustainable PEFC-certified forest/controlled wood sources. Learn more at PEFC.org.

ISBN: 978-1-4236-2465-3
Library of Congress Control Number: 2013948579

Visit us on the Web at MaryJanesFarm.org. MaryJane's personal blog can be found at RaisingJane.org. Follow MaryJane's backyard milk cow movement at HeritageJersey.org.

Dedicated to my growing
herd of grandgirls,
America's future milkmaids.

cow school bus, circa 1920

How do I love thee?

Let me count the ways ...

- butter
- Cheddar
- yogurt
- milk
- buttermilk
- cream
- kefir
- sour cream
- ice cream
- clotted cream
- cottage cheese
- Swiss
- coffee creamer
- Asiago
- Colby-Jack
- Parmesan
- Brie
- blue cheese
- Monterey Jack
- mozzarella
- Gruyère
- cream cheese
- chocolate milk ...

AND

- garden fertilizer!

Author's Note

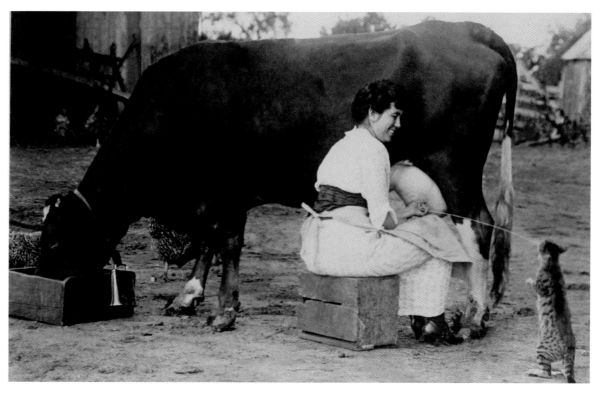

Hi MaryJane,

"I'm amazed to hear you're writing a book about cows. Here's why. I woke up wondering about milking cows. I'm not kidding/joking (sometimes you'll post something on your blog that I was just thinking about—happens a lot!). Anyway, since I have the early-morning-riser thing down pat :-), I was wondering if I had to milk a cow by hand/s? About how long would that take and how much milk does a cow usually share for the day? Also, remember hearing or reading somewhere that if you don't milk the cow every day, bad things happen to the cow? Is the cow then ruined for future milking? I take it the young lady pictured in your post is carrying a milking machine? It looks rather heavy. How long does it take to milk a cow with a machine? What about hook-up time? Are these some of the topics you talk about in your new book? It just so happens I have a great love for cheese, cream, milk, and most things dairy. Oh, and I'm quite fond of cows in general. And so is hubby. I can see us caring for a cow as a pet one day … along with an elephant and giraffe … but that's another story."
– Elizabeth

My response to Elizabeth? "You're the reason I'm writing a book about cows. Your questions will be answered within its pages, already numbering close to 400 (lots to tell). I've been up several times in the night with a new baby calf. Mother and son doing well."

"Why cow? How cow? What cow?" people have asked me over the years. By the time you get to the last page, I hope your questions have turned into one simple statement: "Now cow!"

As someone who has been hopelessly beguiled by cows and incontestably wooed by things like hand-whipped cream, I also feel charged with helping you get to where I am, bringing you into the herd, so to speak, of cow owners and dairy lovers. Here's a recipe to get you started on your journey into all things cow—something you're going to love …

Can you guess what it is?

It's **clotted cream,** an old English indulgence.

Arising from necessity (as good things so often do) rather than epicureanism, it is thought that clotted cream was originally made by dairy farmers in England to reduce the amount of waste from their milk. But it was so undeniably delicious, it's become a much-loved tradition slathered on scones and scooped into afternoon tea.

Clotted cream is very similar to *kajmak*, a Near Eastern delicacy made using buffalo milk, which shares its characteristic golden-hued "clouts" and top crust.

Considered nutritionally superior to raw cream in the 19th century, clotted cream was said to facilitate digestion and store longer than either churned butter or unprocessed cream. Plus, it had a reputation for a sweeter taste than dairy products created by churning.

While it's tough, if not impossible, to find authentic clotted cream in the U.S., it isn't difficult to make.

Here's how. You'll need one pint of quality cream. If you don't have your own cow yet (I hope to fix that problem), Straus Family Creamery organic whipping cream works best because it isn't ultra-pasteurized and doesn't have added thickeners. Preheat oven to 180°F. Pour cream into an 8" x 8" oven-proof glass baking dish and bake uncovered for 12 hours (many modern ovens turn off automatically at 12 hours—mine does). Cool at room temperature, and then refrigerate until thoroughly chilled. Pour off any remaining liquid (preferably into a batch of scones you're about to whip up). Scoop the clotted cream—so thick it won't need to be churned or whipped—and serve, no, *devour*, on biscuits, pancakes, scones or ... by the spoonful (I have no idea who would do that).

As you sit at your table **dining on the divine,** why not invite the following "advices of an old farmer" into your life?

MaryJane ♡

Your fences need to be horse-high, pig-tight & bull-strong.

Keep skunks and bankers at a distance.

Life is simpler when you plow around the stump.

A bumblebee is considerably faster than a John Deere tractor.

Words that soak into your ears are whispered ... not yelled.

Meanness don't jes' happen overnight.

Forgive your enemies; it messes up their heads.

Do not corner something that you know is meaner than you.

It don't take a very big person to carry a grudge.

You cannot unsay a cruel word.

Every path has a few puddles.

When you wallow with pigs, expect to get dirty.

The best sermons are lived, not preached.

Most of the stuff people worry about ain't never gonna happen anyway.

Don't judge folks by their relatives.

Remember that silence is sometimes the best answer.

Live a good, honorable life ... then when you get older and think back, you'll enjoy it a second time.

Don't interfere with somethin' that ain't bothering you none.

Timing has a lot to do with the outcome of a rain dance.

If you find yourself in a hole, the first thing to do is stop diggin'.

Sometimes you get, and sometimes you get got.

The biggest troublemaker you'll probably ever have to deal with watches you from the mirror every mornin'.

Always drink upstream from the herd.

Good judgment comes from experience, and a lotta that comes from bad judgment.

Lettin' the cat outta the bag is a whole lot easier than puttin' it back in.

If you get to thinkin' you're a person of some influence, try orderin' somebody else's dog around.

Live simply. Love generously. Care deeply. Speak kindly.

– Author Unknown

Contents

chapter one
Let's Talk Milk   12
ABCs of Milk & Cheese Making
For Starters (making butter, buttermilk,
  sour cream, yogurt & kefir)
Cheese Making
Farmstyle Recipes Using Dairy

chapter two
Let's Talk Cows   194
You Bought What?!
All Tied Up
Inspiring Milkmaids
Milking (hand & machine)
Milking a Mini-cow
Housing
Fencing
Feed
Hay/Straw Storage
Cow-trough Gardening
Sh@t Happens (manure management)
Pest Control
Birth & Delivery

chapter three
Let's Talk Bull   300
Artificial Insemination
Semen Collection
Breeding
Trich Test
  (managing trichomoniasis)
Bull Rings
Steers

chapter four
Let's Talk Vet Care   310
Hoof Trimming
Vaccinations
Ear Tags
Dehorning
Castration
Vet-care Kit
Life & Death

chapter five
Let's Talk Cowpanions
322
Milk Cow Companionship

chapter six
Let's Talk Business
330
Legalities of Selling Raw Milk
Entre*manure*ship
Changing Zoning Codes
   to Allow for Backyard Cows
Selling Milk

chapter seven
Let's Talk Farm Equipment
346
Not Your Daddy's Tractor
Cattle Trailers

chapter eight
Let's Learn Cow Speak
354
Unmasking Insider Nuance

chapter nine
Let's Do Cow Décor
360
Milk Cow Décor
Milk Paint
Milkmaid Fashion
Baling Twine Re-use

Heritage Jersey Organization   390

Acknowledgments   392

Index   393

About the Author   400

> ❝ We all have **hometown** appetites.
> Every other person is a **bundle** of
> **longing** for the **simplicities** of good
> **taste** once enjoyed on the **farm** or
> in the **hometown** left behind. ❞
> – Clementine Paddleford

Let's Talk Milk

Old King Cole was a merry old soul. His eyes were full of laughter. Said He,"Drink all the Milk you can, If Health is what you're after."

" If happiness truly
consisted in physical
ease and freedom from
care, then the happiest
individual would not
be either a man or a
woman; it would be, I
think, an American cow. "

– William Lyon Phelps

In This Chapter

• ABCs of Milk & Cheese Making.......p. 14

• For Starters (making butter, buttermilk,
sour cream, yogurt, and kefir).........p. 32

• Cheese Making ....p. 52

• Farmstyle Recipes Using Dairy......p. 104

ABCs of MILK & CHEESE MAKING

Because milk is the most important ingredient in our recipes, it's important to use the real deal, as in high-quality, pure, tasty, good-for-you milk. For me, that means organic if store-bought, or locally–produced–on–a–small–scale, or ideally, milk that is homegrown, right outside your back door.

Here are a few things to look for:
If you don't have your own cow and need to buy milk, read the label carefully. Don't buy milk that says things like ultra-pasteurized or the "words" UHT (ultra-high-temperature or ultra-heat-treated) or ESL (extended shelf life).

Either pasteurized milk (145°F for 30 minutes) or HTST milk (high temperature short time, 161°F for 15 seconds) will work in our recipes.

Why not UHT or ESL?
There are a variety of things that make ultra-pasteurized, ultra-high-temperature, and extended-shelf-life-milk undesirable for making things like yogurt and butter, and unsuitable for making cheese. The high temperatures used for these methods affect how the milk coagulates when making cheese, often resulting in poor curd formation, or if a curd does form, it breaks apart easily, turning into grainy flecks. In addition, the high heat used in these methods not only wipes out any bacteria that may be harmful, it also wipes out the beneficial bacteria and enzymes in the milk and destabilizes the whey proteins.

Did you know that ESL milk in an unopened aseptic carton will last 6–9 months without being refrigerated? The cartons could be sitting on a grocery shelf right next to cans of soup, but marketing experts have discovered that placement is everything, so ESL milk is usually found in the milk cooler.

ultra Pasteurized

With that being said, not all heat-treating is bad news—in fact, we prefer to heat-treat our milk before using it—at a much lower temperature, however.

I made the decision to heat-treat our milk when I was going through the process of getting my small-scale dairy approved by the state of Idaho. Once we had our mechanized system all set up for raw milk production (legal in the state of Idaho) and everything was perfectly white and sparkly clean, we sent off a sample of raw milk to be tested for bacteria and … failed the test. What?! I couldn't believe it.

I re-examined our procedures, found a few minor things we could change, and passed the next test. Okay. What did we change? Not much. Rather than hang the hoses to the milking machine in a loop on a hook on the wall after cleaning and sterilizing them, we rigged up a system where they hung straight down so that moisture wasn't getting trapped in the top of the loop overnight. And we started sanitizing our counters and some of our equipment with a spritz of 200 ppm bleach.

Also, I was of the opinion that our first equipment rinse, before we started to really clean and sterilize everything, needed to be done using hot water. As it turns out, hot water can cause some of the milk proteins to stick to the sides of the stainless-steel containers. Who knew?

All along, we'd been checking regularly for mastitis using a quick procedure called the California Mastitis Test (CMT). I felt we were good to sell milk, and then … we failed another test. Granted, Idaho's standard for bacterial count in raw milk is strict, but my level of anxiety was off the charts at that point. I'd had a milk cow on and off since 1980 and never heat-treated the milk that my family and I drank, but expanding that circle beyond my immediate family was challenging my strident belief in raw milk. I was being motivated to learn a whole lot more about bacteria.

My local veterinary dairy inspector heeded my call for help, and during a site visit, pointed out a few more places where bacteria might be lurking. To this day, we've never failed another test. As I explain in more detail on p. 230, we failed the "other bacteria" part of the test, not the coliform or the somatic cell count part of the test (that would indicate our cows had a bacterial infection such as mastitis). In other words, we weren't getting our equipment, hands, etc. clean enough. The reason milk needs to be so clean is because it's the perfect breeding ground for rapid bacterial growth—a little turns into a lot in no time at all.

I think the real culprit that has changed the nutritional value of milk is the process of homogenization—done mostly for cosmetic reasons. It eliminates the cream line in milk. During homogenization, cream is removed from the milk and forced through tiny holes at high pressure, which causes the fat globules to permanently shrink in size.

The smaller size, once the cream is put back into the milk, prevents them from floating to the top. Instead, they are evenly dispersed throughout the milk. Once the correct percentage of cream is put back into the milk (p. 20), it's pasteurized. As more and more people claim to be allergic to milk or have trouble digesting it, I'm wondering if it's the homogenization that makes milk difficult to digest. We deliver milk to a family in town with a child who can drink our heat-treated, non-homogenized milk without getting a tummy ache but can't drink pasteurized milk that's also been homogenized.

The best explanation I've come across is that homogenization breaks the cell walls of the fat globules, which, in turn releases xanthine oxidase (XO), a free radical. Free radicals are responsible for DNA mutations. Worse, these altered fat molecules refuse normal digestion and are capable of ending up in the bloodstream. There, XO wreaks havoc by damaging the walls of our arteries. Our bodies' defense systems react to the harm by telling the liver to produce cholesterol in an attempt to coat the damage the XO causes, resulting in a build-up of arterial plaque.

Because of the expensive equipment needed for homogenization, small dairies never homogenize their milk. Actually, cream-top milk is considered superior among milk aficionados.

The other reason we heat-treat our milk is because we like to make lots of tasty cultured milk products. Rather than making just butter, for instance, we like to culture it. (You know, probiotics, the guardians of your intestinal tract.) And my family's ability to consume yogurt (and once in a while, Greek yogurt) is unparalleled. Depending on the type of cultured product you want to make, you're culturing it at temperatures that undesirable bacteria love, and for that reason, the "critters" you want to rule sometimes can't (too much competition from the critters that you don't want). For example, when making buttermilk or sour cream, cultured buttermilk from a previous batch of buttermilk is simply added to skim milk (to make more buttermilk) or cream (to make sour cream) and left at room temperature to culture for about 24 hours, but that only works, every time without fail, if the milk has been heat-treated first. Yogurt is cultured with cultured yogurt from a previous batch. First, the milk is scalded (180°F), then it's rapidly cooled to 112°F, culture is added, and the temperature is held at 110°F for several hours. The yogurt-making process is slightly more involved than for buttermilk or sour cream, but you get the idea.

We also like to make aged cheese with our milk, and lots of it. As far as the USDA is concerned, cheese made with raw milk is acceptable to sell, as long as it has been aged for at least two months. The USDA's guidelines, stating that aged (hard) cheese made with raw milk must be aged a minimum of two months before being sold, gives the cultures and salt (added during cheese making) time to conquer and destroy any bad bacteria that may be lurking in raw-milk cheese. But there are hard cheeses my family loves like Asiago and Gruyère that taste better when eaten before two months' time is up. Heat-treating the milk beforehand eliminates the need for us to wait two months.

Another reason for heat–treating our milk is that it increases the shelf life of the milk, and in turn, the shelf life of our cultured dairy products. Each batch often yields more than can be consumed within a few days. Heat-treating the milk before making cultured products gives us several extra days before our hard-earned treasures spoil.

The process we use doesn't officially pasteurize the milk, according to the USDA. We use a process called thermization that does minimal damage to the milk proteins, beneficial bacteria, and enzymes in the milk. To thermize milk, you heat it to 150°F for 15 seconds and then cool it to 40°F within two hours. Afterward, it needs to be stored in a refrigerator that reads a constant 36°F.

When food is heated, there are nutrient losses, but they can be small in comparison to the large amount still present. Like any food we eat that we heat first, the nutrients that are left are quantifiable.

You can easily heat-treat your milk using a 2-gallon capacity Kleen-Flo stainless-steel pasteurizer (if you choose to thermize your milk, you can change the setting to 150°F), available at HambyDairySupply.com. You can buy a 3.5-gallon pasteurizer, available at PartsDeptOnline.com.

In thermized milk, soluble calcium is decreased by less than 5%. This was evidenced by the fact that when we were working on recipes for aged and pressed cheeses, we found that we needed to add calcium chloride to pasteurized milk in order for it to curd—not so with thermized milk; no calcium chloride was ever needed. Adding calcium chloride restores the delicate, natural balance between calcium and casein (protein). B vitamins are decreased by 5-8% in thermized milk, and vitamin C anywhere from around 10-20%. But I don't think of milk as a dietary source of vitamin C anyway. Regarding digestive enzymes, Dr. John Whitaker, former Dean of Food Science at UC Davis, says, "Every enzyme is different and some are more stable at higher temperatures than others, but most enzymes will not become completely inactive until food temperatures exceed 140°F–158°F in a wet state." For me, putting the kibosh on harmful bacteria that may be present outweighs the small amount of nutrients lost when I thermize my milk.

If you have someone local who is selling raw milk but you're not sure they're a trusted source, heat-treating it before use can be a safeguard against any harmful bacteria.

If you milk your own cow, it's easy enough to know that it's a "trusted source." If you choose to buy raw milk from someone local, I urge you to make a site visit during milking and handling to make sure their protocol has your good health in mind. Also ask how they train their substitutes if they are unable to do the milking themselves. Several years ago, before I offered milk for sale, I was injured and couldn't milk for a few days. My replacement, a family member, said he knew my protocol, but as it turns out, he forgot to strip each teat before milking. Those first few squirts of milk are full of bacteria. People make mistakes. There isn't any reason to take a chance. Healthy, bone-building milk, cultured products like yogurt and kefir, delicious cheeses like Manchego and Brie, are a pleasure to "know" and "trust." And like everyone is saying these days, know your food! I'm going to add to that, know your dairy-ist.

Here's what the back of our label says:

RAW UNPASTEURIZED

Heat is used in the processing of
this product, but it is considered
RAW UNPASTEURIZED by the
Idaho State Dept. of Agriculture.

MaryJane's Creamery
P.O. Box 8691
Moscow, ID 83843

ISDA Permit #RCM041

Here's a general rule of thumb to remember from all that I've said: As long as milk is not overly heated—pasteurized milk is heated to 145°F for 30 minutes and HTST (high temperature short time) milk is heated to 161°F for 15 seconds—store-bought milk will work for cheese making. The most noticeable difference will be in the curd formation. Cheese made with pasteurized or HTST milk doesn't make a firm curd. That's why our recipes call for the addition of calcium chloride if you're using pasteurized or HTST milk to make cheese. Thermized milk is heated to 150°F for 15 seconds and DOES NOT require the addition of calcium chloride.

But the absolute ultimate in milk is found in the bucket of pure, raw milk you bring through your back door every day. Let's get busy transforming your liquid treasure into all things dairy!

Store-bought pasteurized or HTST milk (again, read the label—you don't want milk that says ultra-pasteurized, UHT, or ESL) is acceptable for cheese making (this may be all you have available). The ultimate in store-bought milk is organic, 100% grass-fed, non-homogenized, pasteurized, cream-top milk.

Straus Family Creamery puts their organic, non-homogenized, pasteurized, cream-top milk in a returnable bottle. And they power their entire dairy from the methane gas their cows produce.

meet Maizy
at 2 years of age

- one gallon 1% milk: approx. 1/2 c cream + 15 1/2 c skim
- one gallon 2% milk: approx. 3/4 c + 15 1/4 c skim
- one gallon whole milk: approx. 1 1/2 c cream + 14 1/2 c skim

- one quart half-and-half:
  2 c cream + 2 c skim
  OR
  1 c cream + 3 c whole

Skim Milk (also known as non-fat or fat-free milk), 1% Low-fat Milk, 2% Reduced-fat Milk, Whole Milk, and Cream-line Milk ...

What do they mean?

Skim Milk (also referred to as non-fat milk or fat-free milk) refers to milk that has had the cream removed. It means the cream was taken out and NONE of the cream was put back in. (It ends up being sold as whipping cream.) If it's store bought, it was then pasteurized. If it comes from a local dairy or your own cow, it means that you've mechanically skimmed off as much of the cream that has floated to the top as you can, either with a cream separator or a ladle.

1% Low-fat Milk is 99% milk and 1% butterfat. This means that one gallon of 1% milk has approximately 1/2 cup cream in it. It means the cream was taken out and then 1/2 cup cream was added to 15 1/2 cups skim milk to make one gallon. If it's store bought, it was then homogenized and pasteurized. If it comes from a local dairy or your own cow, it means that you've mechanically skimmed the cream off the top and then added 1/2 cup cream to 15 1/2 cups skim milk and given it a good shake right before using it.

2% Reduced-fat Milk is 98% milk and 2% butterfat. This means that one gallon of 2% milk has approximately 3/4 cups cream in it. It means the cream was taken out and then 3/4 cups cream was added to 15 1/4 cups skim milk to make one gallon. If it's store bought, it was then homogenized and pasteurized. If it comes from a local dairy or your own cow, it means that you've mechanically skimmed the cream off the top and then added 3/4 cups cream to 15 1/4 cups skim milk and given it a good shake right before using it.

Whole Milk contains anywhere between 3.25% and 4% butterfat, depending on the cow (different cows give different cream content). If whole milk contains 3.5%, there is approximately 1 1/2 cups cream in it. It means the cream was taken out and then 1 1/2 cups cream was added to 14 1/2 cups skim milk to make one gallon. If it's store bought, it was then homogenized and pasteurized. If it comes from a local dairy or your own cow, it means that you've mechanically skimmed the cream off the top and then added 1 1/2 cups cream to 14 1/2 cups skim milk and given it a good shake right before using it.

Cream–line milk is milk that has all of the cream left in it and hasn't been homogenized. It can be used in place of whole milk in any recipe as long as you shake it first. Usually cream-line milk is only available from local dairies or your own backyard cow. Because it hasn't been homogenized, it will have a visible cream line if put into a clear container and left to separate on its own. Depending on your breed of milk cow, it will probably have more cream (butterfat) in it than store-bought whole milk.

In cheese making, the percentage of fat in the milk has a large impact on the final product. Generally, the higher the fat content, the higher the yield and the creamier the texture. Expect to get about 3/4 pound of cheese for every gallon of skim milk, and 1 to 1 1/4 pounds of cheese for every gallon of whole milk. Using whole milk in place of other reduced-fat milks in a recipe will produce a much richer, creamier cheese. (The reason you want your own cow.) Some of our cheese recipes have the option of using skim milk (non-fat milk). It produces a drier, crumblier cheese than cheese made from milk with a higher fat content. Think about the difference between feta (made with skim milk) and Monterey Jack (made with whole milk).

Like brewing your own wine or beer, cheese making can seem like taking a giant leap into the unknown.

Many of the terms are alien and some of the ingredients are unfamiliar. In essence, cheese making is pretty straightforward: milk is warmed to just the right temperature for a particular culture to thrive; a coagulant is added, which is in most cases rennet; and then the whey (leftover liquid) is expelled from the milk solids either through draining or pressing. Even though the process can be broken down into these simple steps, it still feels like a science experiment when reading a recipe, ingredient list, and equipment list for the first time. Everything is timed and precisely measured, and there are a number of ingredients that need to be sought out in advance and often ordered especially for cheese making, but don't sweat—many of these specialty ingredients will last through several batches of cheese and we've reworked our recipes dozens of times to make sure they're fail-proof.

Here's a rundown of **ingredients that commonly crop up in cheese making**—some of them common, and others not so common.

Don't start making a list yet! I've made one for you that includes purchasing information on p. 25–27.

The majority of our recipes for making cheese call for distilled water. **Distilled water** is preferred in cheese making because of its purity. It's ideal to have total control over what goes into your cheese, and the use of distilled water is a great place to start. Once you've experienced success using distilled water, you can test other types of purified water. We have a counter-top distiller. Distilled water is readily available in grocery stores.

In the home dairy, **cultured buttermilk** can be used **to inoculate certain cheeses.** It's simply heat-treated skim milk that has been cultured either from a previous batch or a freeze-dried starter. Store-bought pasteurized buttermilk may also be used for cheese making or to culture store-bought pasteurized skim milk in preparation for making more cultured buttermilk. Just make sure that it says "cultured" on the label and that it's fresh (check the expiration date). The culture used to make buttermilk is a mesophilic culture, which thrives in temperatures between 70–90°F.

It's simple to maintain a constant supply of cultured buttermilk. Buttermilk starter is added to heat-treated skim milk and then left out at room temperature to culture. It couldn't be easier! Just be sure to make a fresh batch at least every seven days.

So this leads to another question: What is the difference between the buttermilk that you buy in the store (or culture at home) and the liquid left over from butter making? Buttermilk is a cultured dairy product made using skim milk. The liquid that is released from cream during butter making is often referred to as buttermilk, but the commercialization of the dairy industry has made it a less familiar product. For the purpose of easily distinguishing between these two, cultured buttermilk is aptly named "cultured buttermilk" in our recipes and the liquid released during butter making is called "old-fashioned buttermilk."

So, what is "old-fashioned buttermilk"? It's called buttermilk, but this name is deceptive. It does not refer to the thick and tangy buttermilk you're familiar with. Old-fashioned buttermilk is closer to whey than anything else. It can be used to replace the liquid in baked goods. Whey is also good for outside gardens and flowerbeds (it's rich in nutrients).

In the home dairy, cultured yogurt can be used to inoculate certain cheeses. It's simply heat-treated skim milk (or whole milk if you love cream the way we do) that has been cultured either from a previous batch or a freeze-dried starter. Store-bought pasteurized plain yogurt may also be used in cheese making or to culture store-bought pasteurized milk in preparation for making more cultured yogurt. Just make sure that it's plain, fresh, and free of additives. The culture used for yogurt is a thermophilic culture, which thrives in temperatures between 90–112°F. As with cultured buttermilk, fresh yogurt can be made with yogurt from a previous batch. It requires a little more care than making cultured buttermilk, but it's well worth the effort! Like cultured buttermilk, a fresh batch should be made at least every seven days.

The great thing about using buttermilk and yogurt as a culture in our cheese recipes is that a fresh batch can be made from previous batches, so you have a constant supply of starter culture.

Rennet is indispensable in cheese making. It's used to coagulate the milk, a step that makes cheese making possible. Rennet is most commonly available in two forms: tablet or liquid. Rennet can be animal- or microbial- (sometimes referred to as "vegetable") based.

Animal rennet (liquid) is extracted from the stomach of young calves. The origins of this type of rennet can be problematic, but it's difficult to mimic both its ability to coagulate milk as well as give superior flavor to the final product.

Microbial rennet is derived from fungi. It's often sold as vegetable rennet (I know, confusing, right?), as a vegetarian alternative to animal rennet. Since it's likely that microbial rennet contains GMOs, it's best to avoid non-organic microbial rennet. Often, microbial rennet is much more potent in its coagulating abilities, but the label should say how many times stronger it is than traditional animal rennet. Our recipes that call for microbial ("vegetable") rennet were made using **organic microbial "vegetable" rennet (double-strength)** and our recipes reflect that.

In addition, all of our recipes specify if animal or microbial rennet is used, so if you use a different type of rennet, you will have to experiment with the amounts. It's a common opinion that microbial rennet gives aged cheeses a bitter flavor. It doesn't make the cheese inedible, but it's not our preference. In our trials, this only happened in cheeses that were aged longer than three weeks. For this reason, most of our fresh cheeses are made using **organic microbial "vegetable" rennet (double-strength)**, and the aged cheeses are made using **liquid animal rennet**.

Lipase powder is an animal–based enzyme that is responsible for giving cheeses like feta, Manchego, and Parmesan the sharper flavor that is traditionally expected in these cheeses. Four different flavors are available: mild lipase, sharp lipase, traditional pecorino lipase, and sharp pecorino lipase. We think the **mild lipase powder** provides enough flavor, but if a sharper flavor is desired, you might want to try the other strengths of lipase.

Propionibacteria is a bacteria added to cheeses like Swiss, Gruyère, and Asiago. Most notably, it gives these cheeses a sweet, nutty flavor that is characteristic to each cheese. It is also partially responsible for the eye formation (air holes) in cheeses.

Penicillium roqueforti is the mold used for making blue cheese. It's added to the milk during cheese making, and after the cheese has drained and dried, holes are poked through the cheese to create passages for the mold to grow in. Penicillium roqueforti is responsible for the creamy texture and tart flavor of blue cheese.

Penicillium camemberti is white mold that is used for making Brie. The mold is added to the milk during cheese making and grows on the outside of the cheese during aging. It's responsible for the creamy texture and rich flavor of Brie.

Fermentation-produced chymosin rennet (FPC rennet) is a combination of the rennin-producing DNA from an animal and a bacterial host. The animal DNA then produces chymosin, the enzyme found in animal rennet responsible for coagulating milk. After a little cultivation and fermentation, rennet is produced that closely mimics the favorable properties of animal rennet. This type of rennet is sold as a vegetarian alternative to animal rennet, but some may take issue with the process, considering that it begins with animal DNA. There's also a big gray area when it comes to the genetic manipulation used in the production of this type of rennet. Since just the chymosin is removed and sold as the final product, any GMOs used in the production of this rennet have been removed, so it's not labeled GMO on a technicality. This type of rennet is sold as vegetable rennet, but if it's FPC "vegetable" rennet, it will be sold as such, or sold as chymosin rennet. True microbial "vegetable" rennet can be identified by the label and is our preference. We do not recommend FPC rennet (aka vegetable rennet or chymosin rennet).

23

Vinegar has a couple of different uses in cheese making. It can be used as a coagulant, as it is in our recipe for soft cheese, and it's also very useful in eliminating mold growth from the surface of hard cheeses. To make a vinegar solution, mix equal parts organic distilled white vinegar with water, rather than using any chemicals or cleaners that might be absorbed by the cheeses and affect their flavor.

Make sure that the vinegar you use is labeled as 100% grain-based, as distilled white vinegars that aren't labeled as grain-based may be petroleum-based. In other words, it's not what you want. Spectrum Organic Distilled White Vinegar is made from non-GMO organic corn and rye.

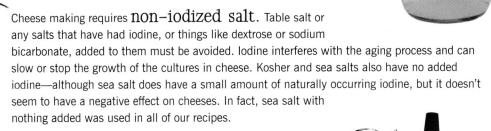

Citric acid is used in making mozzarella. It's responsible for acidifying the milk, which makes it possible to stretch the cheese.

Cheese making requires non-iodized salt. Table salt or any salts that have had iodine, or things like dextrose or sodium bicarbonate, added to them must be avoided. Iodine interferes with the aging process and can slow or stop the growth of the cultures in cheese. Kosher and sea salts also have no added iodine—although sea salt does have a small amount of naturally occurring iodine, but it doesn't seem to have a negative effect on cheeses. In fact, sea salt with nothing added was used in all of our recipes.

Calcium chloride has a couple of important uses in cheese making. The addition of calcium chloride to saturated brine (p. 78) helps cheeses retain their shape and texture. Without it, cheeses tend to get a little slimy and soft in the brine, especially softer cheeses like feta.

Calcium chloride can also be added to pasteurized milk to help with curd formation and something we refer to as a "clean break" (p. 63). Waiting for a clean break can be one of the more anxiety-inducing moments in cheese making. What if it doesn't work? The amount of rennet added to make it happen seems so small that it's hard to believe it will actually do the trick. If you're using store-bought pasteurized milk, our recipes call for adding calcium chloride to the milk before adding the culture (the general rule of thumb is to dilute 1/4 t calcium chloride in 1/4 cup of distilled water for every gallon of milk being used). Note: this will only help if you are using pasteurized or HTST milk, never UHT or ESL milk (p. 14). Thermized milk does not need the addition of calcium chloride.

Cheese Coloring (double strength), aka liquid annatto is a natural colorant used in making Cheddar and Colby-Jack cheese. It's not a necessary ingredient; it just gives Cheddar its familiar yellow-orange color and is responsible for the marbled look of Colby-Jack cheese.

Ingredients ✓ List

- ☐ skim milk
- ☐ 1% low-fat milk
- ☐ 2% reduced-fat milk
- ☐ whole milk
- ☐ cream-line milk
- ☐ distilled water
- ☐ cream
- ☐ cultured fresh buttermilk or freeze-dried buttermilk starter*
- ☐ cultured fresh yogurt or freeze-dried yogurt starter (Bulgarian)*
- ☐ animal rennet (liquid)*
- ☐ organic microbial "vegetable" rennet* (double-strength)

- ☐ lipase powder (mild)*
- ☐ propionibacteria*
- ☐ penicillium roqueforti*
- ☐ penicillium camemberti*
- ☐ vinegar, organic distilled white**
- ☐ citric acid*
- ☐ non-iodized salt*
- ☐ calcium chloride*
- ☐ cheese coloring (double-strength),* aka liquid annatto

Resources
*Available at CulturesForHealth.com
**Available at Amazon.com

General Equipment ✓ List

- ☐ food processor or stand mixer
- ☐ 8-qt, 12-qt, and 16-qt stainless-steel pots w/lids that nest inside of each other
- ☐ two 4-qt stainless-steel pots w/lids
- ☐ assorted sizes of wide-mouth canning jars w/lids and rings (1/2-gal, 1-qt, 1-pt, and 8-oz jars are always good to have on hand)
- ☐ plastic canning jar lids (plastic storage caps, wide mouth)
- ☐ stainless-steel measuring cups
- ☐ stainless-steel measuring spoons (make sure the set has a 1/8 teaspoon—that measurement pops up a lot in our recipes)
- ☐ 7-qt stainless-steel colander
- ☐ 7.5" standard mesh strainer
- ☐ 5-qt stainless-steel bowl
- ☐ 4-qt glass bowl
- ☐ small bowl
- ☐ 6-oz ramekins
- ☐ cutting board
- ☐ stainless-steel cooling rack

- ☐ baking sheet
- ☐ stainless-steel perforated spoon
- ☐ kitchen scale
- ☐ wire whisk
- ☐ wooden spoon
- ☐ cheese planer
- ☐ stainless-steel wide-mouth funnel
- ☐ ladle small enough to fit inside a wide-mouth canning jar, p. 34
- ☐ thin dishtowels
- ☐ paper towels
- ☐ aluminum foil
- ☐ wax paper/plastic wrap
- ☐ latex gloves (or nitrile if allergic to latex)*
- ☐ dishwashing gloves, p. 30*
- ☐ small containers for dispensing salt, optional

Resources

*Amazon.com

Special Equipment ✓ List

This is your shopping list.

For more detailed descriptions, see Special Equipment Check List Details, p. 28–31, or page numbers as noted.

☐ cheesecloth*
☐ butter muslin cloth*
☐ cheesecloth (coarse)**
☐ Euro Cuisine cotton bag (12" x 12")****
☐ curd knife***
☐ stainless-steel skewer****
☐ stainless-steel 12" skimmer****
☐ floating dairy thermometer, glass***
☐ thermometer (stainless-steel
    2" dial w/8" stem)**
☐ 240 mm white wrap*
☐ plastic mesh (fine), 1 yard**
☐ Tupperware 12" pie carrier****
☐ cheese wax (clear, no color)*
☐ cheese wax brush*
☐ 2-qt stainless-steel bowl****
☐ microwavable grill****
☐ cheese press
    ☐ exercise weights
    (see DIY instructions on p. 85)
☐ Camembert and Blue Cheese Mold*
    (order four)

☐ Manchego Molds**
    (order the Manchego "125")
☐ Tomme Molds**
    (order both the 4.9" and 7.5")
☐ hydrometer (h-b instrument salt brine plain
    form hydrometer, 0–100% range)****
☐ 12" hydrometer test jar****
☐ silicone mini-loaf pan (6-cavity butter
    mold), optional, p. 37
☐ pasteurizer, optional, p. 30
☐ distiller, optional, p. 31
☐ cheese (fridge) cellar, optional, p. 31
☐ plastic mesh (large), 4 yards,
    optional, p. 31**
☐ hygrometer, optional, p. 31

Resources

*CulturesForHealth.com
**BobWhiteSystems.com
***Lehmans.com
****Amazon.com

27

Special Equipment ✓ List Details

Cheesecloth

There are two types of cloth that are used frequently in cheese making: **cheesecloth** and **butter muslin**. The primary difference between the two is the thread count. Cheesecloth is used to line molds for pressing hard cheeses. Butter muslin has a much higher thread count than cheesecloth, and is well suited for tasks like draining whey from soft cheeses or cultured dairy products. With both of these, quality is important. Cheesecloth should have about 60 threads per inch and butter muslin should have around 90 threads per inch. For cheese making, cheesecloth should be thin and have a smooth surface with secure fibers.

We also use a third type of cheesecloth to line a colander when draining curds—**coarse cheesecloth** with finished edges. Any high-quality cheesecloth may be used in its place, but we like the finished edges on the cloth because it eliminates the possibility of fibers sneaking their way into the cheese, and the cloth is much more durable than typical cheesecloth.

Curd Knife

A **curd knife** is a long stainless-steel knife with a rounded tip and a blunt edge. The rounded tip makes it easier to smoothly cut the curds and easily reaches to the bottom of large pots.

Dairy Thermometer (glass)

The **floating dairy thermometer** used throughout my book reads temperatures between -10–222°F.

Thermometer (stainless steel)

The stainless-steel **thermometer** you see throughout my book is used primarily to monitor the temperature of the water bath surrounding the milk. It reads temperatures between 0–220°F.

White Wrap

White wrap is specifically designed for wrapping aging "white mold ripened cheeses." It has an inner layer of thin paper to absorb excess moisture and an outer layer of thin perforated plastic that allows the cheese to breathe while it's aging. It comes in two sizes: 240 mm x 240 mm and 420 mm x 420 mm. We prefer the **240 mm white wrap** sheets because they're large enough to wrap a 4" wheel of cheese.

Plastic Mesh

The small squares that cover the tops of the molds in the feta, blue cheese, and Brie recipes are a **"fine" mesh**. One yard will give you a good replacement supply of the 5" x 5" squares you'll need to cut. Start out by cutting four from the yard you buy. The **"large" mesh** proved to be useful in lining the racks of the refrigerator that we converted into a **cheese (fridge) cellar, optional, p. 31.** This eliminated wide lines being imprinted on cheese wheels and kept the smaller wheels from getting stuck in between the bars.

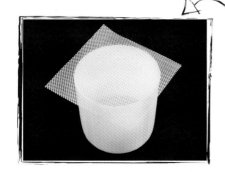

Microwavable Grill

The **"draining tray"** we use to catch whey when cheese is pressed is actually intended for "grilling" bacon and other foods in a microwave. These trays are deep enough to hold a reasonable amount of whey, and the grill pattern keeps the cheese above the whey that has drained off. They are also easy to keep clean and sanitize. They are perfect for drying or ripening cheeses, eliminating the need for what is called a cheese **"ripening mat"** made from bamboo. Before we came up with the idea of using these handy microwave grills, we became thoroughly frustrated with the bamboo draining mats everyone in the cheese world promotes. They tend to leave a wooden flavor on cheeses, and if a cheese begins to grow mold while it's drying or ripening, mold also grows in between the small dowels, and when that happens, the mats are nearly impossible to get clean again, even if they're boiled.

Cheese Molds

There are two general types of cheese molds: molds for pressed cheeses and molds for drained cheeses. The molds for pressed cheeses are two-piece molds. The first piece is the base that holds the cheese and the second is a "follower" that fits inside the mold. Weight is applied to the follower, and the follower puts even pressure on the cheese inside the mold to slowly remove the whey. These molds are often sold as a set that includes the mold and the follower. Molds for drained cheeses are one-piece molds with open tops and a lot more holes for whey to drain through, since they rely on gravity for draining.

The companies where you need to buy what you'll need for our recipes don't have very good search functions. Make sure you type the exact name we gave you in our shopping list on p. 27. If our list says Manchego Molds, type that in exactly. Manchego Mold (singular) won't bring up anything.

If you follow our shopping list to a T, you'll end up with:

- **four 3.5" cheese molds for making feta, blue cheese, and Brie**
- **one 5" cheese mold with a 2.8-lb capacity for making Manchego**
- **one 4.9" cheese mold with a 2.2-lb capacity for making Colby-Jack and Gruyère**
- **one 7.5" cheese mold with a 4.4-lb capacity for making Monterey Jack, Cheddar, Swiss, Parmesan, and Asiago**

Hydrometer (H-B Instrument Durac Salt Brine Plain Form Hydrometer)

A hydrometer is an easy way to test the salinity of a brine solution, which is even more important if the brine is being reused. It's simple to use—just warm the brine to 60°F and drop the hydrometer into the brine (it's kind of long, so a 1/2-gallon jar full of brine will work, but we prefer testing our brine in a **12" hydrometer test jar** that's really a tall test tube w/stand.) The hydrometer will float, and the percentage of saturation can be read at the water line. When purchasing a hydrometer, note that there are two different types: hydrometers that read percentage of saturation (they have a range of 0–100%), and hydrometers that read salt concentration (they have a range of 0–26%). Salt saturation refers to the percentage of salt that has been absorbed by the water. At the highest level of saturation, the water will no longer absorb salt crystals. This would be 100% salt saturation. Salt concentration refers to how much salt is in the brine in proportion to water. A brine is saturated (will not absorb any more salt) when it is 26% salt and 74% percent water by weight. To test the salinity of our brine, we chose a hydrometer that reads the percentage of saturation. For more details, see p. 78.

Gloves

Most of the gloves used during cheese making are basic **latex gloves** (or nitrile, if you're allergic to latex). While not entirely necessary, they do help ensure cleanliness any time cheese or cheese curds come into direct contact with hands. In addition, they are also very useful in protecting your hands while waxing cheese—trust us on this one, wax burns hurt! If gloves are used, they add a layer of protection between your skin and the wax.

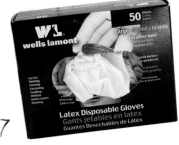

For our mozzarella recipe, we tried heavy-duty rubber gloves but they were too stiff to stretch mozzarella. We found that Playtex Living Drip-Catch Cuff **dishwashing gloves** worked fine. Our hands get a little warm, but not hot. Gloves are necessary because the curds are dipped into 175°F whey, and then stretched by hand.

Pasteurizer, optional

We use the stainless-steel Kleen-Flo pasteurizer to heat-treat our milk. It's basically a 2-gallon electric double boiler (you can also process smaller amounts) that you set at the desired temperature. After straining the milk into the inside container of the pasteurizer, we fill the outside container with water up to the full line, plug the unit into a wall socket, and wait. When it's done, a buzzer goes off and we unplug it. If you set it at 150°F, you'll be thermizing the milk, not pasteurizing it (p. 16). It takes about 15–20 minutes to reach 150°F. The Kleen-Flo pasteurizer is very simple to use and can be purchased at HambyDairySupply.com.

Distiller, optional

We have a countertop Tribest Purewise Water Distiller, available at NaturesAlternatives.com or Virtuvites.com.

Cheese (Fridge) Cellar, optional

For a simple, inexpensive cheese cellar, look no further than that second refrigerator you have sitting on your back porch—you know, the one you only turn on when company arrives. But because a regular refrigerator, even on its warmest setting, is too cold for use as a cheese cellar (you want 55°F), we had to make some adjustments. There are several devices on the market that are designed to override a refrigerator's thermostat. We choose the A419 Digital Thermostat Unit made by Johnson Controls, available at Amazon.com for around $70. The unit is a switch that gives power to the appliance only when its sensing probe senses the temperature set points you've selected. We mounted the unit on the side of the fridge with adhesive after drilling a 3/8-inch hole so we could locate the temperature sensing probe on the interior. NOTE!!!! It's extremely important before drilling any hole through your refrigerator to be certain you will not damage a line carrying refrigerant. These coils are seen on the back or under or on top of older refrigerators, but were a chore to keep free of lint and dust, so in newer models, they've been encased. Most modern refrigerators and freezers now hide the condenser coils just under the skin of the appliance. It's important to locate these coils to avoid drilling through them, and this is possible by turning the refrigerator to the coldest setting and feeling its outer skin. In several minutes, as the compressor hums along, you will feel a zone or two of the surface that is much warmer. Mark these areas and don't drill there! Be sure to also know where the probe will be entering the interior—you want a location that will not be obstructed by a shelf. Once you've drilled the hole through the wall of the refrigerator, the probe can be held in place using sealant or caulk that will seal the orifice. Detailed setup instructions are included with the Digital Thermostat Unit.

Then, the only thing left to control was the humidity (you want 70%), which we accomplished by keeping a bowl of water in the fridge. Easy! We also purchased a hygrometer (Amazon.com) to monitor the humidity of our "cheese (fridge) cellar," but that's optional. And we lined our shelves with plastic mesh (large), p. 27.

Mold happens ...

Try as you might, there's no way to fully rule out the chance that unwanted mold might grow on your precious pressed cheeses. Don't fret; it can be remedied. As long as you keep a watchful eye on your cheeses during the aging process and spot mold before it gets out of hand, it can easily be removed. To remove mold from unwaxed cheeses, simply wipe it away using a cloth dampened in a saltwater or vinegar solution. For waxed cheeses, scrape the wax off where you see mold (this rarely happens on waxed cheeses), wipe it away, let it dry, and reapply wax. To make a saltwater solution, heat 2 cups of distilled water in a small saucepan and dissolve 3 T of non-iodized salt in the water. To make a vinegar solution, mix equal parts organic distilled white vinegar and water. We keep ours in a spray bottle.

FOR STARTERS ...

Let's get churning. Yes, "churning." As in butter. I know—for you non-farm dwellers, butter churning might conjure images of someone's floral-frocked "meemaw" perched on the edge of her porch's rocking chair, squinting against the effort that requires plunging a dasher through gallons of cream over and over again. But you don't need a fancy churn, a floral frock, or even much space to churn your own butter. In fact, it's as simple as standing in your kitchenette with a jar or food processor full of cream, and the flavor will blow your biscuit-lovin' mind. Of course, when you spread just-churned butter over those biscuits for Sunday dinner, you won't be the only one who notices the difference.

Aside from my methods on the following pages, there's another method, using a jar and two marbles (no, I haven't lost mine), that will give you a workout (not designed for those who already have gym memberships), a conversation piece, and a novel way to entertain kids. Start with two cups of cream—this will make 1/4 pound of butter and 1 1/2 cups buttermilk (there's buttermilk and then there's old-fashioned buttermilk. For an explanation see p. 22). Let your cream "ripen" at room temperature for 12 hours. This makes the cream slightly sour, which yields richer, faster-whipping butter. Just don't forget to drape a clean towel over the top to keep out opportunistic kitty cats.

Put the cream into a quart jar so it's half full. Drop in both marbles and ... shake! That's it. It will take about 10 minutes to make butter, depending on how much you rock and roll. The cream will go from frothy to firm and heavy, then coarse and grainy, and then butter! If you're not sure that it's happened, it hasn't. The cream's final separation is a dramatic, hallelujah moment, with a butter island suddenly emerging in a sea of splashing buttermilk. (I know of one woman whose family put the butter jar into a padded, but roomy, box in the trunk of their car when they traveled to town. Back and forth it rocked, until ... butter!)

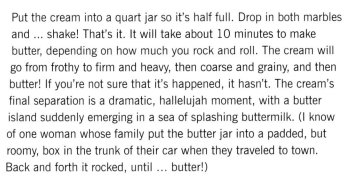

Drain the butter in a cheesecloth-lined colander, applying pressure with a wet, wooden spoon to squeeze out any extra milk. And for Pete's sake, catch and save the buttermilk that runs off to use in tomorrow's pancakes or waffles! After you've squeezed out all you can, massage the butter under icy cold water until it runs clear. Be diligent, 'cause poorly washed butter is sour and unappetizing. Put your butter into a bowl and press it to one side, squeezing out the water. Thoroughly mix in 1/4 to 1/2 teaspoon of fine or flaked salt, pack the butter into an airtight container or crock, and store it in the refrigerator or freezer for use later on.

If there's one thing I don't need to tell you, it's how to use your butter—once you try a little off the spoon, you'll come up with plenty of your own ideas. But I can't resist interjecting my humble opinion that nothing beats the flavor of warm, homemade bread spread with just-churned butter. Why not whip up some buttermilk biscuits ASAP (p. 139), fork-split 'em while they're hot from the oven, and slather on your fresh-churned butter?

No meemaw necessary, I promise.

Churning Butter

The cheapest cream separator is a 7 1/2" mini soup ladle ($2 each). Unless you're milking dozens of cows, there isn't any need to buy an expensive cream separator. It takes only a few seconds to skim the cream from the top of cream-line milk using the right-size ladle.

The melamine ladles I use come in a riot of happy colors (Gourmac.com). I give one to all my first-time home delivery customers. In stores, I put them (handle side down) into a quart canning jar by the dairy cooler. Each one has a tag with a UPC code and price. In other words, the jar serves as a vase for a colorful bouquet of "cream separators."

Whenever I'm out and about antiquing, I always look for functional butter churns to add to my collection. The one pictured at right turns my cream into butter in no time at all. If you can't find a vintage one in good shape, you can buy a new, vintage-inspired, hand-cranked butter churn at Lehmans.com.

For making more butter than your vintage churn or food processor (p. 37) can handle, you can purchase a clever, 2-gallon cream capacity churn that's really just a 5-gallon plastic bucket and a stainless steel paddle that's powered by a drill from BobWhiteSystems.com. All you do is attach your drill to the paddle and power it up. Easy peasy.

Antique Butter Churn

Bucket & Drill

- **Level:** Beginner

- **Prep Time:**
  15 minutes

- **Makes:**
  about 1/2 lb

- **Ingredients:** (p. 25)
  - 4 cups **cream**
  - 1/4 t non-iodized salt

- **Equipment Needed:**
  (p. 26–31)
  - food processor or
    stand mixer
  - stainless-steel
    measuring cups
  - 7.5" standard mesh strainer
  - 4-qt glass bowl
  - wooden spoon
  - cutting board
  - paper towels
  - wax paper/plastic wrap
  - butter mold, optional
  - kitchen scale, optional

1. Place cream into a food processor or stand mixer and beat on high (don't fill food processor past the max fill line). The cream will whip, continue to thicken with little pieces in it, then start to form into butter and release whey. This whole process takes 5–10 minutes, depending on the method.

2. After the butter has formed, place a colander over a bowl to separate the butter from the liquid.

3. Wash the butter under cold running water while moving it around in the colander. Continue until the water is clear after passing through the butter.

4. Thinly spread butter out on a cutting board and work out any additional liquid, using a wooden spoon. Sop liquid up with a paper towel.

5. Sprinkle salt over the butter and work it in. Mold into your desired shape and wrap in wax paper/plastic wrap to store.

Note: The liquid released from the cream during butter making is old-fashioned buttermilk (p. 22)—save it for use in pancakes or waffles.

Quick tip

Butter Molds:

Silicone pans for baking work great as butter molds. They're easy to keep clean, flexible, and come in limitless shapes and sizes. My favorite is a silicone mini loaf pan (6-cavity), Amazon.com. It holds just over 1/2 cup in each cavity, perfect for making standard-sized sticks of butter, with a little assistance from a kitchen scale. Wrap in wax paper or plastic wrap. To mark tablespoons, simply measure how long the mold is, and divide that by 8, then make a mark with a permanent marker.

37

Cultured Butter

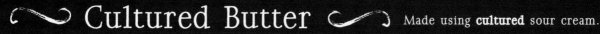

Made using **cultured** sour cream.

Level: Beginner

Prep Time:
15 minutes

Makes:
about 1/2 lb

Ingredients: (p. 25)
- 4 cups **cultured** sour cream (p. 45)
- 1/4 t non-iodized salt

Equipment Needed:
(p. 26–31)
- food processor or stand mixer
- stainless-steel measuring cups
- 7.5" standard mesh strainer
- 4-qt glass bowl
- wooden spoon
- cutting board
- paper towels
- wax paper/plastic wrap
- butter mold, optional, p. 37
- kitchen scale, optional

1. Pour sour cream into a food processor or stand mixer and beat on high (do not fill food processor past the max fill line). The cream will whip and thicken with little pieces in it, then start to form into butter and release whey. This whole process takes 5–10 minutes, depending on the method.

2. After the butter has formed, place a colander over a bowl to separate the butter from the liquid.

3. Wash the butter under cold running water while moving it around in the colander. Continue until the water is clear after passing through the butter.

4. Thinly spread butter out on a cutting board and work out any additional liquid, using a wooden spoon or butter paddle. Sop liquid up with a paper towel.

5. Sprinkle salt over the butter and work it in. Mold into your desired shape and wrap in wax paper/plastic wrap to store.

Note: The liquid released from the sour cream during butter making is old-fashioned buttermilk (p. 22)—save it for use in pancakes or waffles.

Quick tip

The difference between Sweet Cream Butter & Cultured Butter:

Sweet cream butter is made from pasteurized fresh cream. Cultured butter is made from pasteurized cream that has been cultured into sour cream and then made into butter. The primary difference between the two is that sweet cream butter tastes sweet, while cultured butter has a slightly tangy taste. Cultured butter tends to outlast sweet cream butter, but both keep very well, especially if they are thoroughly rinsed during the butter-making process and stored in the freezer until ready to use.

Blue Cheese & Green Onion

Prep Time: 10 minutes
Makes: 3/4 cup

- 1/2 cup butter, softened
- 2 green onions, minced
- 1/4 cup blue cheese

1. In a small bowl, combine butter, green onions, and blue cheese. Roll into a log, wrap in wax paper or plastic wrap, and refrigerate until ready to use.

Raspberry & Honey Butter

Prep Time: 15 minutes
Makes: 3/4 cup

- 1/2 cup butter, softened
- 2 T raspberry preserves
- 2 T raspberry fruit leather, finely diced
- 2 T honey
- 1 cardamom pod, seeds removed and pulverized

1. In a small bowl, combine butter, raspberry preserves, fruit leather, honey, and ground cardamom seeds. Roll into a log, wrap in wax paper or plastic wrap, and refrigerate until ready to use.

Roasted Garlic & Sun-dried Tomato Butter

Prep Time: 15 minutes
Cook Time: 15 minutes
Makes: 5/8 cup

- 4 garlic cloves
- 1/8 t olive oil
- 1/2 cup butter, softened
- 2 T Parmesan
- 1 T sun-dried tomatoes, minced
- 1 T chives, minced

1. Preheat oven to 400°F. Place garlic cloves on a piece of foil, drizzle with olive oil, and wrap up; roast for about 15 minutes, or until garlic is tender. Remove from oven and let cool. When cool enough to handle, mash into a paste.
2. In a small bowl, combine butter, Parmesan, sun-dried tomatoes, chives, and roasted garlic. Roll into a log, wrap in wax paper or plastic wrap, and refrigerate until ready to use.

Cranberry Merlot Butter

Prep Time: 10 minutes
Cook Time: 5–7 minutes
Makes: 5/8 cup

- 1/2 cup butter, softened
- 1/4 cup dried cranberries, minced (orange-juice sweetened)
- 1/3 cup Merlot wine

1. In a small bowl, combine butter and cranberries; set aside.
2. In a small pan, bring Merlot to a simmer, reduce heat to low, and cook for 5–7 minutes, until wine is reduced in half.
3. Cool for a few minutes, then add Merlot to the bowl with the butter and cranberries and mix well. Roll into a log, wrap in wax paper or plastic wrap, and refrigerate until ready to use.

Fig, Maple & Vanilla-bean Butter

Prep Time: 15 minutes
Makes: 5/8 cup

- 1/2 cup butter, softened
- 3 T dried figs, minced
- 1 T maple syrup
- 1 vanilla bean, seeded
- 1/4 t cinnamon
- zest from half an orange

1. In a small bowl, combine butter, figs, maple syrup, vanilla-bean seeds, cinnamon, and orange zest. Roll into a log, wrap in wax paper or plastic wrap, and refrigerate until ready to use.

Cultured Buttermilk

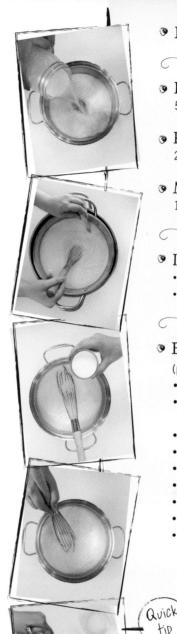

① Heat milk in pot to room temperature (64–73°F); whisk in cultured buttermilk.

② Using funnel, pour into sanitized 1-qt canning jar, cover with cheesecloth, and secure cloth with a canning jar ring.

③ Culture at room temperature for 24 hours. Remove cheesecloth and jar ring; cover with a plastic canning-jar lid. Refrigerate and use within 7 days.

• If you can't find good-quality, fresh buttermilk, a freeze-dried starter can be purchased at CulturesForHealth.com. After following the directions on the package for the initial batch, homemade buttermilk can then be re-cultured indefinitely using our recipe.

Level: Beginner

Prep Time: 5 minutes

Ripening Time: 24 hours

Makes: 1 quart

Ingredients: (p. 25)
• 3 1/2 cups **skim** milk
• 1/2 cup cultured buttermilk

Equipment Needed: (p. 26–31)
• 4-qt stainless-steel pot
• stainless-steel measuring cups
• wire whisk
• floating dairy thermometer
• 1-qt canning jar
• stainless-steel funnel
• cheesecloth
• canning-jar ring
• plastic canning-jar lid

Did you know?
Buttermilk is a broad term that describes a plethora of dairy products. Today, buttermilk is most commonly skimmed milk that has been inoculated with culture to impart it with its characteristic tang and thick, smooth texture. The term buttermilk can also refer to the liquid that is left over after making butter, particularly cultured butter. This is old-fashioned buttermilk, complete with flecks of real butter floating around. Delicious in things like pancakes and waffles! Use this up fast—it spoils quickly.

Quick tip

Cultured Buttermilk:
In this book, buttermilk is a vital ingredient in many of the recipes. Buttermilk and yogurt provide the source of culture for most of our cheese recipes. Be sure to purchase cultured buttermilk, ideally organic. From there, it can be propagated using this simple recipe. Buttermilk should always smell pleasantly tangy—never sour.

Food for thought:

Why does *sour* cream
have an expiration date?

In a hurry?
Add 1 t fresh lemon
juice to 1 cup cream.
Whisk. Voilà! Rich,
thick faux sour cream.

44

Cultured Sour Cream

1. Heat cream in pot to room temperature (64–73°F). Using a funnel, pour into a sanitized 1/2-gal jar and add cultured buttermilk. Cover jar with a plastic canning-jar lid and gently shake to combine.

2. Remove plastic lid. Cover jar with cheesecloth, and secure with a canning-jar ring.

3. Culture at room temperature for 24 hours. Remove cheesecloth and jar ring; cover with a plastic canning-jar lid. Refrigerate and use within 7 days.

Level: Beginner

Prep Time: 8 minutes

Ripening Time: 24 hours

Makes: 1 quart

Ingredients: (p. 25)
- 4 cups **cream**
- 1/2 cup cultured buttermilk (p. 43)

Equipment Needed: (p. 26–31)
- 4-qt stainless-steel pot
- stainless-steel measuring cups
- floating dairy thermometer
- assorted canning jars
- stainless-steel funnel
- plastic canning-jar lid
- cheesecloth
- canning-jar ring

 Quick tip

Cheese & Dairy Products:

When we began making cheese and dairy products, one of the most surprising things was the long list of ingredients on commercial labels to make a product that is simply delicious with just two ingredients—fresh cream and cultured buttermilk.

sweet treat

For a special treat, dip strawberries in sour cream and roll them in brown sugar.

Most yogurt problems are caused by poor temperature control and/or length of incubation time. Heating the milk too much during incubation or over-incubating it can cause the bacteria to misbehave. Often, this makes the yogurt too acidic, causing it to curdle. The best incubation temperature for your yogurt depends on your starter. If the yogurt you're making is curdling, try lowering the incubation temperature. You may need to go as low as 100°F. Also, if your yogurt doesn't thicken to your desired consistency, try incubating it longer than the recommended 6 hours, up to 9 hours. **We've come around to incubating our yogurt at exactly 110°F for 8 hours.**

⑨ **Level:** Beginner

⑨ **Prep Time:**
15 minutes

⑨ **Culturing Time:**
8 hours (timing will vary
depending on method)

⑨ **Makes:**
about 6 1/2 cups

⑨ **Ingredients:** (p. 25)
- 6 cups **skim** milk
- ice water
- 1/2 cup cultured
  plain yogurt

⑨ **Equipment Needed:**
(p. 26–31)
- 4-qt stainless-steel pot
- wire whisk
- stainless-steel
    measuring cups
- floating dairy thermometer
- yogurt incubator

① Heat milk in pot to 180°F. Place pot in ice water and cool to 112°F.

② Once milk has cooled, take out 1/2 cup and mix it with the cultured yogurt in a small bowl. Now add that to the rest of the milk and whisk.

③ Transfer mixture to a yogurt incubator, and set timer for 8 hours, or until yogurt has reached your desired consistency.

- If you can't find good-quality, plain, fresh yogurt, a freeze-dried yogurt starter (Bulgarian) can be purchased at CulturesForHealth.com. After following the directions on the package for the initial batch, homemade yogurt can then be re-cultured indefinitely using our recipe.

Flavored Yogurt

To make flavored yogurt right in the yogurt containers for quick and easy snacks, reduce the milk in this recipe to 4 cups and the cultured yogurt to 1/3 cup. This will leave enough room after the yogurt has cultured to add flavorings, fruit, and granola. To sweeten, try honey, maple syrup, or fruit preserves. For flavoring, try a touch of instant coffee powder, cinnamon, nutmeg, vanilla beans, vanilla, or any other flavored extract. Top it all off with some fresh fruit, replace the lids, and refrigerate until ready to use.

Quick tip

My favorite brand of yogurt incubator is Donvier (Amazon.com) because it's simple and easy to use. I like that the containers the yogurt "yogs" in have snap-on lids, making it so you can toss a yogurt right into your lunchbox or purse. Confession: I've tried making yogurt in a slow cooker with water surrounding the jars, in a box with a heat lamp, in my oven near the pilot light, and on a heating pad in the bottom of an insulated cooler. Call me frustrated. The only alternative method that worked consistently for me was the heating pad/ insulated cooler idea (p. 49). If you're serious about making yogurt routinely, get a yogurt maker.

Cultured Greek Yogurt

After making Cultured Plain Yogurt (p. 47), proceed with the following:

1. Line colander with butter muslin and place colander over a bowl.

2. Pour yogurt into the colander and let drain for 4 hours in the refrigerator (or on a countertop if a more sour yogurt is desired).

3. Remove drained yogurt from butter muslin and use within 7 days.

Level: Beginner

Prep Time: 5 minutes

Draining Time: 4 hours

Makes: about 3 1/2 cups

Ingredients: (p. 25)
- 5 cups Cultured Plain Yogurt (p. 47)

Equipment Needed: (p. 26–31)
- 7.5" fine mesh colander
- butter muslin
- 5-qt stainless-steel bowl

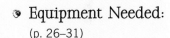

Quick tip

With cultured dairy products, you get back exactly what you put in. Think of it this way: when you add culture to milk or cream, you are attempting to create an optimal environment for that culture to thrive and multiply. A substandard culture will yield a mediocre final product. Choose only the freshest, organic, plain yogurt you can find without a laundry list of additives.

DIY Yogurt Incubator

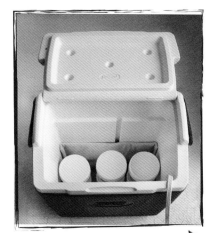

If you have a heating pad, put it in the bottom of an insulated cooler and turn it on medium (you're shooting for a temperature of 108–115°F). The cooler I had on hand held six 8-oz canning jars (with plastic storage lids). Close the lid (it won't close entirely because of the heating pad electrical cord). After six hours, I had six jars of yogurt.

Flavoring Kefir

Use stevia, raw honey, or puréed fresh fruit to sweeten. Add vanilla extract for additional flavor. Kefir is great for smoothies, pancakes, popsicles, and for making salad dressing.

Kefir: ka-**fear**, Russian (In English, often **kee**-fir—think Kiefer Sutherland; French children call it "kee-fee.")

1 package makes 2 qts

① Create a double boiler by putting the milk in the smaller pot and water in the larger pot. Heat the milk to 86°F.

② Remove from heat and whisk in one packet of starter culture until fully dissolved.

③ Pour into sanitized 1-qt canning jar, using a funnel, and loosely place the lid on.

④ Incubate at 70–78°F for 12–48 hours or until desired consistency and flavor are reached. Refrigerate.

Re-culturing Kefir (next batch)
Once you've made a batch of kefir from starter, you can re-culture fresh batches by mixing 1/2 cup plain kefir with 3 1/2 cups whole milk, and following steps 3–4. How many times this process can be repeated varies, but if kefir is not reaching desired consistency within 48 hours, start over again by making a batch using fresh starter.

Why not make kefir using raw milk?
Making kefir using raw milk can be done, but it's fussy. You start with kefir grains instead of kefir starter (CulturesForHealth.com) and use pasteurized milk for the first batch. With each batch thereafter, you gradually decrease the amount of pasteurized milk and replace it with raw milk (still using the grains that were at the bottom—not really "grains," but lumps of "culture"). You can make a batch of kefir with kefir starter using raw milk, but trying to make subsequent batches from it is difficult because the bacteria you *don't* want has become more prevalent.

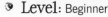

◉ **Level:** Beginner

◉ **Prep Time:**
5 minutes

◉ **Incubating Time:**
12–48 hours

◉ **Makes:**
1 quart

◉ **Ingredients:** (p. 25)
• 1 quart **whole** milk
• kefir starter

◉ **Equipment Needed:**
(p. 26–31)
• 4-qt stainless-steel pot
• 8-qt stainless-steel pot
• floating dairy thermometer
• wire whisk
• stainless-steel funnel
• 1-qt canning jar with plastic canning-jar lid
• incubator

We like the Brod & Taylor Folding Bread Proofer and Yogurt Maker, BrodAndTaylor.com, for incubating our kefir (and large batches of yogurt). This multifunctional kitchen tool also creates a consistently humid, warm environment for rising your favorite bread-dough recipes; can be used to temper and hold chocolate; and even keeps chips, crackers and cookies crisp longer. Best of all, it folds away easily for drawer or cabinet storage.

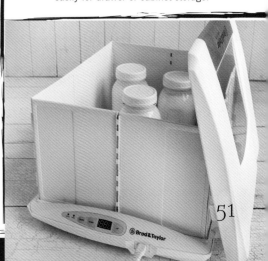

51

CHEESE MAKING

soft
- Soft Cheese
- Cream Cheese
- Cottage Cheese
- Mozzarella

pressed, brined & aged
- Monterey Jack
- Cheddar
- Colby-Jack
- Feta (drained & brined)
- Manchego
- Gruyère
- Swiss
- Parmesan
- Asiago

mold-ripened
- Blue Cheese
- Brie

pick your cheese

Before you dive into cheese making ...

First, a word about cultural differences. Cheese is all about different cultures—adding diversity, mixing and matching this with that. When you add organisms (culture) to milk, you're enlisting them to do some muscle work: digest lactose and produce lactic acid. This helps make the cheese more acidic and is the first step in curd formation and development of the flavor profile of a particular cheese. As the cultures trapped in the cheese die off, they release enzymes that digest proteins and fats within the cheese, creating its final flavor and texture.

In other words, it's all about the "bugs" you add. Swiss cheese is made using a specific critter, Brie yet another. You can just imagine how all the different cheeses we enjoy today were happy accidents that happened long before refrigeration. Cheese came about as a way to preserve the nutritional benefits of milk, back before we had aseptic milk cartons and things like ultra-pasteurization.

If you stop to think about it, there are probably more cheeses waiting to be invented—you know, from specific places where specific bacteria hang out. Tomato-vine cheese, anyone? How about date sap cheese? (The tree, silly, not the guy from DateHookUp.com.) Can't you just picture the teats of someone's ewe brushing the leaves of a particular plant indigenous to Greece centuries ago, resulting in curdled milk (Miss Muffet's curds and whey), but this time the curds were different, no, *mo' bettah,* so the shepherd exclaimed, "Feta!"

There are two groups of *primary* cultures that are used in cheese making:

Thermophilic cultures multiply at 90–112°F and can be heat tolerant up to 140–150°F (opinions vary).
Mesophilic cultures multiply at 70–90°F and can be heat tolerant up to 105–110°F (opinions vary).

Are you staying with me so far? Think of cheese making the same way you approach gardening. You're trying to *grow* specific plants—say, tomatoes, not pigweed or bindweed. In order to get good tomatoes, you take certain steps to promote what it is you *do* want—same thing with cheese making. You want specific things to do well and multiply, others you don't. And just like a tomato plant, cheese cultures mustn't get too hot or too cold, otherwise they die.

"Give me some examples!" you say. Most yogurt is made using a thermophilic culture, which is the reason you have to keep it warm (incubate it) for X amount of time. You're keeping it warm so the darling little therms can multiply to the point that you have the perfect storm (intersection of different factors) and then, *voilà!*—yogurt. (Dairy products are a bowl of complicated chemistries.) If your homemade yogurt is curdled, it got too warm. If it's watery, it wasn't warm enough. And then to keep you on your toes, cultures like to test your patience when you keep yogurt at the perfect warmth but it stayed warm too long. Are they ever happy? Most definitely, but just like raising a family or growing a garden, it takes a while to get the hang of it.

One more thing: You know how the human family is diverse to the point you can't keep track of it all? I'm going to put this out there and you can do with it what you will: There are some not–so–common gourmet yogurts you can make using mesophilic cultures instead of thermophilic. Meso-ing around with your head, right? Viili, piimä, matsoni, and filmjölk yogurt starters are all mesophilic cultures that multiply at room temperature.

Fine then, be confusing. **But make note of this: They don't make the kind of yogurt you're used to.** And you can't use this kind of yogurt when one of our cheese recipes calls for the addition of yogurt (thermophilic culture) because recipes that call for yogurt require higher temperatures in order to create an ideal environment for the heat-loving thermophilic culture and those temperatures are too toasty for mesophilic cultures (mesos dead on arrival). If you make yogurt using one of those cultures, I'm just saying, it can't be used in our recipes calling for the addition of yogurt in order to add some primary culture to things. **FYI, almost all store–bought yogurts are made using thermophilic culture; their labels will list it in the ingredients.** (Phew. Glad I got that out of the way.)

- Here's an example of a label from Straus Organic Plain Yogurt. Ingredients: Pasteurized Organic Whole Milk, Organic Sweet Cream Buttermilk, Living Yogurt Cultures: *L. acidophilus, L. bulgaricus, S. thermophilus* and *Bifidobacterium lactis*.

Now, wrap your brain around this: **In most of our cheese recipes, we have you adding yogurt, for the thermo of it all, NOT for probiotics** (a term I know you're familiar with). **Probiotics are cultures added to fresh dairy products** and some fruit-flavored concoctions, even coconut water, but most notably yogurt (they'll be listed on the label). Why? They're strains that have the ability to survive digestion and head on down to your colon, etc. Remember, **the only way you can get nutrition from the food you eat is when little bugs are there in abundance to digest whatever it is you've eaten so the tiny micro–nutrients can end up in your bloodstream.** (That pizza you ate didn't just end up in your bloodstream because you chewed each bite 30 times.) However, they're sensitive little critters and need to be eaten in their fresh form, and can't be heated too high. So yeah, when we have you adding *cultured* yogurt to one of our cheese recipes, it's for the thermophilics that multiply during the ripening stage of our recipes, not for the probiotics—they aren't going to survive the heat required to make curd (cheese). Most cheese recipes require the purchase of "packets of direct-set thermophilic starter" in addition to the unique *secondary* cheese-specific cultures like *Propionic shermanii* needed for Swiss cheese.

My daughter-in-law and I decided early on when working on our cheese recipes, why bother buying so many *packets of direct-set thermophilic starters* (one-time use/keep in the freezer/oh no! I'm in the mood to make cheese and I'm out, or my packet is expired and it takes several days for more to arrive) when you can grab a container of yummy cultured yogurt, use a small amount to make your cheese, and then eat the rest? Turns out, we were right.

And that's what makes our cheese recipes so unique and simple to make— we've taken care of all the scientific details (that are all over the map when you consult the Internet).

Why should you have to know the difference between *Lactobacillus delbrueckii subsp. bulgaricus* (LB) and *Lactobacillus helveticus* (LH)? Not only that, but the scientific community recently renamed members of the genus *Streptococcus* to *Lactococcus*. For instance, *Streptococcus thermophilus* is now *Lactococcus thermophilus*. "Uncle!" we cried!!!!

So in some of our recipes, we put our bright idea to the test and started adding cultured buttermilk (mesophilic culture). Again, success! And who doesn't think having buttermilk around to add to baked goods improves the flavor and texture?

So the next time you hear, "Hey you, get some culture, why don't ya?" you'll be ready. With most of our cheese recipes, yogurt and buttermilk are going to become your consummate companions. What a wonderfully diverse and *yummy* world we cheese makers live in!

If you have questions as you work with our recipes, go to our chatroom on HeritageJersey.org to ask for help. After my daughter-in-law and I got our recipes to the point we thought they were perfect, they were tested two to three more times using someone other than ourselves. But putting our creations out into the world creates a mountain of variables. For example, our French Toast Casserole is a regular breakfast staple we serve to our B&B guests. When I decided to include it in this book, I wanted to be sure of the baking time. You know how it is with a tried and true recipe, pinch of this, pat of that? The first time it burned on the bottom and was soggy in the middle. What!? I was using a new oven so I blamed the oven and bought an oven thermometer—nope, spot on. I tried it again and adjusted the times. Same thing. In order to get it done in the center and browned on the top, the bottom and edges burned. My daughter baked one in her oven—perfection. As it turns out, I was using a white ceramic baking dish my daughter-in-law had recently purchased. My daughter had used glass like we always use for our B&B. So when I finally tested it in a clear glass dish, perfection, just like we were used to. Ugh, right? Get in touch if you're frustrated. We'd like to help you troubleshoot.

Stay tuned for the possibility of a cheese-making sequel because after this book is done, I'm free to play around with virtuoso, around-the-world cheeses like Morbier, Paneer, Pavé, Valençay, Halloumi, Gouda, Port Salut, Époisses, Taleggio, Reblochon, Cambozola, Caerphilly, Gorgonzola, Brie de Coulommiers, cocoa-rubbed, herb-encrusted, love-encased, flower-wrapped cheeses ... *oh my*. Another reason why I *love* my cows.

Sterilizing Equipment

Whether raw milk, pasteurized milk, or thermized milk is used, the importance of cleanliness when handling milk cannot be stressed enough. Don't forget, it's the perfect medium for growing tiny unmentionables.

Maintaining a super-clean work space ensures that any unwanted bacteria or molds have been eliminated from work surfaces and equipment. It also keeps the various different types of cultures you're going to use from cross-contaminating new batches of cheese.

To make sure your equipment is good to go, wash it with soap and water, then sanitize it by dipping it into boiling water or a sanitizing rinse (this uses chemicals, so it's not my choice) or by washing it in a dishwasher with a "sanitize" setting. I prefer dipping everything into boiling water. Here's how:

1. Fill a large stockpot with hot water and put all the tools you'll be using to make a particular type of cheese into the water. This includes plastic cheese molds called for in your recipe or cheesecloth you've laundered and are re-using, as well as the tips of thermometers. Bring the water to a rolling boil.

2. Put a clean hand towel on the counter. Using a pair of tongs, remove your tools one by one and place them on the towel to dry.

3. To sanitize something big, like a colander or a lid, put it in your sink and pour the leftover hot water all over it. Then set it to dry along with the other tools.

4. It's a drag to make a batch of cheese and have it fail because you didn't take a few minutes to sanitize your equipment. Everyone knows it's important to sanitize jars and tools when canning jams, etc. Making cheese isn't any different.

Soft Cheese

Can be made using **thermized** or **pasteurized** or **raw** milk/cream.

1. Heat milk and cream in pot to 125°F.

2. Remove pot from heat and add vinegar in a steady stream while whisking constantly. Let the mixture sit undisturbed for 20 minutes. The mixture will separate into curds and whey.

3. Line a colander with cheesecloth and place colander over a bowl. Pour the curds and whey into the colander and let drain for 4 hours (alternatively, it can be covered and placed in the refrigerator to drain overnight).

4. Discard whey, remove cheese from cheesecloth, and transfer to a bowl. Serve plain or stir in your choice of flavor blend.

5. For presentation, line small molds or ramekins with damp cheesecloth and press cheese into mold. Turn upside down onto serving plate and remove cheesecloth.

• Fig–Walnut Flavor Blend

- **Level:** Beginner

- **Prep Time:**
  5 minutes

- **Cook Time:**
  10 minutes

- **Draining Time:**
  4 hours

- **Makes:**
  1 1/2 cups

- **Ingredients:** (p. 25)
  - 1 quart **whole** or **cream-line** milk
  - 1 cup **cream**
  - 1/4 cup organic distilled white vinegar (don't substitute other vinegars because they impart a strange flavor)

- **Equipment Needed:**
  (p. 26–31)
  - 4-qt stainless-steel pot
  - stainless-steel measuring cups
  - wire whisk
  - floating dairy thermometer
  - 7.5" fine mesh colander
  - cheesecloth
  - 5-qt stainless-steel bowl
  - 6-oz ramekins (we used a 5-oz vintage gelatin mold)

Flavor Blends

Garlic–Dill Blend
- 2 T garlic, peeled and minced
- 2 T fresh dill, minced
- 1/2 t salt
- 1/2 t pepper

Mix well, stir into 1 1/2 cups soft cheese.

Garlic–Herb Blend
- 2 T garlic, peeled and minced
- 1 T fresh thyme, minced
- 1 T fresh rosemary, minced
- 1/2 t salt
- 1/2 t pepper

Mix well, stir into 1 1/2 cups soft cheese.

Fig–Walnut Blend
- 1/2 cup walnuts, chopped
- 1 cup dried figs, stemmed and finely chopped
- 1/3 cup water
- 1/3 cup kalamata olives, pitted and minced
- 1 T capers, diced
- 2 T olive oil
- 1 T balsamic vinegar
- 1 1/2 t fresh thyme, minced

1. Preheat oven to 350°F. Toast walnuts on a baking sheet for about 10 minutes, or until fragrant (watch closely—they burn quickly).

2. In a medium skillet, combine figs and water; cook over medium-high heat for about 5 minutes, or until water is absorbed and figs are soft. Drain.

3. Mix together walnuts, figs, and remaining ingredients; mix well. Stir into 1 1/2 cups soft cheese.

With three simple ingredients, soft cheese is the perfect beginner recipe. It provides a creamy, rich cheese with a texture similar to ricotta, but with a lot more flavor.

In many of the recipes for fresh cheese (any cheese that is not aged), vegetable rennet is an acceptable replacement for animal rennet. Both are excellent for coagulating milk, but beware, often vegetable rennet is much more potent than animal rennet, and it coagulates milk with 2–3 times less rennet. Cream cheese is the exception to the rule. It uses animal rennet despite being a fresh cheese because of the miniscule amount of rennet needed for the recipe. Even 1 drop of double-strength vegetable rennet in this recipe is too much. It produces a dry, crumbly cheese that is not at all like cream cheese.

Cream Cheese

Level: Beginner

Prep Time:
15 minutes

Ripening Time:
1 hour, 30 minutes

Draining Time:
6 hours

Makes:
about 24 ozs

Ingredients: (p. 25)
- 2 cups **whole** or **cream-line** milk
- 6 cups **cream**
- 1/2 cup cultured buttermilk (p. 43)
- 2 drops liquid animal rennet
- 2 T distilled water

Equipment Needed:
(p. 26–31)
- 4-qt stainless-steel pot with lid
- stainless-steel measuring cups
- assorted canning jars
- wire whisk
- floating dairy thermometer
- 7.5" fine mesh colander
- 5-qt stainless-steel bowl
- cotton bag
- ladle
- large plastic container

1. Heat milk and cream in pot to room temperature (64–73°F); whisk in cultured buttermilk.

2. Dilute rennet in distilled water and add to cream mixture. Whisk in, using a back-and-forth motion.

3. Cover pot with lid and let sit undisturbed at room temperature for 1 1/2 hours, or until mixture has a custard-like consistency.

4. Place colander inside a bowl, line with a cotton bag, and pour or ladle the mixture into it. Gather up the edges of the bag by pulling the drawstring. Suspend the bag over a large bowl to catch the whey as it drains off.

5. Let drain for 6 hours, or until the whey is no longer dripping from the bag. Remove cheese from the sack, put in a sanitized container, and refrigerate. Enjoy immediately or use within 7 days.

61

Cottage Cheese

Can be made using **thermized** or **pasteurized** or **raw** milk.

If using pasteurized milk, add calcium chloride, p. 24.

① Create a double boiler by putting the milk in the smaller pot and water in the larger pot. Heat the milk to 84°F.

② Add cultured buttermilk and whisk to incorporate. Cover and let ripen for 45 minutes, holding the temperature at 84°F.

③ Dilute rennet in distilled water and add it to the milk. Whisk in, using a back-and-forth motion. Cover and let sit undisturbed until a clean break forms (p. 63)—about 30 minutes.

④ Cut into 1/2" cubes, using a curd knife. Let curds rest for 10 minutes.

⑤ Slowly heat curds to 114°F (this should take about 25 minutes), stirring constantly with a perforated spoon.

⑥ Once the curds start to sink to the bottom of the pot, spoon a few out. If they are firm to the touch, they are ready.

⑦ Prepare an ice-water bath in a bowl. Line colander with cheesecloth and pour curds into the colander. Lift the corners of the cloth to encourage whey to drain off. Still in the cheesecloth, transfer to ice water and swirl around for about 5 minutes to set curds.

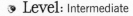

- ◉ **Level:** Intermediate

- ◉ **Prep Time:**
  2 hours, 15 minutes

- ◉ **Makes:**
  32 ozs

- ◉ **Ingredients:** (p. 25)
  - 1 gal **2%** milk
  - 3/4 cup cultured buttermilk (p. 43)
  - 1/4 t liquid vegetable rennet
  - 1/4 cup distilled water
  - ice water
  - 1 1/2 cups cultured Greek yogurt (p. 49)
  - 3/4 t non-iodized salt

- ◉ **Equipment Needed:**
  (p. 26–31)
  - 8-qt stainless-steel pot with lid
  - 12-qt stainless-steel pot
  - stainless-steel measuring cups
  - stainless-steel measuring spoons
  - assorted canning jars
  - wire whisk
  - floating dairy thermometer
  - thermometer
  - curd knife
  - stainless-steel perforated spoon
  - 7-qt stainless-steel colander
  - cheesecloth
  - 4-qt glass bowl

8. Once the curds are set, place them in a bowl. Mix in the Greek yogurt and salt; use within 7 days.

Clean Break

The clean break stage in cheese making is when the milk has coagulated and is roughly the consistency of gelatin. At this point, if a curd knife is inserted into the curd, it will cut in a clean line that will be visible even after the knife is removed.

Cutting the Curd

After a clean break has formed, it's time to cut the curd into smaller squares (curds) in a size specified by the recipe. To cut the curds, first cut lines that are the width specified in the recipe, and then cut in the opposite direction to form a grid pattern. After that, insert the knife at a 45° angle and cut in between all of the grid lines.

Making cottage cheese is a good way to get familiar with the skills you'll need to make more advanced pressed cheeses. Plus it's simple and delicious—who doesn't love cottage cheese?

Mozzarella

Can be made using **thermized** or **pasteurized** or **raw** milk.

If using pasteurized milk, add calcium chloride, p. 24.

If using pasteurized milk, add calcium chloride, p. 24.

Level: Intermediate

Prep Time: 1 1/2 hours

Makes: 1 lb

Ingredients: (p. 25)
- 1 gal **whole** milk or **cream-line** milk
- 1 1/2 t citric acid
- 1/2 cup distilled water, divided
- 1/4 cup cultured plain yogurt (p. 47)
- 1/8 t liquid animal rennet
- 1 1/2 T non-iodized salt, divided
- ice water

Equipment Needed:
(p. 26–31)
- 8-qt stainless-steel pot with lid
- stainless-steel measuring cups
- stainless-steel measuring spoons
- assorted canning jars
- wire whisk
- floating dairy thermometer
- curd knife
- stainless-steel perforated spoon
- stainless-steel skimmer
- 4-qt glass bowl
- latex gloves
- dishwashing gloves
- cutting board

1. Pour milk into pot. Dissolve citric acid in 1/4 cup distilled water; whisk into milk.

2. Heat milk to 90°F. Whisk in cultured yogurt, cover, and let ripen for 10 minutes.

3. Dilute rennet in remaining distilled water; add to milk. Whisk in, using a back-and-forth motion. Cover and let sit undisturbed until a clean break forms (p. 63)—about 8 minutes.

4. Cut the curd into 1" cubes, using a curd knife, and let them rest for 5 minutes.

5. Heat the curds to 110°F, stirring occasionally.

6. With a perforated spoon, remove the cheese curds from the whey and place in a bowl. Wearing latex gloves, squeeze any excess whey back into the pot.

7. Heat the whey to 175°F.

8. Once the whey is hot, place about half of the curds in a skimmer and dip into the hot whey for 30 seconds at a time.

9. Continue dipping while kneading the curd between each dip using a perforated spoon. Repeat this process several times until the curd is malleable.

10 Wearing rubber gloves, stretch the heated curd on a cutting board (the second half of the batch is still in the bowl) and fold it over on itself several times, working in 1/2 the salt (3/4 T) as the cheese is stretched.

11 Form the cheese into a ball and place it in a bowl of ice water to set. Repeat this process with remaining curds and salt, reheating the whey if necessary.

12 Refrigerate, covered in water, up to 3 days, or once cooled, grate and store in freezer.

Mozzarella is a fresh, stretched curd cheese with a sweet, delicate flavor. Making a fresh batch of mozzarella is a quick and simple process and the end result is a deliciously soft, creamy cheese.

Monterey Jack cheese is a mild cheese with a smooth, creamy texture. The process of making Monterey Jack differs from most other cheeses because it's a washed-curd cheese. After the curds are cut and heated, some of the whey is removed and replaced with distilled water. This cuts back on the acidity of the cheese, and helps create its mild flavor.

Monterey Jack

Can be made using **thermized** or
pasteurized or **raw** milk.

If using pasteurized milk, add calcium chloride, p. 24.

Level: Intermediate

Prep Time:
3 hours

Pressing Time:
18 hours, 15 minutes

Aging Time:
2–3 months

Makes:
2 to 2 1/2 lbs

Ingredients: (p. 25)
- 2 gals **whole** or **cream-line** milk
- 3/4 cup cultured buttermilk (p. 43)
- 1/2 t liquid animal rennet
- 4 1/4 cups distilled water, divided
- 3 1/2 T non-iodized salt

Equipment Needed:
(p. 26–31)
- 12-qt stainless-steel pot with lid
- 16-qt stainless-steel pot
- stainless-steel measuring cups
- stainless-steel measuring spoons
- assorted canning jars
- wire whisk
- floating dairy thermometer
- thermometer
- curd knife
- stainless-steel perforated spoon
- ladle
- cheesecloth
- 7-qt stainless-steel colander
- latex gloves
- 7.5" cheese mold
- draining tray
- cheese press with exercise weights: 8 (board)+10+2 1/2
- 4-qt stainless-steel pot
- 2-qt stainless-steel bowl dedicated to cheese wax
- cheese wax
- cheese wax brush

1. Create a double boiler by putting the milk in the smaller pot and water in the larger pot. Heat milk to 90°F; whisk in cultured buttermilk. Cover and let ripen for 45 minutes.

2. Dilute rennet in 1/4 cup distilled water and whisk into the milk, using a back-and-forth motion. Cover and let sit undisturbed until a clean break forms (p. 63)—about 30 minutes.

3. Cut the curds into 1/2" cubes, using a curd knife. Let them rest for 20 minutes.

4. Slowly heat the curds to 100°F, gently stirring with a perforated spoon. Using a ladle, drain off the whey until it's level with the curds; add remaining 4 cups of distilled water.

5. Reheat to 100°F and hold this temperature for 30 minutes, stirring occasionally.

6. Pour the curds into a colander lined with cheesecloth to drain off the whey. Work quickly so the curds don't cool off. Lift the corners of the cheesecloth to encourage the whey to drain faster. Once most of the whey has drained, mix in salt.

(continued)

(continued from p. 67)

⑦ Quickly transfer curds to the cheese mold lined with cheesecloth.

⑧ Place cheese mold onto a draining tray and press, using 8 lbs pressure for 15 minutes (p. 85). Remove cheese from press, flip over, and redress (p. 89). Press, using the same amount of pressure, for 30 minutes.

⑨ Remove cheese from press, flip, and redress. Press the cheese again, using 20 1/2 lbs pressure for 1 1/2 hours. Remove cheese from press, flip, and redress. Press again, using the same amount of pressure, for 16 hours.

⑩ Remove cheese from mold and cheesecloth; place on a draining tray to dry. Flip cheese over several times a day. A small fan on low placed nearby on the counter can speed up the drying process. It should take 1–3 days for the cheese to dry out. It's ready for waxing once the surface is dry to the touch. If mold appears on the surface of the cheese during drying, wipe it away with a cloth dampened in a saltwater solution or vinegar (p. 31).

⑪ Once cheese is dry to the touch, apply two even coats of wax. Age the cheese at 55°F and 70% humidity for 2–3 months.

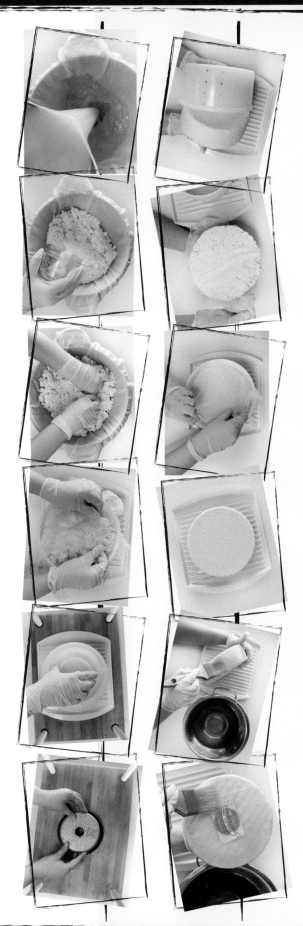

Waxing Cheese

Most cheese wax is a mixture of paraffin and microcrystalline wax. It comes in a variety of colors, usually red, black, yellow, or natural. We prefer to use the clear, no color wax.

Waxing cheese is a simple enough process. The wax is melted, and can be either brushed onto the cheese using a cheese wax brush, or the cheese can be dipped directly into the wax. You'll want a small bowl or pan dedicated to cheese wax that will nestle into a larger pan to form a double boiler. Never put wax over direct heat, as it's highly flammable. Also, the wax should be heated just enough to melt and should never be left unattended.

Generally, it's better to brush the wax onto the cheese rather than dip the cheese into the wax. There are a few different reasons for this: it's easier to control the thickness of the wax when it's brushed on; it's easier to ensure that all small imperfections in the cheese are filled in with wax to create an airtight seal (which prevents the growth of mold); and if the cheese is dipped in wax, the wax in the bowl tends to collect particles of cheese, so brushing on the wax keeps the leftover wax in the bowl clean and pristine and ready to be heated up again the next time you need it. It's also advisable to apply a label to the cheese after the first coat is applied, essentially embedding it in the wax. This makes it much easier to keep track of cheese types and aging times.

Cheddar cheese gets its name from the village of Cheddar in Southwestern England, where it originated, and from the process that has traditionally defined the cheese: cheddaring. This is a step in a lengthy process that starts once the curds are heated to 100°F. After heating, the whey is drained, and the temperature is held at 100°F. The curds compress and knit together. This mass is cut into slabs, which are then stacked on top of each other—this stacking of the slabs is called "cheddaring." After cheddaring, the slabs are cut back into curds and pressed. Purists believe that cheddaring is what gives the cheese its distinct flavor, but the process is lengthy and not well suited for small batches of cheese made at home. Ours is a condensed version of this cheddaring process.

Cheddar

Can be made using **thermized** or **pasteurized** or **raw** milk.

If using pasteurized milk, add calcium chloride, p. 24.

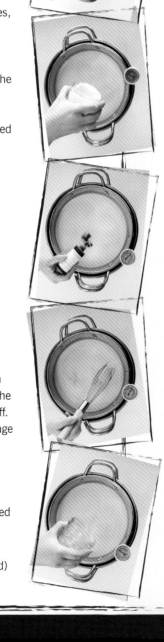

1. Create a double boiler by putting the milk in the smaller pot and water in the larger pot. Heat the milk to 86°F and whisk in cultured buttermilk. Cover and let ripen for 30 minutes, holding the temperature at 86°F.

2. Add annatto to the milk, and whisk in until the color is even. Dilute rennet in distilled water and add to the milk. Whisk in, using a back-and-forth motion. Cover and let sit undisturbed until the curd gives a clean break (p. 63)—about 30 minutes.

3. Cut the curd into 1/2" cubes, using a curd knife, and let them rest for 10 minutes.

4. Slowly heat the curds to 100°F (this should take 20–25 minutes), gently stirring with a perforated spoon. Let the curds rest for 10 minutes.

5. After the curds have rested, pour them into a colander lined with cheesecloth to drain off the whey. Work quickly so the curds don't cool off. Lift the corners of the cheesecloth to encourage the whey to drain faster. Once most of the whey has drained, mix in salt.

6. Quickly transfer curds to the cheese mold lined with cheesecloth.

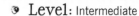

Level: Intermediate

Prep Time:
2 hours, 30 minutes

Pressing Time:
17 hours, 45 minutes

Aging Time:
2 months for mild,
12–24 months for sharp

Makes:
2 to 2 1/2 lbs

Ingredients: (p. 25)
- 2 gals **whole** or **cream-line** milk
- 3/4 cup cultured buttermilk (p. 43)
- 20 drops liquid annatto for color (optional)
- 1/2 t liquid animal rennet
- 1/4 cup distilled water
- 2 1/2 T non-iodized salt

Equipment Needed:
(p. 26–31)
- 12-qt stainless-steel pot with lid
- 16-qt stainless-steel pot
- stainless-steel measuring cups
- stainless-steel measuring spoons
- assorted canning jars
- wire whisk
- floating dairy thermometer
- thermometer
- curd knife
- stainless-steel perforated spoon
- cheesecloth
- 7-qt stainless-steel colander
- latex gloves
- 7.5" cheese mold
- draining tray
- cheese press with exercise weights: 8 (board)+25+10+10+5+2 1/2
- 4-qt stainless-steel pot
- 2-qt stainless-steel bowl dedicated to cheese wax
- cheese wax
- cheese wax brush

(continued)

71

(continued from p. 71)

⑦ Place cheese mold onto a draining tray and press, using 23 lbs pressure for 15 minutes (p. 85). Remove cheese from the mold, flip over, and redress (p. 89). Press again, using the same amount of pressure for 30 minutes.

⑧ Remove cheese from mold, flip, and redress. Press again, this time using 55 1/2 lbs pressure for 1 hour. Remove cheese from press, flip, and redress. Press again, using the same amount of pressure for 16 hours.

⑨ Remove cheese from mold and cheesecloth; place on a draining tray to dry. Flip cheese over several times a day. A small fan on low placed nearby on the counter can speed up the drying process. It should take 1–3 days for the cheese to dry out. It's ready for waxing once the surface is dry to the touch. If mold appears on the surface of the cheese during drying, wipe it away with a cloth dampened in a saltwater solution or vinegar (p. 31).

⑩ Once cheese is dry to the touch, apply two even coats of wax (p. 69). Age the cheese at 55°F and 70% humidity for 2 months for mild Cheddar or 12–24 months for sharp.

Did you know?

Annatto is a natural yellow/orange food coloring made from seeds of tropical achiote trees. It was first used in modern cheese making in the 16th century in England to replicate the color of the best Gloucester cheese, which got its color naturally from high levels of carotene in the area's grass.

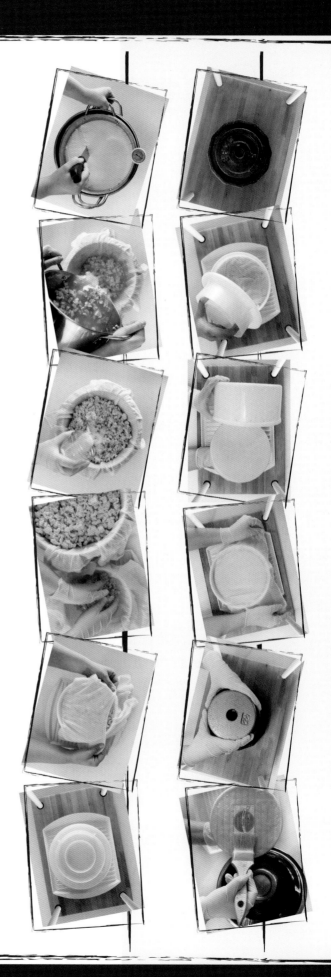

72

Colby-Jack cheese is the combination of two distinctly American cheeses. Colby is dense and slightly squeaky, and Monterey Jack is creamy and moist. Both cheeses are washed-curd cheeses (see Monterey Jack), and the colby is dyed with annatto to create the marbled look of Colby-Jack cheese.

Can be made using **thermized** or **pasteurized** or **raw** milk.

If using pasteurized milk, add calcium chloride, p. 24.

Level: Intermediate

Prep Time:
2 hours, 20 minutes

Pressing Time:
18 hours, 15 minutes

Aging Time:
2–3 months

Makes:
1 to 1 1/4 lbs

Ingredients: (p. 25)
- 1 gal **whole** or **cream-line** milk
- 1/4 cup cultured buttermilk, divided (p. 43)
- 5 drops liquid annatto
- 1/4 t liquid animal rennet, divided
- 2 1/4 cups distilled water, divided
- 1 T non-iodized salt

Equipment Needed:
(p. 26–31)
- two 4-qt stainless-steel pots with lids
- 8-qt stainless-steel pot
- 12-qt stainless-steel pot
- stainless-steel measuring cups
- stainless-steel measuring spoons
- assorted canning jars
- wire whisk
- floating dairy thermometer
- thermometer
- kitchen knife
- stainless-steel perforated spoon
- ladle
- cheesecloth
- 7-qt stainless-steel colander
- latex gloves
- 4.9" cheese mold
- draining tray
- exercise weights: 5+2 1/2+1 1/4 directly on follower
- 4-qt stainless-steel pot
- 2-qt stainless-steel bowl dedicated to cheese wax
- cheese wax
- cheese wax brush

1. Create two double boilers, putting 1/2 gal of milk into each of the smaller pots and water in the larger pots. Heat milk to 90°F. Add 2 T of cultured buttermilk to each of the double boilers. Cover and let ripen for 30 minutes.

2. Add annatto (for color) to one of the double boilers, and whisk in until the color is even.

3. In two separate 8-oz canning jars, dilute 1/8 t rennet in 2 T distilled water. Add one jar of diluted rennet to each of the double boilers. Whisk in, using a back-and-forth motion. Cover and let sit until a clean break forms (p. 63)—about 30 minutes.

4. Using a kitchen knife rather than a curd knife, cut the curds into 1/2" cubes. Let them rest for 10 minutes.

5. Slowly heat the curds to 100°F, gently stirring with a perforated spoon. Using a ladle, remove some of the whey from both of the pots so it's level with the curds. Add 1 cup distilled water to each pot.

6. Reheat to 100°F and hold this temperature for 10 minutes, stirring occasionally.

(continued)

(continued from p. 75)

7. Pour the curds from both pots into a colander lined with cheesecloth to drain off the whey. Work quickly so the curds don't cool off. Lift the corners of the cheesecloth to encourage the whey to drain faster. Once most of the whey has drained off, add salt and gently mix the two colors of curds together.

8. Quickly transfer to the cheese mold lined with cheesecloth.

9. Place cheese mold onto a draining tray and press, using 2 1/2 lbs pressure, by placing the weight directly on top of the cheese mold follower, for 15 minutes. (You don't need a cheese press for this recipe, p. 85.) Remove cheese from press, flip over, and redress (p. 89). Press, using the same amount of pressure, for 30 minutes.

10. Remove cheese from mold, flip, and redress. Press the cheese again, using 8 3/4 lbs pressure for 1 1/2 hours. Remove cheese from mold, flip, and redress. Press again, using the same amount of pressure, for 16 hours.

11. Remove cheese from mold and cheesecloth; place on a draining tray to dry. Flip cheese over several times a day. A small fan on low placed nearby on the counter can speed up the drying process. It should take 1–3 days for the cheese to dry out. It's ready for waxing once the surface is dry to the touch (p. 69). If mold appears on the surface of the cheese during drying, wipe it away with a cloth dampened in a saltwater solution or vinegar (p. 31).

12. Once cheese is dry to the touch, apply two even coats of wax. Age the cheese at 55°F and 70% humidity for 2–3 months.

Brine

Simply put, brines are saltwater solutions that you soak cheese in to make it salty ... and delicious! But beware, brines can be finicky little devils. If the salt drops too much, there's the worry that nasty bacteria can sneak in. If the brine is too salty, cheeses can soak up way too much salt, making them inedible. In softer cheeses (like feta), they can go from just salty enough to tasting like a salt lick in no time at all. The trick is finding that perfect balance. All of the brining times in our recipes are based on fresh brines with a 73% salt saturation at 60°F (don't worry, I'll explain saturation in a bit). After brining each cheese, the saturation of the brine was tested again, and on average, the saturation level dropped 2–3% before straining and re-boiling the brine. The catch is that this is just an average, and the numbers can vary greatly after brining and again after the brine is strained and boiled to sanitize (which should happen after each use). It is for this reason that a hydrometer (more on these handy contraptions in a minute) is your best friend when preparing and maintaining brines. We can't tell you what percentage of saturation your brine is at after you've used it once; consequently, we can't tell you how much salt to add, but your hydrometer can!

Just to make matters more confusing, there are two ways of measuring brine strength: salt saturation and salt concentration. Water can only absorb so much salt. When it has absorbed all of the salt it can, the brine is 100% saturated. Salt concentration is all about the ratio of salt to water. You can buy hydrometers that measure either. If it measures salt saturation, it will have a range from 0–100. If it measures the concentration, it will have a range from 0–26 (meaning your solution is 0–26% salt by weight). We recommend a hydrometer that measures salt saturation, p. 27 (fewer cumbersome decimals and headaches).

"What is the target salt saturation of my brine and how do I test it?" A hydrometer looks like a glass thermometer, and it tests the salt saturation of a brine. Typically, this is done by filling a 1/2–gallon canning jar or test jar that is taller than the hydrometer with brine that is a specified temperature, 60°F. The hydrometer will float, and the percentage of saturation is read at the water line. Ideally, for our recipes, brine should have a 72–74% salt saturation, which is in the 19% salt concentration (the ratio of salt to water in the brine solution) range.

"If I use my brine for Swiss and then for Parmesan, do I need to worry about transferring bacteria or cultures?" Brines can be stored and reused for long periods of time as long as they are properly cared for, but there's definitely the possibility that unwanted bacteria and cultures could exist in reused brines. To reduce the chances of this, after each use, strain your brine through butter muslin to remove any particles and then bring it to a boil to sanitize it. Never let the salt saturation drop below 72% and remember to store it below 40°F (in your fridge) to prevent the growth of bacteria. As for the cultures, they could still be in the brine, so if it's a concern, keep separate brines for different cheeses.

It's also a good idea to sterilize your brine container periodically. It's also advised to test the salinity of a fresh batch of brine as well as again after straining and sanitizing used brine. The target percentage is 73%, but allowing 1/2–1% in either direction is acceptable. Dissolve small amounts of salt in the brine if it needs more salt, or add small amounts of distilled water if it's too salty. Honestly, the easiest thing to do? Make a fresh batch of brine each time.

Prep Time: 5 minutes

Cook Time: 5 minutes

Makes: 8 cups (1/2 gal)

Ingredients:

- 7 1/3 cups distilled water*
- 14 ozs (1 1/2 cups) non-iodized salt*
- 1/8 t calcium chloride

Equipment Needed:

- 4-qt stainless-steel pot
- stainless-steel measuring cups
- stainless-steel measuring spoons
- wire whisk
- glass dairy thermometer (to measure temperature of brine before using hydrometer—needs to be 60°F)
- 1/2-gal canning jar
- plastic canning-jar lid
- hydrometer, p. 27
- hydrometer test jar, p. 27
- kitchen scale

Note: Don't let the mixture boil; heat just until brine is clear and salt has dissolved. In other words, get in and get 'er done! If you keep it on the heat too long, you'll be evaporating too much of your water, and then your brine will have a higher salt saturation than our recipes call for.

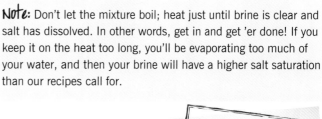

1. In a 4-qt pot over medium heat, heat water and salt, stirring constantly, until salt is dissolved.

2. Cool to 60°F and stir in calcium chloride. Test with hydrometer. Store in refrigerator in a 1/2-gal canning jar with lid.

*When preparing brine, always measure accurately! When measuring the water, be careful not to overfill the cup and spill it into the pot. Add salt by weight instead of volume. All salts are different, and the only way to get accurate results is to add the required salt by weight.

Note: Test the saturation of your brine using the hydrometer test jar. Why? When you make a fresh batch, the brine will come up to the top of a 1/2-gallon canning jar, which will work fine for floating the hydrometer. But if you're testing brine you've already used and want to re-process, it won't come up to the top of the jar, hence the handy-dandy test jar. Just pour some brine in and test, making sure the water is 60°F.

Feta

Can be made using **thermized** or **pasteurized** milk. Why not raw? p. 15–17

If using pasteurized milk, add calcium chloride, p. 24.

1. Dissolve lipase powder in 1/4 cup distilled water and allow it to rehydrate.

2. Create a double boiler by putting the milk in the smaller pot and water in the larger pot. Heat the milk to 86°F.

3. Add rehydrated lipase powder and cultured buttermilk; whisk to incorporate. Cover and let ripen for 45 minutes, holding the temperature at 86°F.

4. Dilute liquid rennet in 1/4 cup distilled water and pour into the milk. Whisk in, using a back-and-forth motion. Cover and let sit undisturbed until the curd gives a clean break (p. 63)—about 30 minutes.

5. Cut the curd into 1/2" cubes, using a curd knife. Let them rest for 10 minutes, and then stir for 15 minutes with a perforated spoon to firm up the curds and release more whey. **(Stirring for 15 minutes produces a softer feta than sold in stores, but I prefer it. If you prefer a firm feta, simply stir for 20–25 minutes, depending on your preference. Experiment with this until you get your feta the way you like it.)** During stirring, the curds will shrink and be similar in size to cottage-cheese curds. Using a ladle, drain off some of the whey until it's level with the curds.

- **Level:** Intermediate

- **Prep Time:**
  2 hours, 30 minutes

- **Draining Time:**
  19 hours

- **Brining Time:**
  2 hours

- **Makes:**
  1 1/2 lbs

- **Ingredients:** (p. 25)
  - 1/4 t mild lipase powder
  - 1/2 cup distilled water, divided
  - 1 gal **skim** milk
  - 3/4 cup cultured buttermilk (p. 43)
  - 1/4 t liquid organic vegetable rennet
  - saturated brine (p. 78)

- **Equipment Needed:**
  (p. 26–31)
  - 8-qt stainless-steel pot with lid
  - 12-qt stainless-steel pot
  - stainless-steel measuring cups
  - stainless-steel measuring spoons
  - assorted canning jars
  - wire whisk
  - floating dairy thermometer
  - thermometer
  - curd knife
  - stainless-steel perforated spoon
  - ladle
  - baking sheet
  - stainless-steel cooling rack
  - three 3.5" cheese molds
  - plastic mesh
  - latex gloves
  - thin dishtowels
  - 4-qt glass bowl

6. Place a cooling rack on top of a baking sheet, and place the three cheese molds on top of the cooling rack. Spoon the curds into the molds and cover each mold with a square of mesh. Cover with a thin dishtowel and let drain on the counter for 1 hour.

7. Gently flip the molds over so the mesh is covering the bottom of the molds and drain for 2 more hours.

8. Flip the molds back over and drain on the counter for 16 hours.

9. Remove feta from the molds and place in a 4-qt glass bowl, cover with saturated brine (p. 78), and soak in saturated brine for 2 hours, refrigerated. (For a feta that is less salty, brine for 1 1/2 hours, more salty, 2 1/2 hours.)

10. Remove feta from brine and eat within 10 days.

❧ Here's our system for selling 8 ozs of feta cheese. The top round label is a laser/inkjet 3" removable white label, 6 labels to a sheet. The clear plastic container is a "tamper evident lid" that locks as soon as the lid is attached to the container (FreundContainer.com, item #2332T11). They stack easily, and our dairy customers think they're a total class act. We charge $8 for 8 ozs of feta cheese.

Feta is characteristically a tangy, salty, crumbly cheese. Though feta is traditionally made with a combination of sheep and goat's milk, cow's milk versions are becoming more commonplace, owing their tangy flavor to the addition of lipase powder.

Manchego: man-**chay**-go, Spanish

Manchego cheese originates in the La Mancha region of Spain and is made with Manchega sheep's milk. Traditionally, Manchego cheese has a zigzag pattern on the rind, created by the molds of esparto grass and wooden presses placed on the top and bottom of the cheese. Lipase powder is used in our cow's milk version of the cheese to give it some of the piquancy that true Manchego is famous for.

Can be made using **thermized** or **pasteurized** or **raw** milk.

If using pasteurized milk, add calcium chloride, p. 24.

- **Level:** Intermediate
- **Prep Time:**
  2 hours, 15 minutes
- **Pressing Time:**
  3 hours, 15 minutes
- **Brining Time:**
  3 1/2 hours
- **Aging Time:**
  2–3 months
- **Makes:**
  about 1 lb

- **Ingredients:** (p. 25)
  - 1/4 t mild lipase powder
  - 1/2 cup distilled water, divided
  - 1 gal **whole** or **cream-line** milk
  - 1/4 cup cultured buttermilk (p. 43)
  - 1/4 cup cultured plain yogurt (p. 47)
  - 1/4 t liquid animal rennet
  - saturated brine (p. 78)

- **Equipment Needed:**
  (p. 26–31)
  - 8-qt stainless-steel pot with lid
  - 12-qt stainless-steel pot
  - stainless-steel measuring cups
  - stainless-steel measuring spoons
  - assorted canning jars
  - wire whisk
  - floating dairy thermometer
  - thermometer
  - stainless-steel perforated spoon
  - cheesecloth
  - 7-qt stainless-steel colander
  - latex gloves
  - 5" cheese mold
  - draining tray
  - cheese press with exercise weights: 8 (board)+25 +5+2 1/2+1 1/4
  - 4-qt glass bowl
  - thin dishtowels

1. Dissolve lipase powder in 1/4 cup distilled water and allow it to rehydrate.

2. Create a double boiler by putting the milk in the small pot and water in the larger pot. Heat milk to 86°F; whisk in lipase, cultured buttermilk, and cultured yogurt. Cover and let ripen for 45 minutes, holding the temperature at 86°F.

3. Dilute liquid rennet in remaining distilled water and pour into the milk. Whisk in, using a back-and-forth motion. Cover and let sit undisturbed until the curd forms a clean break (p. 63)—about 30 minutes.

4. Using a wire whisk, "cut" the curds until they're approximately 1/4". Let the curds rest for 15 minutes.

5. Slowly heat the curds to 104°F (this should take about 20 minutes), stirring with a perforated spoon.

6. Let the curds rest for 5 minutes. Then, pour the curds into a colander lined with cheesecloth to drain off the whey. Work quickly so the curds don't cool off. Lift the corners of the cheesecloth to encourage the whey to drain faster. Transfer curds to the cheese mold lined with cheesecloth.

(continued)

(continued from p. 83)

(7) Place cheese mold onto a draining tray and press, using 16 3/4 lbs pressure for 15 minutes (p. 85). After 15 minutes, remove the cheese from the mold, flip it over, and redress (p. 89).

(8) Press the cheese again, this time using 33 lbs pressure for 3 hours.

(9) After 3 hours, remove cheese from mold and cheesecloth, and place into saturated brine (p. 78) for 3 1/2 hours, refrigerated.

(10) Remove from brine and pat dry. Enjoy immediately or age at 55°F and 70% humidity for 2–3 months. If mold appears on the surface of the cheese during aging, wipe it away with a cloth dampened in a saltwater solution or vinegar (p. 31).

Weights

It seems that everyone has a set of old weightlifting weights that are abandoned, collecting dust in the back of a closet or lonely corner. As it turns out, those are exactly the kind of weights that are perfect for pressing cheese. In this circumstance, function definitely trumps aesthetics. Even if they're the oldest, ugliest set, it doesn't matter—pressing cheese gives them purpose again. Once you determine the weight of your top cutting board (ours weighed 8 lbs), you can cow-culate what size of weights you'll need to stack on top based on the amount of pressure stated in each of our recipes. With an 8-lb cutting board, we needed one 25-lb, two 10-lb, four 5-lb, three 2 1/2-lb, and one 1 1/4-lb weights (common barbell weights) for all of our cheese recipes.

Note: The cheeses you press will always sit on top of a draining tray to catch the whey.

84

Cheese Press

A cheese press is a simple device that helps apply a specified amount of pressure to cheese to expel excess whey and help create just the right balance of moisture in the cheese. There are several different types of cheese presses, including a Dutch press, which operates on a lever system and is very useful in applying large amounts of constant pressure with a limited amount of weight. Other cheese presses use a spring and board combination where the pressure is adjusted by tightening springs that put pressure on a board that sits on top of the cheese mold, which in turn puts pressure on the cheese. The amount of pressure is usually measured on a scale where the fractions of inches that the pressing board is lowered are equal to a specified weight. The primary problem with these types of presses is that as the cheese compresses and loses whey, the amount of pressure changes and needs to be adjusted constantly. The type of cheese press we prefer is a simple press that has a stationary cutting-board base and four rods attached to it at all of the corners, with another cutting board that sits on top and can be removed. The cheese mold is placed in between these boards on top of a draining tray and weights are placed onto the top board to press the cheese, applying constant and consistent pressure. This type of press is quick, simple, and inexpensive to make.

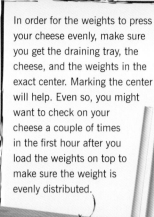

In order for the weights to press your cheese evenly, make sure you get the draining tray, the cheese, and the weights in the exact center. Marking the center will help. Even so, you might want to check on your cheese a couple of times in the first hour after you load the weights on top to make sure the weight is evenly distributed.

Making Your Own Cheese Press

- two 4" C-clamps
- two large wooden cutting boards
   (preferably 12" x 18", weighing 8 lbs ea)
- corded drill or drill press
- 7/8" spade drill bit
- hacksaw
- 5' of 1/2" PVC pipe
- four 1/2" PVC slip caps
- four 1/8"-thick by 13/16"
   inner-diameter O-rings

1. With C-clamps, securely clamp both boards together, making sure that all four sides of both boards are flush. Measure and mark 1 1/2" squarely in from each corner of the top board. Using a corded drill or drill press, drill 7/8" holes through both boards on all four measured marks.

2. Using a hacksaw, cut the PVC pipe into four 15"-long pieces.

3. Attach a slip cap to the end of each pipe, and insert capped pipes through all four holes in one of the boards, with the capped ends on the bottom (these will be the feet of the press).

4. On the other side of the board, place an O-ring at the base of each pipe to keep the pipes in place. Insert pipes through the holes in the second board and drop down.

   Note: The weight of the top cutting board will be part of the weight specified for pressing the cheeses in our recipes. For example, if your top board weighs 8 lbs and the recipe says to press the cheese using 33 lbs of pressure, you will need to use 25 lbs of weight in addition to the cutting board.

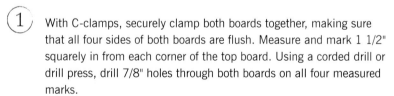

Gruyère: grew-**yair** (think "chair"), Swiss

To be perfectly honest, I haven't liked the flavor of the store-bought Gruyère cheeses I've tried. They taste "aged" all right, but not in a good way. But homemade Gruyère? Everyone who tastes it remarks enthusiastically, "Now, *that* is good-tasting cheese." Also, most store-bought Manchego cheeses are hard like Parmesan. Homemade Manchego (our recipe) is softer and out-of-this-world divine.

Ready to eat in just 3 weeks, Gruyère has one of the shortest aging times of all of the ripened cheeses in our book. Don't be afraid to age it longer—with proper aging practices, the flavor will improve and intensify over time.

If using pasteurized milk, add calcium chloride, p. 24.

① Create a double boiler by putting the milk in the smaller pot and water in the larger pot. Heat the milk to 90°F. Whisk in cultured yogurt. Remove about 1/2 cup of milk from the pot, and mix in propionibacteria. Pour back into the milk and whisk to incorporate. Cover and let ripen for 45 minutes, holding the temperature at 90°F.

② Dilute liquid rennet in distilled water and pour into the milk. Whisk in, using a back-and-forth motion. Cover and let sit undisturbed until a clean break forms (p. 63)—about 30 minutes.

③ Cut curds into 1/2" cubes with a curd knife and let them rest for 10 minutes.

④ Heat curds to 120°F, stirring frequently with a perforated spoon (this should take about 30 minutes). Once 120°F is reached, the curds should be small and rubbery (it's okay if they begin to melt together). If the curds aren't rubbery, hold them at 120°F until they are.

⑤ Pour the curds into a colander lined with cheesecloth to drain off the whey. Work quickly so the curds don't cool off. Lift the corners of the cheesecloth to encourage the whey to drain faster.

(continued)

◉ Level: Advanced

◉ Prep Time:
2 hours, 15 minutes

◉ Pressing Time:
4 hours

◉ Brining Time:
2 1/2 hours

◉ Aging Time:
3 weeks
(2 months if using raw milk)

◉ Makes:
about 1 lb

◉ Ingredients: (p. 25)
- 1 gal **whole** or **cream-line** milk
- 1/2 cup cultured plain yogurt (p. 47)
- 1/4 t propionibacteria
- 1/4 t liquid vegetable rennet
- 1/4 cup distilled water
- saturated brine (p. 78)

◉ Equipment Needed:
(p. 26–31)
- 8-qt stainless-steel pot with lid
- 12-qt stainless-steel pot
- stainless-steel measuring cups
- stainless-steel measuring spoons
- assorted canning jars
- wire whisk
- floating thermometer
- thermometer
- curd knife
- stainless-steel perforated spoon
- cheesecloth
- 7-qt stainless-steel colander
- latex gloves
- 4.9" cheese mold
- draining tray
- cheese press with exercise weights: 8 (board)+10+2 1/2
- 4-qt glass bowl
- thin dishtowels

(continued from p. 87)

6. Quickly transfer to the cheese mold lined with cheesecloth.

7. Place cheese mold onto a draining tray and press, using 8 lbs pressure for 15 minutes (p. 85). Remove cheese from press, flip over, and redress (p. 89). Press, using the same amount of pressure, for 15 minutes. Remove cheese from mold, flip, and redress.

8. Press, using 20 1/2 lbs pressure for 30 minutes. Remove cheese from press, flip, and redress. Press, using the same amount of pressure, for 3 hours.

9. After 3 hours, remove cheese from mold and cheesecloth and brine (p. 78) for 2 1/2 hours, refrigerated.

10. Remove from brine and pat dry. Age the cheese at 55°F and 70% humidity for 3 weeks (2 months if using raw milk). If mold appears on the surface of the cheese during aging, wipe it away with a cloth dampened in a saltwater solution or vinegar (p. 31).

Redressing

The process of flipping and redressing cheese is simple: After the first pressing, the cheese will be pressed into a shape that is solid enough to be handled. At this point, using gloved hands, you will remove the weights from the press and remove the mold (this is also a good time to empty the whey from the draining tray to avoid spills). Lift the follower and remove the cheese from the mold and then remove the cloth. Set the wheel aside (likely on the draining tray), and line the mold with the same cheesecloth used in the previous pressing. Flip the cheese over so the side that was on the top is now on the bottom, and cover the top with the cheesecloth (keep the cloth as flat as possible—it will imprint into the cheese, so the smoother the cloth is laid, the smoother the surface of the cheese will be), then place the follower over the cheesecloth. At this point, the cheese is ready for its next pressing.

The primary reasons for flipping and redressing the cheese are that it helps create a uniform shape and texture, and it prevents the cheesecloth from becoming embedded in the surface of the cheese (not so much fun). The purpose of producing a wheel of cheese with a smooth, even surface is more than cosmetic—cheeses with fewer surface imperfections are less likely to have cracks and crevices that invite unwanted mold.

We expect to see holes throughout a slice of Swiss cheese, but do you know why? The holes in Swiss cheese are produced by gas that is released after the cheese is pressed and brined. The holes are called "eyes," and the eye size is used to describe the cheese. Lacey Swiss is laced with small holes. Baby Swiss has slightly larger eyes and is made with whole milk. Traditional Swiss cheeses have even larger eyes, particularly those made in Switzerland. Blind Swiss has no eyes. This recipe makes a Lacey Swiss cheese.

Swiss

Can be made using **thermized** or **pasteurized** or **raw** milk.

If using pasteurized milk, add calcium chloride, p. 24.

1. Create a double boiler by putting the milk in the smaller pot and the water in the larger pot; heat milk to 90°F. Add cultured yogurt and whisk to incorporate. Remove about 1/2 cup of milk from the pot. Stir in the propionibacteria and pour back into the pot. Whisk for another 2 minutes to make sure the yogurt and propionibacteria are fully incorporated.

2. Cover and hold the temperature at 90°F for 30 minutes to ripen.

3. Dilute rennet in distilled water and pour into the milk. Whisk in using a back-and-forth motion. Cover and let sit undisturbed until a clean break forms (p. 63)—about 30 minutes.

4. Cut the curd into 1/2" cubes, using a curd knife. Let the curds rest for 10 minutes.

5. Stir the curds, using a perforated spoon, for 20 minutes, holding the temperature at 90°F.

6. Slowly heat the curds to 120°F, stirring constantly (this should take about 30 minutes).

7. Once 120°F is reached, hold the temperature to cook the curds until they hold together when squeezed (using latex gloves), but will readily break apart into small pieces.

(continued)

- **Level:** Advanced
- **Prep Time:** 3 hours
- **Pressing Time:** 20 hours, 15 minutes
- **Brining Time:** 3 hours
- **Aging Time:** 3 months
- **Makes:** 2 to 2 1/2 lbs

- **Ingredients:** (p. 25)
  - 2 gal **whole** or **cream-line** milk
  - 1 cup cultured plain yogurt (p. 47)
  - 1 t propionibacteria
  - 1/2 t liquid animal rennet
  - 1/4 cup distilled water
  - saturated brine (p. 78)

- **Equipment Needed:** (p. 26–31)
  - 12-qt stainless-steel pot with lid
  - 16-qt stainless-steel pot
  - stainless-steel measuring cups
  - stainless-steel measuring spoons
  - assorted canning jars
  - wire whisk
  - floating dairy thermometer
  - thermometer
  - curd knife
  - stainless-steel perforated spoon
  - cheesecloth
  - 7-qt stainless-steel colander
  - latex gloves
  - 7.5" cheese mold
  - draining tray
  - cheese press with exercise weights: 8 (board)+25+10+2 1/2
  - 4-qt glass bowl
  - thin dishtowels
  - 4-qt stainless-steel pot
  - 2-qt stainless-steel bowl dedicated to cheese wax
  - cheese wax
  - cheese wax brush

(continued from p. 91)

8. Once the curds are sufficiently cooked, pour the curds into a colander lined with cheesecloth to drain off the whey. Work quickly so the curds don't cool off. Lift the corners of the cheesecloth to encourage the whey to drain faster. Once most of the whey has drained, transfer curds to the cheese mold lined with cheesecloth.

9. Place cheese mold onto a draining tray and press, using 35 1/2 lbs pressure for 30 minutes (p. 85).

10. Remove cheese from mold, flip over, and redress (p. 89). Press, using 45 1/2 lbs pressure for 4 hours. Remove cheese from mold, flip, and redress. Press again, using the same amount of pressure, for 16 hours.

11. After 16 hours, remove cheese from mold and cheesecloth; brine for 3 hours, refrigerated (p. 78).

12. Remove cheese from brine and pat dry. Place on a draining tray to dry. Flip cheese over several times a day. A small fan on low placed nearby on the counter can speed up the drying process. It should take 1–3 days for the cheese to dry out. It's ready for waxing (p. 69) once the surface is dry to the touch. If mold appears on the surface of the cheese during drying, wipe it away with a cloth dampened in a saltwater solution or vinegar (p. 31).

13. Once cheese is dry to the touch, apply 2 even coats of wax. Age the cheese at 55°F and 70% humidity for 3 months.

If you have a calf born in the winter, you can get out your knitting needles (we thought our little Charlie looked dapper in blue) or you can buy a calf blanket (similar to a nylon horse blanket) from UdderTechInc.com. They offer a couple of different colors, including a pink version! Their calf blankets are Velcro-free (no yucky matted straps) and washable.

93

Parmesan is a hard, dry cheese. Traditional Parmesan cheese (Parmigiano-Reggiano, which is made exclusively in Italy) is aged for 24 months before the wheels are cut and sold. The wheels of cheese are so dense that they need to be cut with a saw. Don't be intimidated by this long aging time—our Parmesan tastes great after aging for 2 months, although it may be aged longer to develop a stronger flavor. For an even stronger flavor use cream-line milk. Parmesan cheese made with home-grown cream-line milk has an exquisite flavor and texture.

Parmesan

Can be made using **thermized** or **pasteurized** or **raw** milk.

If using pasteurized milk, add calcium chloride, p. 24.

1. Dissolve lipase powder in 1/4 cup distilled water and allow it to rehydrate.

2. Create a double boiler by putting the milk in the smaller pot and water in the larger pot. Heat the milk to 90°F. Stir in cultured yogurt and dissolved lipase. Cover and let ripen for 45 minutes, holding the temperature at 90°F.

3. Dilute rennet in remaining distilled water and pour into the milk. Whisk in, using a back-and-forth motion. Cover and let sit undisturbed until a clean break forms (p. 63)—about 45 minutes.

4. Cut the curd into 1/4" cubes, using a curd knife.

5. Heat curds to 124°F, stirring frequently with a perforated spoon (this should take about 45 minutes). Once 124°F is reached, the curds should be small and rubbery (it's okay if they begin to melt together). If the curds aren't rubbery at this point, hold them at 124°F until they are.

6. Pour the curds into a colander lined with cheesecloth to drain off the whey. Work quickly so the curds don't cool off. Lift the corners of the cheesecloth to encourage the whey to drain faster. Once most of the whey has drained, transfer curds to the cheese mold lined with cheesecloth.

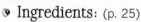

- **Level:** Advanced
- **Prep Time:**
  3 hours
- **Pressing Time:**
  12 hours, 35 minutes
- **Brining Time:**
  5 hours
- **Aging Time:**
  minimum of 2 months
- **Makes:**
  1 1/2 lbs

- **Ingredients:** (p. 25)
  - 1/4 t mild lipase powder
  - 1/2 cup distilled water, divided
  - 2 gals **whole** milk or **cream-line** milk
  - 1 cup cultured plain yogurt (p. 47)
  - 1/2 t liquid animal rennet
  - saturated brine (p. 78)

- **Equipment Needed:**
  (p. 26–31)
  - 12-qt stainless-steel pot with lid
  - 16-qt stainless-steel pot
  - stainless-steel measuring cups
  - stainless-steel measuring spoons
  - assorted canning jars
  - wire whisk
  - floating dairy thermometer
  - thermometer
  - curd knife
  - stainless-steel perforated spoon
  - cheesecloth
  - 7-qt stainless-steel colander
  - latex gloves
  - 7.5" cheese mold
  - draining tray
  - cheese press with exercise weights: 8 (board)+25+10+10+2 1/2
  - 4-qt glass bowl
  - thin dishtowels

(continued)

(continued from p. 95)

⑦ Place cheese mold onto a draining tray and press, using 28 lbs pressure for 15 minutes (p. 85). Remove cheese from mold, flip over, and redress (p. 89).

⑧ Press the cheese again, this time using 55 1/2 lbs pressure for 20 minutes. Remove cheese from mold, flip, and redress. Press again, using the same amount of pressure, for 12 hours.

⑨ Remove cheese from mold and cheesecloth; place in saturated brine (p. 78) for 5 hours, refrigerated.

⑩ Remove cheese from brine and pat dry. Age the cheese at 55°F and 70% humidity for at least 2 months. If mold appears on the surface of the cheese during aging, wipe it away with a cloth dampened in a saltwater solution or vinegar (p. 31).

Asiago

Can be made using **thermized** or **pasteurized** milk. Why not raw? p. 15–17

If using pasteurized milk, add calcium chloride, p. 24.

1. Create a double boiler by putting the milk in the smaller pot and water in the larger pot. Heat the milk to 94°F. Whisk in cultured yogurt. Remove about 1/2 cup of milk, whisk in propionibacteria, and pour back into the pot. Cover and let the milk ripen for 30 minutes.

2. Dilute rennet in the distilled water and pour into the milk. Whisk in, using a back-and-forth motion. Cover and let sit undisturbed until a clean break forms (p. 63)—about 30 minutes.

3. Cut the curds into 1/4" cubes, using a curd knife, and let them rest for 30 minutes.

4. Using a perforated spoon, gently stir the curds for 15 minutes to release more whey. Slowly heat the curds to 120°F, continuing to stir.

5. Pour the curds into a colander lined with cheesecloth to drain off the whey. Work quickly so the curds don't cool off. Lift the corners of the cheesecloth to encourage the whey to drain faster. Once most of the whey has drained, transfer curds to the cheese mold lined with cheesecloth.

6. Place cheese mold onto a draining tray and press, using 11 3/4 lbs pressure for 30 minutes (p. 85). Remove cheese from mold, flip, and redress (p. 89).

Level: Advanced

Prep Time:
2 hours, 30 minutes

Pressing Time:
4 1/2 hours, plus 24 hours weightless in draining tray

Brining Time:
8 hours

Aging Time:
at least 3 weeks

Makes:
2 to 2 1/2 lbs

Ingredients: (p. 25)
- 2 gals **whole** or **cream-line** milk
- 1/4 cup cultured plain yogurt (p. 47)
- 1/8 t propionibacteria
- 1/4 t liquid vegetable rennet
- 1/4 cup distilled water
- saturated brine (p. 78)

Equipment Needed:
(p. 26–31)
- 12-qt stainless-steel pot with lid
- 16-qt stainless-steel pot
- stainless-steel measuring cups
- stainless-steel measuring spoons
- assorted canning jars
- wire whisk
- floating dairy thermometer
- thermometer
- curd knife
- stainless-steel perforated spoon
- cheesecloth
- 7-qt stainless-steel colander
- latex gloves
- 7.5" cheese mold
- draining tray
- cheese press with exercise weights: 8 (board)+10+ 5+2 1/2+1 1/4
- 4-qt glass bowl
- thin dishtowels

7. Press the cheese again, using 25 1/2 lbs pressure for 1 hour. Remove cheese from press, flip, and redress, using the same amount of pressure, for 3 more hours. After 3 hours, remove the weights and let the cheese sit for 24 hours.

8. Remove cheese from mold and cheesecloth; place in saturated brine (p. 78) for 8 hours, refrigerated.

9. Remove cheese from brine, pat dry, and age the cheese at 55°F and 70% humidity for at least 3 weeks. If mold appears on the surface of the cheese during aging, wipe it away with a cloth dampened in a saltwater solution or vinegar (p. 31).

Quick tip

Asiago is a semi-dry Italian cheese with a texture that is reminiscent of Parmesan, but its flavor is nuttier and sweeter. The nutty flavor can be credited to the propionibacteria used to make the cheese. This is the same bacteria responsible for the eye formation in Swiss cheese. Asiago may develop a few eyes, but its shorter aging time and the small amount of the bacteria used in this recipe limit their growth. Asiago may be aged beyond 3 weeks; the texture of the cheese will become drier over time, and the flavors will intensify.

Asiago: ah-see-**ah**-go (ah—I see!), Italian

Blue Cheese

Can be made using **thermized** or **pasteurized** or **raw** milk.

If using pasteurized milk, add calcium chloride, p. 24.

1. Create a double boiler by putting the milk in the smaller pot and water in the larger pot. Heat milk to 80°F; whisk in cultured buttermilk. Cover and let ripen for 30 minutes.

2. Add penicillium roqueforti; cover and let ripen for an additional 30 minutes.

3. Dilute rennet in distilled water and add to the milk, whisking in a back-and-forth motion. Cover and let sit undisturbed until a clean break forms (p. 63)—about 30 minutes. Cut the curd into 1/2" cubes, using a curd knife, and let them rest for 10 minutes.

4. Place a cooling rack on top of a stainless-steel bowl, and place the molds on top of the cooling rack. Using a perforated spoon, transfer the curds to the molds (if all of the curds don't fit, wait until the curds in the mold have drained, then spoon in remaining curds). Cover each mold with squares of mesh and a thin dishtowel; drain on the counter for 1 hour.

5. After an hour, gently flip the molds over so the mesh is covering the bottom of the molds and let cheese drain for 2 1/2 hours.

6. Flip the cheese over one more time and allow it to drain overnight, still sitting on the counter.

Level: Advanced

Prep Time: 2 hours

Draining Time: 19 1/2 hours

Aging Time: 2–4 months

Makes: 1 1/2 to 2 lbs

Ingredients: (p. 25)
- 2 gals **whole** or **cream-line** milk
- 3/4 cup cultured buttermilk (p. 43)
- 1/4 t (one packet) penicillium roqueforti
- 1/2 t liquid animal rennet
- 1/4 cup distilled water
- 1 T non-iodized salt

Equipment Needed: (p. 26–31)
- 12-qt stainless-steel pot with lid
- 16-qt stainless-steel pot
- stainless-steel measuring cups
- stainless-steel measuring spoons
- assortment of canning jars
- wire whisk
- floating dairy thermometer
- thermometer
- curd knife
- stainless-steel perforated spoon
- stainless-steel cooling rack
- 5-qt stainless-steel bowl
- four 3.5" cheese molds
- fine plastic mesh
- thin dishtowels
- stainless-steel skewer
- latex gloves
- baking sheet
- pie carrier
- cheese planer
- aluminum foil

7   After the cheese has drained overnight, place cooling rack on top of a baking sheet, remove cheese from molds, rub the entire surface with salt, and place on the cooling rack. Cover with a thin dishtowel and let the cheese air dry to form a rind, periodically flipping cheese over and lightly sprinkling with salt.

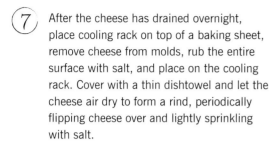

8   Once a rind has formed on the outer layer of the cheese wheels (1–2 days), poke holes through the cheese using a small, sterile, stainless-steel skewer (the number of holes you poke depends on the size of the wheel, and how much blue you want to see in your cheese).

A little extra care is needed when making this cheese—too much moisture during aging or aging the cheese for too long can easily cause the cheese to spoil. For this reason, it's important to scrape the mold off of the surface of the cheese as instructed in the recipe, and pay attention to the color of the mold. It should always be blue-green, never yellow or brown.

9   Place cheese in a sanitized, airtight container (a plastic pie carrier works well) with plenty of room to breathe (the container should be large enough that the wheels don't touch each other). Age the cheese at 55°F and 70% humidity.

10   Flip the cheese daily for the first week, then every other day the following week. After two weeks, mold should appear on the surface of the cheese. Using a cheese planer, scrape off the mold, and once again store it in an airtight plastic container at 55°F and 70% humidity for 4 weeks.

11   During these 4 weeks, flip the cheese twice a week and scrape off any mold that appears on the surface of the cheese.

12   After 4 weeks, scrape the surface of the cheese again (if needed), but this time, wrap each wheel in foil and store it in your kitchen refrigerator (36°F) to age for 30–90 days (length of time depends on how strong you want the flavor to be).

Brie

Made using **thermized** or **pasteurized** milk/cream.
Why not raw? p. 15–17

If using pasteurized milk, add calcium chloride, p. 24.

1. Create a double boiler by putting the milk and cream in the smaller pot and water in the larger pot. Heat the milk to 86°F. Whisk in buttermilk and the penicillium camemberti. Cover and ripen for 10 minutes.

2. Dilute rennet in distilled water and whisk into the milk. Cover for 45 minutes or until a clean break forms (p. 63).

3. Cut the curd into 1/2" cubes, using a curd knife, and let them rest for 10 minutes.

4. Place a cooling rack on top of a stainless-steel bowl, and place the four molds on top of the cooling rack. Using a perforated spoon, transfer the curds to the molds (if all of the curds don't fit, wait until the curds in the mold have drained, then spoon in remaining curds). Cover each mold with squares of mesh and a thin dishtowel; drain on the counter for 2 hours.

5. After 2 hours, gently flip the molds over so the mesh is covering the bottom of the molds, wait another 2 hours, and flip again. Drain overnight, still sitting on the counter.

6. After the cheese has drained overnight, place cooling rack on top of a baking sheet, remove cheese from molds, rub the entire surface with salt, and place on the cooling rack. Cover with a thin dishtowel and let the cheese air dry for 8 hours, periodically flipping cheese over and lightly sprinkling with salt.

- **Level:** Advanced
- **Prep Time:** 1 hour, 30 minutes
- **Draining Time:** 20 hours
- **Aging Time:** 1 month
- **Makes:** 2 1/2 to 3 lbs

- **Ingredients:** (p. 25)
  - 3 qts **whole** or **cream-line** milk
  - 1 qt **cream**
  - 1/4 cup cultured buttermilk (p. 43)
  - 1/8 t penicillium camemberti
  - 16 drops animal rennet
  - 2 T distilled water
  - 1 T non-iodized salt

- **Equipment Needed:** (p. 26–31)
  - 8-qt stainless-steel pot with lid
  - 12-qt stainless-steel pot
  - stainless-steel measuring cups
  - stainless-steel measuring spoons
  - assortment of canning jars
  - wire whisk
  - floating dairy thermometer
  - thermometer
  - curd knife
  - stainless-steel perforated spoon
  - stainless-steel cooling rack
  - 5-qt stainless-steel bowl
  - four 3.5" cheese molds
  - fine plastic mesh
  - thin dishtowels
  - latex gloves
  - baking sheet
  - pie carrier
  - white wrap

7. Place cheese in a sanitized, airtight container (a plastic pie carrier works well) with plenty of room to breathe (the container should be large enough that the wheels don't touch each other). Refrigerate at 36°F (in other words, your kitchen refrigerator) for 10 days, flipping every other day.

8. After 10 days, the surface of the cheese should be covered in white mold. At this point, wrap each wheel of cheese in white wrap, put back in the airtight container (sanitized again), and place in your kitchen refrigerator to age for 3 weeks, flipping cheese over every couple of days until ripe.

"My mother always said that if she had cows, she'd name them after cheeses," Amy Hetrick (p. 208) said to me when I showed up at her home, trailer in tow, to pick up her heifer, "Brie." (Amy's mother never ended up with cows, but her daughter, Amy, sure did! In addition to Jerseys, she also raises Scottish Highlands.) Brie's sister is named Cheddar. Brie was coming to my farm for a "connubial" session with one of my bulls.

The "Queen of Cheeses," our homemade Brie can be eaten at room temperature. But it softens and tastes divine when heated. Preheat your oven to 350°F. Slice off the top rind. Place on a baking sheet lined with foil and bake for 8–10 minutes. Serve with crackers, wine, and sliced fresh fruit. Also good served with chutney or preserves.

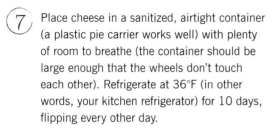

FARMSTYLE RECIPES USING DAIRY

- Milk Syrups — p. 107
- Coffee Creamers — p. 109
- Stuffed Pepper Scramblers — p. 111
- Creamy Garlic Breakfast Potatoes — p. 113
- Blueberry French Toast Casserole — p. 115

- Grilled Cheese & Pear Sandwiches — p. 117
- Eggplant Parmesan Rounds — p. 119
- Butternut Squash Gnocchi — p. 121
- Beet & Plum Salad — p. 123
- Buttermilk Ranch Dressing — p. 125
- Creamy Blue Cheese Dressing — p. 127
- Caesar Dressing — p. 129
- Roasted Red Pepper Tzatziki — p. 131
- Cabbage Soup with Blue Cheese — p. 133
- Greek Meatloaf — p. 135
- Hors d'Oeuvres — p. 137

- Buttermilk Biscuits   p. 139
- Farm Kitchen Gravy   p. 141
- Cauliflower Crust Pizza   p. 143
- Pastor's Pie   p. 145
- Stuffed Portobellos   p. 147
- Easy Cheese-y Macaroni   p. 149
- Four-cheese Macaroni   p. 151
- Macaroni & Cheese Dinner   p. 153
- Lasagna   p. 155
- White Chili with Chicken   p. 157
- Chicken & Cream Mexicana   p. 159
- Chorizo Burgers   p. 161
- Scalloped Potatoes   p. 163
- Sweet Corn Casserole   p. 165
- Make-ahead Spaghetti Pie   p. 167
- Chili with Lime Cream   p. 169
- Vegetable Galette   p. 171

- Flourless Chocolate Cake   p. 173
- Caramel Apple Cheesecake   p. 175
- Caramels   p. 177
- S'more Pie   p. 179
- Peach Crisp   p. 181
- Pastor's Wife's Pie   p. 183
- Ice Cream   p. 185
- Ice Cream Sandwiches   p. 191

FARMSTYLE RECIPES
~ Breakfast ~

Got
(chocolate)
Milk?

Chocolate Milk Syrup

Prep Time: 5 minutes
Cook Time: 8 minutes
Makes: 1 1/4 cups (approx. 13 servings)

- 2/3 cup cocoa powder
- 1 cup sugar
- 2/3 cup water
- 1/4 t salt
- 1/2 t vanilla extract

1. In a medium saucepan, whisk together cocoa powder, sugar, water, and salt.

2. Bring to a simmer over medium heat, whisking frequently. Simmer for 3 minutes, then remove from heat. Whisk in vanilla. Store in refrigerator in sealed container.

To make chocolate milk, add 1 1/2 T syrup to 1 cup cold milk and stir.

Strawberry Milk Syrup

Prep Time: 5 minutes
Cook Time: 8 minutes
Makes: 1 2/3 cups (13 servings)

- 1/2 cup organic whole food strawberry powder, Activz.com
- 3/4 cup sugar
- 1 cup water
- 1/2 t vanilla extract

1. In a medium saucepan, whisk together strawberry powder, sugar, and water.

2. Bring to a simmer over medium heat, whisking frequently. Simmer for 3 minutes, then remove from heat. Whisk in vanilla. Store in refrigerator in sealed container.

To make strawberry milk, add 2 T syrup to 1 cup cold milk and stir.

Sweetened Condensed Milk

Prep Time: 5 minutes
Cook Time: 4 hours
Makes: 3 cups

- 7 cups whole milk
- 2 1/2 cups sugar

1. In a medium saucepan over medium heat, combine milk and sugar. Heat until sugar is dissolved, and steam is rising from milk.

2. Reduce heat to low, and simmer until milk is reduced by more than half (just under 4 hours), whisking every 30 minutes.

3. Strain milk through a fine mesh sieve, and store in the refrigerator or pressure can per conventional wisdom.

The color of homemade sweetened condensed milk tends to be a little darker than its store-bought counterpart. The color is dependent on the amount of cream in the milk. The higher the cream content, the darker it will be, but it doesn't seem to affect the final color of recipes.

How lucky am I? Moda Fabrics (ModaFabrics.com) let me design cow-themed fabric in conjunction with the release of my book. What you see here is an enlarged version that's on my kitchen wall. "Milk Cow Kitchen" cotton fabric is available at your local quilt shop or FatQuarterShop.com.

Coffee Creamers

Can be made using **thermized** or **pasteurized** or **raw** milk.

Moo-ve over, Starbucks!

Coffee Creamer Base

Prep Time: 3 minutes
Cook Time: 5–7 minutes
Makes: 1 pint

- 1 2/3 cups half-and-half (p. 20)
- 2/3 cup sugar

1. In a small saucepan, combine half-and-half and sugar. While stirring constantly, heat on low just until sugar is dissolved, remove from heat, and stir in desired flavor.

Flavors

French Vanilla:
Add 1/2 t organic French vanilla flavor concentrate, NaturesFlavors.com.

Hazelnut:
Add 1 1/2 t organic hazelnut flavor concentrate, NaturesFlavors.com.

Coconut:
Add 1/4 t organic coconut flavor concentrate, NaturesFlavors.com.

Pumpkin Pie:
Add 1/4 t organic pumpkin pie flavor concentrate, NaturesFlavors.com.

Peppermint:
Add 1/2 t organic peppermint extract, FlavOrganics.com.

Mason Jar Travel Lid
With this reusable lid, you'll make any canning jar into a handy travel cup. The "cuppow" lid is super durable, made in the USA, phthalate- and BPA-free, recyclable, and it doesn't break the bank. Available in wide-mouth or regular, Amazon.com.

Mason Jar Recaps
Turn any jar into an on-the-go container with Mason Jar Recaps (Amazon.com), making Mason jars more usable than ever. Available in regular and wide-mouth sizes in silver, black, and pink.

Gluten Free

Stuffed Pepper Scramblers

1. Preheat oven to 350°F.

2. Cut off tops of peppers and remove seeds. Place peppers in an 8" x 8" baking dish; set aside.

3. In a skillet, cook bacon over medium heat, remove 2 T for garnish, add mushrooms to skillet, and cook until tender. Remove from heat and drain, if necessary.

4. In a medium bowl, whisk together eggs, sour cream, salt, and pepper. Add onions, tomato, and feta. Stir in bacon and mushrooms. Divide egg mixture evenly between the peppers. Cover with foil and bake for 70 minutes, or until eggs have set.

5. Sprinkle with Gruyère, top with bacon garnish, and bake an additional 3 minutes, or until cheese is melted.

Prep Time:
10 minutes

Cook Time:
1 1/2 hours

Makes:
6 servings

Ingredients:
- 6 yellow bell peppers
- 6 slices bacon, diced
- 1 cup mushrooms, diced
- 6 eggs
- 2 T sour cream
- 1 t salt
- 1/4 t pepper
- 1/3 cup green onions, sliced
- 1 small tomato, diced
- 1 cup feta
- 1/2 cup Gruyère, shredded

In this recipe

GRUYÈRE, see p. 87
Also: Feta, p. 80, Sour Cream, p. 45

Creamy Garlic Breakfast Potatoes

- **Prep Time:**
  35 minutes

- **Cook Time:**
  45–50 minutes

- **Makes:**
  6 servings

1. Preheat oven to 375°F.

2. In a medium skillet over medium heat, cook bacon about halfway, add garlic, and continue to cook until bacon is crispy. Drain off excess bacon grease and set aside.

3. In a small saucepan, bring wine to a slow simmer. Cook for 3 minutes, then remove from heat. Stir in cream and set aside.

4. Using a mandoline slicer (p. 163), slice potatoes to 1/8" thickness; quarter slices. In a medium bowl, toss potatoes with salt; divide half of the potatoes between six 9-oz oval, cast-iron mini-servers (Amazon.com) or a 10" oven-proof skillet. Divide 1 cup Cheddar and half the bacon and garlic mixture evenly between each dish (or layer in skillet). Top with remaining potatoes.

5. Divide cream mixture evenly between dishes (or add to skillet). Evenly divide remaining Cheddar between dishes (or add to skillet); top with remaining bacon and garlic mixture.

6. Place trays on a baking sheet, cover with foil, and bake for 40–45 minutes, or until potatoes are tender; remove foil and bake for 5 more minutes. (For 10" skillet, bake covered for 1 hour, uncovered for 5 minutes.) *In this recipe*

- **Ingredients:**
  - 1/2 lb bacon, diced
  - 6 garlic cloves, peeled and sliced
  - 1/4 cup white wine
  - 1 1/2 cups cream
  - 2 lbs red potatoes (4 medium-large potatoes), cut into 1/8" slices
  - 3/4 t salt
  - 2 1/2 cups Cheddar, shredded

- CHEDDAR, see p. 71

This dish always gets rave reviews from our B&B guests. It's a regular on our breakfast menu because it's something we can prep the night before and then pop in the oven the next morning. Just make sure you use good quality organic baguettes. The maple cream syrup has a unique flavor—a cross between something caramel-y and maple-y that's as smooth as ice cream melting in your mouth.

1. Generously butter an 8" x 8" clear glass baking dish. (Or use a 9" x 13" clear glass baking dish and double the ingredients for 8 servings.)

2. In a medium bowl, mix together baguette cubes, cream cheese, and blueberries; add to prepared baking dish.

3. In a small bowl, mix together eggs, milk, and syrup. Pour over bread mixture. Using a spatula, press ingredients down into liquid.

4. Cover with plastic wrap and refrigerate overnight.

5. Remove casserole from refrigerator 30 minutes prior to baking. Preheat oven to 350°F.

6. Remove plastic wrap, cover with aluminum foil, and bake for 35 minutes (or 45 minutes for a 9" x 13" baking dish). Remove foil and bake until top is golden brown and mixture is set in the center, about 15 minutes (or 25 minutes for a 9" x 13" baking dish).

7. Serve topped with Maple Cream Syrup.

◈ Prep Time:
20 minutes, plus overnight refrigeration

◈ Cook Time:
50 minutes

◈ Makes:
4 servings

◈ Ingredients:

- 3 cups day-old 1" baguette cubes
- 1/4 cup cream cheese (2 ozs), cut into 1" cubes
- 1/4 cup fresh or thawed frozen blueberries
- 3 eggs
- 1/2 cup milk
- 1 1/2 T maple syrup

Maple Cream Syrup

Cook Time: 15 minutes
Makes: 4 servings (double recipe for 8 servings)

- 1/2 cup maple syrup
- 1 cup cream

In a small saucepan, combine maple syrup and cream. Stir over medium heat until thickened, approximately 15 minutes. Drizzle over French Toast Casserole.

In this recipe →

◈ CREAM CHEESE, see p. 61

FARMSTYLE RECIPES
~ Lunch ~

Prep Time:
15 minutes

Cook Time:
25–30 minutes

Makes:
4 sandwiches

Ingredients:

- 4 slices bacon
- 8 slices bread
- 8 ozs Cheddar, sliced
- 1 Bartlett pear, cored and thinly sliced
- 2 cups clover sprouts
- 1/4 cup butter, melted
- honey mustard

1. Preheat oven to 400°F. Line a baking sheet with foil.

2. Place bacon on baking sheet and bake for 15 minutes, or until cooked to preference. Drain off grease and cut each slice in half.

3. Assemble sandwiches: Divide and layer Cheddar (reserving some for tops of sandwiches), pear, bacon, and clover sprouts on 4 slices of bread. Top with reserved Cheddar, and cover with remaining 4 slices of bread.

4. Brush one side of each sandwich with butter and grill in a skillet or on a griddle over medium-low heat for about 3 minutes, or until golden brown. Flip over and grill for another 3 minutes or until bread is golden brown and cheese is melted.

5. Serve with honey mustard.

To make honey mustard, combine 1/4 cup mayonnaise, 2 T yellow mustard, and 2 T honey in a small bowl. Refrigerate until ready to use.

In this recipe

CHEDDAR, see p. 71
Also: Butter, p. 37

fun fact

Did you know two-thirds of the world's eggplant is grown in New Jersey?

If anyone ever tells you that you put too much Parmesan cheese on your food, stop talking to them. You don't need that kind of negativity in your life.

1. For the topping, combine diced tomatoes, wine, garlic, salt, pepper, Italian seasoning, and brown sugar in a medium saucepan. Cook over medium-low heat until wine is reduced, about 15 minutes. Remove from heat and set aside.

2. Meanwhile, make fried eggplant: Cut eggplant into 1/4"-thick rounds and arrange in a single layer on a baking sheet. Brush with lemon juice, sprinkle with 1/4 t salt, flip over, brush with lemon juice, and sprinkle with 1/4 t salt. Set aside.

3. Combine bread crumbs, Parmesan, basil, garlic, pepper, and remaining 1/4 t salt in a medium bowl. Whisk eggs together in a small bowl.

4. Pat the eggplant dry with paper towels, flip over, and pat the other side dry. Dip eggplant rounds in egg, then coat in bread-crumb mixture.

5. In a large skillet, heat 3 T oil over medium-high heat. Fry breaded eggplant rounds for 3–4 minutes on each side, or until golden brown, adding remaining oil as needed.

6. Divide sliced mozzarella between eggplant rounds, then divide the tomato mixture evenly between the rounds; top with Parmesan.

7. Broil until mozzarella is melted.

- **Prep Time:**
  25 minutes

- **Cook Time:**
  30–35 minutes

- **Makes:**
  about 36 rounds

- **Ingredients:**

Topping
- two 14.5-oz cans diced tomatoes, drained
- 1/2 cup red wine
- 6 garlic cloves, peeled and minced
- 1/2 t salt
- 1/4 t pepper
- 1/2 t Italian seasoning
- 1 t brown sugar
- 8 ozs mozzarella, sliced
- 1/4 cup Parmesan, shredded

Fried Eggplant
- 2 Japanese eggplants
- juice of 1 lemon
- 3/4 t salt, divided
- 1 cup bread crumbs
- 1/4 cup Parmesan, shredded
- 1/4 cup fresh basil, minced
- 4 garlic cloves, peeled and minced
- 1/4 t pepper
- 2 eggs
- 6 T safflower oil, divided

In this recipe

- PARMESAN, see p. 95
  Also: Mozzarella, p. 64

This may seem like a large amount of sage, but it really gives the dish fantastic flavor. If using dried sage, use 2 1/2 T (when substituting dried herbs for fresh in recipes, the general rule of thumb is to use 1/3 of the amount).

Gnocchi: **noh**-kee, Italian, little dumplings

Gluten Free

In this recipe

ASIAGO, see p. 99
Also: Butter, p. 37

1. Preheat oven to 400°F. Line a large baking sheet with parchment paper. Set aside.

2. Peel and cut potato into 1/2" cubes. In a small bowl, toss with 1 t olive oil. Place in a small baking dish and cover with foil.

3. Seed, peel, and cut squash into 1/2" cubes. In a medium bowl, toss with remaining olive oil and 1/2 t of salt. Place in a 9" x 13" baking dish and cover with foil.

4. Roast squash and potato for 35 minutes, or until tender.

5. In a small bowl, combine rice and tapioca flours; set aside.

6. Cool potato and squash for 5 minutes, then measure out 1/2 cup of squash, reserving the rest for step 12.

7. Using a potato ricer, rice measured squash into a medium bowl, then rice potato into same bowl.

8. Add 1/2 t salt, Asiago, brown sugar, curry powder, and egg; mix well. Add flour mixture and mix until dough forms.

9. Dust a clean work surface with rice flour. Remove a small portion of the dough and roll it into a 1/2"-thick rope, dusting with rice flour as needed. Make decorative indentations in the dough by gently rolling a wire whisk along the rope. Cut rope into 1"-long pieces.

10. Carefully transfer gnocchi to prepared baking sheet as they are cut. Repeat this process until all the dough has been cut. Bake gnocchi for 12–15 minutes.

11. Add 1/4 cup of water to a medium saucepan. Add cauliflower and cover. Steam over medium heat until cauliflower is tender. Drain cauliflower and set aside.

12. Melt butter in large skillet over medium heat. Add remaining 1/2 t salt, onion, and sage. Cook until onion is tender. Add gnocchi, cauliflower, and reserved butternut squash. Continue to cook over medium heat until heated through.

- **Prep Time:**
  1 hour

- **Cook Time:**
  55 minutes

- **Makes:**
  6–8 servings

- **Ingredients:**
  - 1 medium russet potato (about 6 ozs)
  - 4 t olive oil, divided
  - 1 small butternut squash (about 2 lbs)
  - 1 1/2 t salt, divided
  - 3/4 cup rice flour, plus more for dusting
  - 1/4 cup tapioca flour
  - 1/4 cup Asiago cheese, shredded
  - 2 T brown sugar
  - 1/4 t curry powder
  - 1 egg, lightly beaten
  - 1 head cauliflower, cut into florets
  - 3/4 cup butter
  - 1 red onion, peeled, quartered
  - 1/2 cup fresh sage leaves, minced

121

"You've got to go out on a limb sometimes because that's where the fruit is."
– Will Rogers

❀ **Prep Time:**
20 minutes

❀ **Cook Time:**
45 minutes

❀ **Makes:**
10 servings

❀ **Ingredients:**
- 6 large or 12 small
  beets, peeled and cut into
  1/2" cubes (about 8 cups)
- 1/2 cup red wine vinegar
- 1 t honey
- 3/4 cup grapeseed oil
- salt and pepper to taste
- 4 cups plums, pitted
  and cut into 1/2" pieces
- 1 medium red onion, peeled and
  thinly sliced into half-rounds
- 4 cups baby spinach
  or tat soi leaves
- 1 cup (8 ozs) Soft Cheese (p. 58)

1. Preheat oven to 375°F. Place beets on a silicone mat or parchment-lined baking sheet and roast until tender, about 45 minutes. Place beets in large bowl to cool.

2. In a blender, blend vinegar and honey; gradually add oil. Add salt and pepper to taste.

3. Add plums and onion to cooled beets; toss with vinaigrette.

4. Serve over baby spinach or tat soi and sprinkle with crumbled cheese.

In this recipe

❀ SOFT CHEESE, see p. 58

Buttermilk Ranch Dressing

1 Whisk together all ingredients in a small bowl.

2 Cover and chill at least 1 hour before serving.

How to Make Spiral Radishes

Insert the corkscrew end into the top of the radish and drill through.

Move the slicing arm around the radish to slice it into a spiral.

Prep Time:
15 minutes, plus
1 hour chilling

Makes:
1 1/2 cups

Ingredients:
- 1/2 cup buttermilk
- 1/2 cup mayonnaise
- 1/4 cup sour cream
- 1 t lemon juice
- 1 T fresh dill, minced
- 1 T fresh parsley, minced
- 1 t fresh chives, minced
- 1 garlic clove, peeled and minced
- 1/4 t salt

The handy-dandy gadget shown here is sold individually as a "spiral slicer vegetable 4404" or in a kit as "garnish kitchen tool set" on Amazon.com.

In this recipe

BUTTERMILK, see p. 43
Also: Sour Cream, p. 45

1) In a small bowl, whisk together buttermilk, mayonnaise, sour cream, vinegar, sugar, and salt. Stir in crumbled blue cheese.

2) Cover and chill at least 1 hour before serving.

* **Prep Time:**
10 minutes, plus
1 hour chilling

* **Makes:**
1 1/2 cups

* **Ingredients:**
  * 1/2 cup buttermilk
  * 1/2 cup mayonnaise
  * 1/4 cup sour cream
  * 2 t white vinegar
  * 2 1/2 t sugar
  * 1/4 t salt
  * 1/2 cup blue cheese, crumbled

Iceberg Lettuce

Okay, fess up. Who doesn't love the occasional crisp, cold salad made from iceberg lettuce? We farmer types grow every lettuce *but*. But. Every now and then ...

Once the most popular lettuce in the U.S., iceberg, a variety of crisphead lettuce, has the fewest nutrients and least flavor of all the lettuces. Before modern refrigeration advances, transporting lettuce from farm to table meant only the hardiest of lettuces could be shipped safely. Iceberg was developed in the 1940s for its uniform leaves; firm, crunchy texture; and long shelf life. After that time, nearly 95% of all lettuce grown and consumed in the U.S. was crisphead lettuce. Because it was grown mostly in California and shipped by train to the rest of the country while packed in ice, it acquired the name "iceberg."

In this recipe

* **BLUE CHEESE**, see p. 100
Also: Buttermilk, p. 43, Sour Cream, p. 45

1. Whisk together all ingredients in a small bowl.

2. Cover and refrigerate at least 1 hour before serving.

Caramelized Honey Meyer Lemons:

Slice a Meyer lemon into 1/4"-thick slices. In a large skillet over medium heat, heat 1 T coconut oil and 1 T honey. Once oil is hot, add lemon slices and cook on each side for 2–3 minutes, or until golden brown.

• **Prep Time:**
10 minutes, plus
1 hour chilling

• **Makes:**
1 1/2 cups

• **Ingredients:**
- 1/2 cup buttermilk
- 1/2 cup sour cream
- 1/4 cup mayonnaise
- 1 T lemon juice
- 2 t anchovy paste
- 1 t honey
- 1/4 t salt
- 1/4 t pepper

Meyer lemons originated in China and are thought to be a cross between a lemon and a mandarin orange. They are sweeter and more fragrant than common lemons and have an intense lemon flavor, perfect for garnishing a salad.

Tip: When hand-squeezing half a lemon, squeeze it into your other hand, letting the juices go through your fingers and into a bowl. You'll end up with a handful of seeds that you can easily toss.

In this recipe

• SOUR CREAM, see p. 45
Also: Buttermilk, p. 43

Tzatziki: zat-**zee**-kee, Greek

Serving Ideas

Tzatziki is a traditional Greek and Turkish cucumber and yogurt sauce, always served cold. Try it on gyros, Greek salads, or our Greek Meatloaf, p. 135. Also good as a veggie or chip dip.

1. Preheat oven to 400°F.

2. Place bell pepper and garlic cloves on a piece of foil, drizzle with olive oil, and wrap up. Roast for 40 minutes, or until a fork easily pierces the pepper.

3. While the pepper is roasting, line a colander with a thin dishtowel and place the colander inside a bowl. Add diced cucumber and sprinkle with 1/4 t salt.

4. Remove pepper from oven and let cool. If the cucumber still has a lot of moisture, wring it out in the dishtowel.

5. In a medium bowl, combine cucumber, remaining salt, yogurt, vinegar, dill, and cayenne pepper.

6. Once pepper is cool enough to handle, peel the skin off and discard. Mash pepper and garlic into a paste; stir into yogurt mixture.

7. Cover and refrigerate for at least 1 hour before serving.

- **Prep Time:**
  50 minutes plus
      1 hour chilling

- **Cook Time:**
  40 minutes

- **Makes:**
  1 3/4 cups

- **Ingredients:**
  - 1/2 red bell pepper, seeded
  - 2 garlic cloves, peeled
  - 1/4 t olive oil
  - 1 cucumber, peeled, seeded, and finely diced
  - 3/4 t salt, divided
  - 1 1/2 cups Greek yogurt
  - 1 T red wine vinegar
  - 1/4 cup fresh dill, minced
  - 1/4 t ground cayenne pepper

In this recipe

GREEK YOGURT, see p. 49

Gluten Free

Cabbage Soup with Blue Cheese

Prep Time:
15 minutes

Cook Time:
40 minutes

Makes:
8 servings

Ingredients:
- 1/2 lb bacon, diced
- 3 medium red potatoes, peeled, and cut into 1/2" cubes
- 1 red onion, peeled and diced
- 8 cups chicken broth
- 1/2 t salt
- 1/2 t pepper
- 1 head purple cabbage, shredded (roughly 6 cups)
- 2 cups blue cheese, crumbled

1. Add bacon to a large stockpot. Cook over medium heat for 5 minutes; add potatoes. Cook for an additional 5 minutes. Add onion and cook until tender (about 5 minutes).

2. Add broth, salt, and pepper. Bring to a boil, cover, and simmer until potatoes are almost tender.

3. Stir in cabbage, cover, and simmer until tender. Serve with crumbled blue cheese.

In this recipe

BLUE CHEESE, see p. 100

Muffin-tin Meatloaf

Who doesn't remember that yummy topping on Granny's meatloaf? The topping you could never get enough of. Well, here's how you can get yummy topping with every bite. In a small bowl, combine 3/4 cup ketchup and 3 T light-brown sugar. Divide your meatloaf into 12 equal portions and shape into balls. Place in muffin cups. Spoon about 1 T topping onto each mini-meatloaf. Bake for 25 minutes, or until the internal temperature reaches 165°F.

Gluten Free

Greek Meatloaf

perfect for gyros

① In a medium bowl, combine lamb, beef, and salt. Cover with plastic wrap and refrigerate for at least 45 minutes.

② Preheat oven to 325°F.

③ Add oregano, rosemary, feta, garlic cloves, onion, pepper, red pepper flakes, and meat mixture to a food processor. Pulse until all of the seasonings are mixed into the meat.

④ Transfer mixture to a loaf pan and firmly press into pan. Bake uncovered for 1 to 1 1/4 hours, or until the internal temperature reaches 165°F.

⑤ Remove meatloaf from oven, place a layer of aluminum foil over the top, and add small weights to compress the meat (we use three 15-oz cans of food). Let meat rest for about 25 minutes before slicing (the longer the meatloaf rests, the easier it will slice).

● Prep Time:
  15 minutes, plus
    45 minutes chilling

● Cook Time:
  1 to 1 1/4 hours, plus
    25 minutes resting

● Makes:
  6–8 servings

● Ingredients:
  • 1 lb ground lamb
  • 3/4 lb lean ground beef
  • 1 t salt
  • 1/4 cup fresh oregano
  • 1 fresh rosemary sprig
  • 3/4 cup feta
  • 3 garlic cloves, peeled
  • 2 T dried minced onion
  • 1/4 t pepper
  • 1/4 t red pepper flakes

In this recipe

● FETA, see p. 80

Hors d'Oeuvres

Salt & Pepper Salmon Chips

Prep Time: 15 minutes
Makes: 25–35 chips

Ingredients:
- 1 cup (8 ozs) cream cheese
- 1 T lemon juice
- 1 bag salt & pepper potato chips
- 4 ozs thinly sliced smoked salmon, cut into bite-size pieces
- 1 T capers

1. In a small bowl, whip together cream cheese and lemon juice. Place mixture into pastry bag.
2. Arrange chips on serving platter and top each chip with one piece of salmon. Add a decorative dollop of cream cheese to the salmon and top with a caper.

In this recipe

CREAM CHEESE,
see p. 61

Soft Cheese Tapenade

Prep Time: 10 minutes
Makes: 2 1/2 cups

Ingredients:
- 1/2 cup (4 ozs) soft cheese
- 1 cup pitted green olives, drained
- 1 cup pitted kalamata olives, drained
- 1/4 cup fresh flat Italian parsley, minced
- 1/2 t red pepper flakes (optional)
- crackers or baguette slices

1. Place cheese in a food processor and pulse until smooth.
2. Add olives, parsley, and pepper flakes. Pulse until mixed but still chunky.
3. Serve on crackers or baguette slices.

In this recipe

SOFT CHEESE,
see p. 58

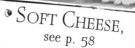

FARMSTYLE RECIPES
~ Dinner ~

Buttermilk Biscuits

1. Preheat oven to 450°F and line a baking sheet with parchment paper.

2. Toss dry ingredients into a bowl, stir them together with your fingers, and work the butter in with your fingertips until it looks like coarse crumbs. Work quickly—for the flakiest biscuits, you want the fat to stay cold and lumpy.

3. Make a valley in the center and pour in the buttermilk; stir.

4. Work the dough with your hands until it just comes together in a sticky mass.

5. Flour your countertop generously and roll the dough just enough to get it into a rough round about 1" thick.

6. Using a biscuit cutter or floured drinking glass, cut biscuits with a firm downward press.

7. Place biscuits on a baking sheet, allowing the sides to touch slightly. At this point, either re-roll the rest of the dough briefly to cut out more biscuits, or just put up with oddly-shaped scraps pushed together into makeshift biscuits. I recommend the second option. They're not as pretty, but they're much flakier than biscuits from dough that has been rolled twice.

8. Bake until the biscuits are tall and golden on top, about 15 minutes.

- **Prep Time:**
  15 minutes

- **Cook Time:**
  about 15 minutes

- **Makes:**
  six 3" biscuits

- **Ingredients:**
  - 2 cups flour
  - 4 t aluminum-free baking powder
  - 1/4 t baking soda
  - 1/4 t salt
  - 4 1/2 T cold butter, cut into pieces
  - 1 cup cold buttermilk

In this recipe

- **BUTTERMILK**, see p. 43
  Also: Butter, p. 37

Okay, I know it's far from the latest health craze, but I also know I'm not the only one who thinks biscuits and gravy once in a while. Gravy isn't about watching your waistline or counting calories (obviously), but if it's savored in moderation, it doesn't have to be. Gravy is the stuff of old-time hearty sustenance, conjuring up notions of cozy country kitchens where families gathered to satisfy belly and soul. The thing that puzzles me in this era of modern quick-fixes is the profusion of powdered gravy mixes on the market, as if somebody is trying to convince us there's a trick—or a lot of time—involved in making gravy. Hogwash! Gravy is a snap to make. It's one of the quickest components of a meal, even when it's simmered from scratch. What's more, homemade gravy is incredibly rich and delicious, lacking that strange chemical bite you'll find in packaged mixes.

Here are five farm kitchen recipes that will warm up all sorts of "down home" family meals. Enjoy them as they are, or get groovy with a splash of wine and a little garlic, or add extra pinches of cayenne, chipotle, and other sizzling spices to kick up the heat.

Basic Pan Gravy
- 2 cups pan drippings from a turkey or chicken, divided (supplemented with extra chicken stock as needed)
- 1/4 cup milk (water or stock can be substituted)
- 1/4 cup flour
- salt and pepper to taste

Pour 1/2 cup of the pan drippings (fat included) into a small bowl and add milk. Whisk in flour, mashing any lumps as you mix. Add remaining 1 1/2 cups of pan drippings to a saucepan and heat over medium heat. Stirring constantly, add flour mixture in a steady stream. Continuing to stir, cook until gravy thickens. To thin, add a few tablespoons of milk or water. To thicken, add a pinch of flour. Cook and stir for about 1 minute. Season to taste.

Giblet Variation
- giblets (liver, heart, and gizzard) and neck from turkey or chicken, cooked with the bird
- 2 cups pan drippings from turkey or chicken, divided (supplemented with extra chicken stock as needed)
- 1/4 cup milk (water or stock can be substituted)
- 1/4 cup flour
- salt and pepper to taste

Dice the giblets and the meat from the neck; set aside. Pour 1/2 cup of the pan drippings (fat included) into a small bowl and add milk. Whisk in flour, mashing any lumps as you mix. Add giblets, neck meat, and remaining 1 1/2 cups pan drippings to a saucepan and heat over medium heat. Stirring constantly, add flour mixture in a steady stream. Continuing to stir, cook until gravy thickens. To thin, add a few tablespoons of milk or water. To thicken, add a pinch of flour. Cook and stir for about 1 minute. Season to taste.

quick tip

When it comes to basic gravy, remember the 4-4-2 rule of thumb: 4 T oil/fat/butter, 4 T flour, 2 cups meat juices or drippings.

Or alternatively, the 4-1 rule: 4 T flour completely dissolved in 1 cup milk or water (a blender works well) added in a slow stream to simmering meat juices while stirring constantly.

Sausage (or Bacon) Gravy
- 1/2 lb sausage or 6 slices bacon
- 1/4 cup flour
- 2 cups milk (or 1 cup milk plus 1 cup water)
- salt and pepper to taste

Brown sausage or bacon in a cast-iron skillet. Remove meat and all but 1/4 cup of drippings from skillet. Add flour to the drippings in skillet. Cook and stir over medium heat until the flour mixture browns. Add 2 cups milk (or 1 cup milk plus 1 cup water) and mix vigorously. Break up sausage or crumble bacon and add to skillet. Continue to cook and stir until thickened. Season to taste.

Roast-beef Gravy
- 2 cups roast-beef drippings (supplemented with extra beef stock as needed)
- 1/4 cup flour
- salt and pepper to taste

Pour 3/4 cup of the drippings (fat included) into a small bowl. Whisk in flour, mashing any lumps as you mix. Add remaining 1 1/4 cups of drippings to a saucepan and heat over medium heat. Stirring constantly, add flour mixture in a steady stream. Continuing to stir, cook until gravy thickens. To thin, add a few tablespoons of water. To thicken, add a pinch of flour. Cook and stir for about 1 minute. Season to taste.

Veggie Gravy
- 1/4 cup olive oil
- 1 T minced garlic
- 1/4 cup flour
- 2 t nutritional yeast
- 1/4 t dried sage
- 2 T soy sauce
- 2 cups vegetable broth
- salt and pepper to taste

Heat oil in a saucepan over medium heat. Sauté garlic until soft and brown, about 5 minutes. Whisk in flour, nutritional yeast, and sage, forming a smooth paste. Slowly whisk in soy sauce and broth; bring to a boil. Reduce heat to simmer, stirring constantly until thickened. Season to taste.

Gluten
Free

142

◉ **Prep Time:**
25 minutes

◉ **Cook Time:**
45 minutes

◉ **Makes:**
one 12" pizza

◉ **Ingredients:**

Crust
- 1 large head cauliflower
- 2 cups mozzarella, shredded
- 2 eggs
- 1/4 t salt
- 1/4 t pepper

Toppings
- 1/2 cup basil pesto
- 2 1/2 cups mozzarella, shredded
- 1 Roma tomato, thinly sliced

① Fill a medium saucepan halfway with water. Cut cauliflower into florets and add to pan. Bring to a boil and cook until tender. Drain cauliflower.

② Using a cheese grater or potato ricer, finely grate cauliflower. Place cauliflower in a thin dishtowel and wring out any extra moisture (after removing excess moisture, there should be about 2 1/4 cups of grated cauliflower).

③ Preheat oven to 450°F. Line a pizza pan with parchment paper.

④ Combine cauliflower, mozzarella, eggs, salt, and pepper in a medium bowl. Spoon mixture onto pizza pan and spread out evenly, forming a raised crust at the edges.

⑤ Bake pizza crust for 20 minutes.

⑥ Spread pesto over the crust; top with mozzarella and tomato.

⑦ Bake for 10–12 minutes, until cheese is melted and bubbling.

In this recipe

◉ MOZZARELLA, see p. 64

fun fact

Ever heard of Pastor's Pie? Aiming to please, the women of a congregation would deliver to their pastor one of their prize-winning best. His favorite, as it turns out, involved a chicken and a Dutch oven. The instructions for this recipe might seem fussy, but trust me, it's well worth the effort. It's the best "chicken pot pie" you'll ever eat.

In this recipe

● BUTTERMILK, see p. 43
Also: Butter, p. 37

144

① Preheat oven to 450°F. Remove the giblet package from the inside of the chicken.

② Stuff the cavity of the chicken with 5 whole, unpeeled garlic gloves, half an onion, and the bottom portion of the celery bunch.

③ Rub the outside of the chicken with 1 t salt and 3/4 t pepper. In a 5-qt lidded Dutch oven, heat olive oil over medium-high heat for 2 minutes.

④ Place the whole chicken into the Dutch oven, uncovered, and sear both sides for 5 minutes each.

⑤ Remove the Dutch oven from heat, cover, and bake, breast side down, at 450°F for 1 hour, or until internal temperature of the legs reaches 160°F.

⑥ Once the chicken is cooked, remove from oven, remove the lid, and allow it to cool for 1 hour.

⑦ Once the chicken has cooled, remove it from the Dutch oven, leaving the pan drippings inside the Dutch oven.

⑧ Preheat oven to 450°F. Remove all of the meat from the chicken and cut it into small pieces.

⑨ Over medium heat, reheat the pan drippings inside the Dutch oven.

⑩ Dice remaining onion and add it to the pan; cook for 3 minutes. Then add sliced celery. Allow mixture to cook for 5 minutes, then stir in the sliced carrots, and cook for an additional 5 minutes.

⑪ In a small bowl, mix cornstarch and water. Slowly pour the cornstarch into the Dutch oven, and cook until mixture has thickened; remove from heat.

⑫ Add the diced chicken, peas, remaining 1 t salt, and remaining 3/4 t pepper to the Dutch oven. Stir to combine.

⑬ To prepare biscuit topping, add flour, baking powder, salt, and baking soda to a medium bowl. Cut in butter using a pastry blender or fork. The mixture should resemble coarse crumbs. Pour in buttermilk and stir until dough forms.

⑭ On a lightly floured surface, roll out biscuit dough to 1/4" thickness. Use the Dutch oven lid to stamp a depression in the dough to make a topping that fits perfectly over the top of the pie.

⑮ Bake at 450°F uncovered for 20 minutes, or until biscuit topping is golden brown.

🕐 **Prep Time:**
1 hour 30 minutes plus
1 hour cooling

🕐 **Cook Time:**
1 hour 45 minutes

🕐 **Makes:**
8 servings

🕐 **Ingredients:**
- 4–5 lb whole chicken
- 5 garlic cloves
- 1 1/2 onions, peeled, divided
- 1 celery bunch bottom
- 2 t salt, divided
- 1 1/2 t pepper, divided
- 2 T olive oil
- 2 cups celery, sliced
- 4 carrots, sliced
  (about 2 cups)
- 2 T cornstarch
- 2 T cold water
- 2 cups peas

Biscuit Topping
- 1 1/3 cups flour, plus
  more for dusting
- 1 t baking powder
- 1/2 t salt
- 1/4 t baking soda
- 3 T butter
- 2/3 cup buttermilk

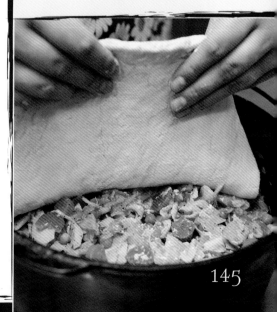

Gluten
Free

146

- **Prep Time:**
  25–28 minutes

- **Cook Time:**
  20–25 minutes

- **Makes:**
  4 servings

- **Ingredients:**
  - 1 cup milk
  - 1/4 cup polenta
  - 1/4 t pepper
  - 1/8 t salt
  - 1/2 cup diced ham
  - 2 T butter
  - 1 onion, peeled and cut in 1/8" slices
  - 4 Portobello mushroom caps, stemmed
  - 4 slices tomato, 1/4" thick
  - 1 cup Swiss, grated
  fresh parsley for garnish

① Preheat oven to 400°F. Lightly butter a 9" x 13" baking dish.

② In a 2-qt saucepan over medium heat, heat milk to just boiling. Whisk in the polenta, pepper, and salt. Cook until thickened; stir in ham. Remove from heat and set aside.

③ In a large skillet, melt butter over medium-high heat. Add onion slices and sauté for 6–8 minutes, until golden brown.

④ To assemble, place the mushroom caps into the prepared baking dish. Place a tomato slice in the bottom of each mushroom cap. Divide the polenta mixture evenly among the mushrooms, followed by the caramelized onions. Divide Swiss cheese evenly among mushrooms.

⑤ Bake for 20–25 minutes, or until the mushroom caps are tender. Top with parsley.

quick tip

What is an Heirloom?

Heirloom varieties are plants that maintain their traits from one generation to the next. Besides boasting lush colors and succulent flavors, heirloom fruits and veggies are also rich in history. Their sacred seeds have been passed down through generations, developing natural disease resistance and acquiring abundant nutrients.

In this recipe

- SWISS, see p. 91
  Also: Butter, p. 37

Easy Cheese-y Macaroni

1. Preheat oven to 350°F.

2. Bring a pot of water to a boil and cook macaroni until al dente; drain.

3. In a large bowl, combine pasta, salt, cheese, and sour cream; set aside.

4. Melt butter in a large skillet and add onion. Cook for about 6 minutes, stirring occasionally, until golden brown; remove from heat.

5. Transfer half of pasta mixture to a 9" x 13" baking dish and layer half of the onion, then remaining pasta mixture. Pour milk over all and top with remaining onion.

6. Cover with foil and bake for 45–50 minutes.

- **Prep Time:**
  30 minutes

- **Cook Time:**
  45–50 minutes

- **Makes:**
  12 servings

- **Ingredients:**
  - 1 lb elbow macaroni
  - 1 t salt
  - 6 cups Colby-Jack, shredded
  - 1 1/2 cups sour cream
  - 3 T butter
  - 1 large yellow onion, peeled and thinly sliced
  - 1 1/2 cups whole milk

in this recipe

COLBY-JACK, see p. 75
Also: Sour Cream, p. 45, Butter, p. 37

Gluten
Free

Words like peerless, unsurpassed, look-no-further, and greatest-tasting-ever have been used to describe this recipe. Be fearless and dive in!

Four-cheese Macaroni

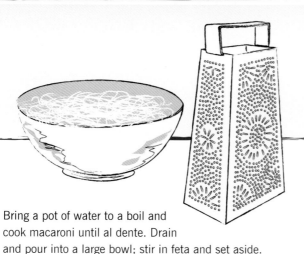

1. Bring a pot of water to a boil and cook macaroni until al dente. Drain and pour into a large bowl; stir in feta and set aside.

2. Meanwhile, in a medium saucepan, melt butter over medium heat. Add onion and cook until golden brown (about 6 minutes). Add dry mustard, salt, pepper, and cream. Bring to a low boil, reduce heat to low, and simmer until the cream is slightly thickened and reduced (about 8 minutes).

3. Preheat oven to 350°F.

4. Stir sour cream into the cream mixture and bring to a slow simmer. In a medium bowl, combine Asiago, Monterey Jack, and Parmesan. Reserve about 1 cup for topping. Slowly stir in remaining cheese to cream mixture.

5. Pour the sauce into the bowl with the macaroni and stir. Pour mixture into an 8" x 8" baking dish, top with reserved cheese, and bake for 30 minutes, or until cheese is golden brown.

☞ **Prep Time:**
20 minutes

☞ **Cook Time:**
30 minutes

☞ **Makes:**
6–8 servings

☞ **Ingredients:**
- 12 ozs brown-rice macaroni
- 1/2 cup feta
- 2 T butter
- 1 yellow onion, peeled and diced
- 2 t dry mustard
- 3/4 t salt
- 1/4 t pepper
- 2 1/4 cups cream
- 1/2 cup sour cream
- 2 cups Asiago, shredded
- 2 cups Monterey Jack, shredded
- 1/2 cup Parmesan, shredded

In this recipe

☞ **ASIAGO,** see p. 99
Also: Feta, p. 80, Butter p. 37, Monterey Jack, p. 67, Parmesan, p. 95, Sour Cream, p. 45

1. Bring a pot of water to a boil and cook macaroni until al dente. Drain and pour into medium bowl; stir in feta and set aside.

2. In a large skillet over medium heat, partially cook bacon (you want it soft and pliable to wrap around asparagus spears). Remove bacon from skillet, leaving bacon grease.

3. Preheat oven to 350°F and line a baking sheet with foil.

4. Wrap bacon around asparagus spears, securing tops and bottoms with toothpicks. Bake until the bacon is crispy, leaving oven on.

5. Carefully remove stems and gills from mushrooms and discard. In a medium bowl, combine flour, mustard, and 1/4 t salt. Dredge mushroom caps in flour mixture and fry in the skillet with bacon grease over medium-high heat for 2–3 minutes on each side.

6. Place mushroom caps on a baking sheet. Evenly divide Brie between mushroom caps. Set aside.

7. In a medium saucepan, melt butter over medium heat. Add yellow onion and remaining 1/4 t salt. Cook until golden brown, about 6 minutes. Add wine and cook until reduced by about half (about 5 minutes).

8. Pour in cream, bring to a simmer, reduce heat to low, and cook for 8–10 minutes, stirring frequently.

9. In a small bowl, combine Monterey Jack and Asiago. Reserve about 1/4 cup for topping. Slowly stir in remaining cheese to cream mixture.

10. Add macaroni to sauce, divide evenly between the mushroom caps, and sprinkle with reserved cheese. Bake for 8–10 minutes, until cheese is golden brown. Serve with bacon-wrapped asparagus.

- **Prep Time:**
  30 minutes

- **Cook Time:**
  1 hour, 10 minutes

- **Makes:**
  4 servings

- **Ingredients:**
  - 1 cup brown-rice macaroni
  - 1/4 cup feta
  - 8 slices bacon
  - 8 asparagus spears
  - 4 Portobello mushrooms
  - 1/4 cup flour
  - 1 t dry mustard
  - 1/2 t salt, divided
  - 1/2 cup (4 ozs) Brie, cut into 1" pieces
  - 1 T butter
  - 1/2 yellow onion, peeled and diced
  - 1/4 cup white wine
  - 1 cup cream
  - 1 cup Monterey Jack, shredded
  - 1 cup Asiago, shredded

In this recipe

- MONTEREY JACK, see p. 67
Also: Feta, p. 80, Brie, p. 102, Butter, p. 37, Asiago, p. 99

Gluten Free

154

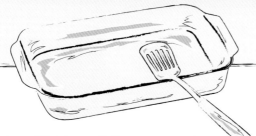

1. In a deep skillet, brown Italian sausage and chorizo. Once meat is browned, add onion, garlic, tomato sauce, diced tomatoes, pepper, bay leaf, Italian seasoning, and red wine. Simmer for 30 minutes.

2. While sauce is simmering, cook lasagna noodles according to package directions. Drain and cool noodles.

3. Preheat oven to 375°F.

4. Remove sauce from heat and discard bay leaf.

5. Spread a thin layer of sauce over the bottom of a 9" x 13" baking dish. Cover the sauce with 3 lasagna noodles. Spread half of the cottage cheese over noodles, spread half of the sauce over cottage cheese, and cover with about 2 cups of mozzarella. Add another layer of noodles, remaining cottage cheese, remaining sauce, and 2 cups of mozzarella. Add a final layer of noodles and sprinkle remaining mozzarella and the Parmesan over the top.

6. Place baking dish on a baking sheet, cover with foil, and bake for 30 minutes, then bake uncovered for 15–20 minutes, until cheese is lightly browned and lasagna is heated through. Let cool for 10–15 minutes before serving. Garnish with basil.

Prep Time:
30 minutes

Cook Time:
1 hour, 45 minutes

Makes:
12 servings

Ingredients:
- 1 lb ground sweet Italian sausage
- 1 lb ground chorizo
- 1 yellow onion, peeled and diced
- 5 garlic cloves, peeled and minced
- two 15-oz cans tomato sauce
- one 14 1/2-oz can diced tomatoes, drained
- 1/4 t pepper
- 1 bay leaf
- 1 1/2 t Italian seasoning
- 1/2 cup red wine
- 9 brown-rice lasagna noodles
- 3 cups cottage cheese
- 6 cups mozzarella, shredded
- 1/2 cup Parmesan, shredded
fresh basil for garnish

In this recipe

COTTAGE CHEESE, see p. 62
Also: Mozzarella, p. 64, Parmesan, p. 95

White Chili with Chicken

Prep Time:
20 minutes

Cook Time:
40 minutes

Makes:
6 servings

Ingredients:

- 1 lb boneless, skinless chicken breasts, diced (2 breasts)
- 1 yellow onion, peeled and diced
- 4 garlic cloves, peeled and minced
- 1 T olive oil
- 1 t chili powder
- 1/2 t cumin
- 1/4 t cayenne pepper
- 1 t salt
- 2 cups chicken broth
- two 15-oz cans white beans, rinsed and drained
- 1 cup corn kernels
- 2 jalapeño peppers, seeded and minced
- 1 cup sour cream
- juice of 1 lime
- 3/4 cup Colby-Jack, shredded

1. In a medium saucepan, combine chicken, onion, garlic, olive oil, chili powder, cumin, cayenne pepper, and salt. Cook over medium heat until chicken is cooked through.

2. Add chicken broth, white beans, corn, and jalapeño pepper.

3. Bring to a simmer, reduce heat to low, and stir in sour cream and lime juice.

4. Top chili with Colby-Jack.

In this recipe

COLBY-JACK, see p. 75
Also: Sour Cream, p. 45

157

- **Prep Time:**
  20 minutes

- **Cook Time:**
  25 minutes

- **Makes:**
  6 servings

- **Ingredients:**
  - 2 T coconut oil
  - 1 1/2 lbs boneless, skinless chicken breasts (about 3 breasts), diced
  - 5 garlic cloves, peeled and minced
  - 1 jalapeño, seeded and minced
  - 1 t salt, divided
  - 1/8 t pepper
  - 1/4 t cayenne pepper
  - 12 button mushrooms, quartered
  - 1 2/3 cups sour cream
  - 3 cups Monterey Jack, shredded
  - fresh cilantro for garnish
  - flour tortillas
  - cooked brown rice

1. In a large skillet over medium heat, combine oil, chicken, garlic, jalapeño, 1/2 t salt, pepper, and cayenne pepper. When chicken is mostly cooked, add mushrooms and cook until mushrooms are tender; remove from heat.

2. While the chicken and mushrooms are cooking, heat sour cream and remaining salt in a large saucepan over medium-low heat; stirring constantly.

3. Once sour cream is hot, slowly begin adding cheese, stirring well after each addition. Stir in chicken and mushroom mixture, including resulting liquid.

4. Serve with flour tortillas and brown rice.

In this recipe

- MONTEREY JACK, see p. 67
Also: Sour Cream, p. 45

159

1. Make pesto: add cilantro, chives, almonds, serrano pepper, garlic, salt, paprika, Manchego, lime juice, and olive oil to a food processor; pulse to combine and set aside.

2. For the burgers, combine chorizo, ground beef, serrano pepper, garlic, salt, and pepper. Shape mixture into 4 patties.

3. In a large skillet, fry burgers over medium heat, flipping after about 6 minutes. Top with sliced Manchego and fry until cooked through (note: the longer your Manchego is aged, the longer it will take to melt).

4. While the burgers are cooking, brush the hamburger buns with butter and broil until golden brown.

5. Serve burgers with cilantro pesto, romaine lettuce, and sliced tomato.

Prep Time:
30 minutes

Cook Time:
12–15 minutes

Makes:
4 burgers

Ingredients:

Cilantro Pesto
- 3 cups cilantro
- 1/4 cup chives
- 2 T slivered almonds
- 1/2 serrano pepper, seeded
- 2 garlic cloves, peeled
- 1/2 t salt
- 1/4 t paprika
- 1/4 cup Manchego, grated
- juice of 1 lime
- 1 t olive oil

Burgers
- 1/2 lb ground chorizo
- 1/2 lb lean ground beef
- 1/2 serrano pepper, seeded and minced
- 2 garlic cloves, peeled and minced
- 1/8 t salt
- 1/4 t pepper
- 4 slices Manchego
- 4 hamburger buns
- 1 T butter, melted
- 4 leaves romaine lettuce
- 1 tomato, sliced

In this recipe

MANCHEGO, see p. 83
Also: Butter, p. 37

Scalloped Potatoes

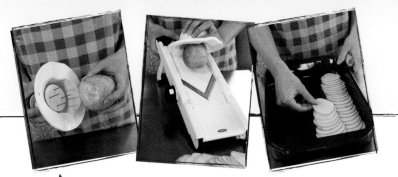

If you haven't discovered a mandoline slicer yet (Amazon.com), it's a fabulous tool!

① Preheat oven to 350°F. Lightly butter a 9" x 13" baking dish.

② In a medium bowl, combine Gruyère, Swiss, and Asiago cheeses; set aside.

③ In a medium saucepan over medium heat, melt butter. Add onion and cook until golden brown, about 6 minutes; stir in flour.

④ Add white wine, milk, cream, salt, and pepper; mix well. Remove from heat.

⑤ Add a layer of potatoes to the casserole dish, overlapping each slice. Pour about 1/2 cup of the sauce over potatoes, and sprinkle about 1/3 cup cheese over top. Repeat with remaining potatoes, sauce, and cheese.

⑥ Cover dish with foil and bake for 1 hour. Remove foil and bake an additional 30 minutes.

For 6 servings, prepare an 8" x 8" baking dish and cut recipe in half. Bake covered at 350°F for 45 minutes, and uncovered for 15 minutes.

- **Prep Time:**
  35 minutes

- **Cook Time:**
  1 hour, 40 minutes

- **Makes:**
  12 servings

- **Ingredients:**
  - 1 1/4 cups Gruyère, grated
  - 1 1/4 cups Swiss, grated
  - 3/4 cup Asiago, grated
  - 4 T butter
  - 1 yellow onion, peeled and diced
  - 2 T flour
  - 1/4 cup white wine
  - 2 cups milk
  - 1 cup cream
  - 1 1/2 t salt
  - 1/2 t pepper
  - 2 1/2 lbs Yukon Gold potatoes, sliced 1/8" thick

In this recipe

GRUYÈRE, see p. 87
Also: Swiss, p. 91, Asiago, p. 99, Butter, p. 37

163

Gluten Free

Sweet Corn Casserole

1. Preheat oven to 350°F. Generously butter an 8" x 8" clear, glass baking dish. (Or use a 9" x 13" clear, glass baking dish and double the ingredients for 12 servings.)

2. Combine 1 cup corn and eggs in a food processor; blend. Transfer to a large bowl. Add butter, sour cream, sugar, and salt; mix thoroughly. Add remaining 1/2 cup corn, green chiles, and ham (optional); mix.

3. In another bowl, combine cornmeal, flour, and baking powder.

4. Combine wet and dry ingredients; stir until just blended.

5. Transfer mixture to prepared baking dish. Bake until casserole is puffed in center, golden brown around edges, and a knife inserted in the center comes out clean, about 50 minutes (60 minutes if doubling the recipe).

Makes a great potluck or breakfast dish!

● **Prep Time:**
20 minutes

● **Cook Time:**
50 minutes

● **Makes:**
6 servings

● **Ingredients:**
- 1 1/2 cups fresh or thawed frozen corn, divided
- 2 eggs
- 1/2 cup butter, melted and slightly cooled
- 3/4 cup sour cream
- 1/2 cup sugar
- 1 t salt
- one 4-oz can diced green chiles (can substitute 1/2 cup fresh poblano chile, finely diced)
- 1/2 cup cooked ham, cut into 1/4" cubes (optional)
- 1 cup cornmeal
- 2/3 cup white rice flour
- 1 T baking powder

In this recipe

● BUTTER, see p. 37
Also: Sour Cream, p. 45

Not only a life-saver on those evenings you want to arrive home and do nothing but pop something yummy into the oven, my Spaghetti Pie is also a hit at potlucks. Who wouldn't want a wedge of perfectly balanced spaghetti flavors in an easy-to-serve shape? Before wheat harvest every year, I used to build a dozen of these and put them in my freezer.

(1) Cook spaghetti according to package directions; drain, and toss with butter. Stir in Parmesan and eggs.

(2) Lightly butter two 9" pie plates. Evenly divide spaghetti mixture between pie plates. Over each dish, spread a layer of cottage cheese, then a layer of spaghetti sauce. Top with mozzarella.

(3) Cover with aluminum foil and freeze for baking at a later date. (Thaw before baking.)

(4) To bake, preheat oven to 350°F. Bake uncovered for 40 minutes. Let sit for 5 minutes before serving.

❧ **Prep Time:**
15 minutes

❧ **Cook Time:**
50 minutes

❧ **Makes:**
12 servings

❧ **Ingredients:**
- 12 ozs spaghetti
- 3 T butter, melted
- 3/4 cup Parmesan, grated
- 3 eggs, whisked
- 2 1/4 cups cottage cheese
- 3 cups spaghetti sauce
- 1 1/2 cups mozzarella, shredded

In this recipe

❧ MOZZARELLA, see p. 64

❧ COTTAGE CHEESE, see p. 62

❧ BUTTER, see p. 37

❧ PARMESAN, see p. 95

Chili with Lime Cream

Prep Time:
25 minutes

Cook Time:
50–55 minutes

Makes:
8–10 servings

① In a large saucepan or Dutch oven, combine olive oil, onion, garlic, bell pepper, carrot, and celery. Cook over medium heat until the vegetables are tender, about 7 minutes.

② Add the black beans, red beans, diced tomatoes, tomato sauce, honey, adobo sauce, coriander, chili powder, cumin and salt.

③ Simmer for 45 minutes, stirring occasionally.

④ In a small bowl, combine sour cream with lime zest and juice. Serve chili with a dollop of lime cream, grated Manchego, and cilantro.

Ingredients:
- 2 T olive oil
- 1 yellow onion, peeled and diced
- 3 garlic cloves, peeled and minced
- 1 red bell pepper, seeded and diced
- 1 carrot, diced
- 1 celery bunch, sliced
- two 15-oz cans black beans, drained and rinsed
- one 15-oz can small red beans, drained and rinsed
- one 14 1/2-oz can diced tomatoes
- three 15-oz cans tomato sauce
- 1 T honey
- 2 t adobo sauce
- 1/2 t ground coriander
- 1 T chili powder
- 1 1/2 t cumin
- 1 1/2 t salt

grated Manchego for garnish
fresh cilantro for garnish

Lime Cream
- 2 cups sour cream
- 1 lime, zest and juice

In this recipe

SOUR CREAM, see p. 45
Also: Manchego, p. 83

169

1. Preheat oven to 400°F. Add sweet potato, beet, parsnip, onion, carrots, and Brussels sprouts to a medium bowl. Add salt and pumpkin seed oil; toss to combine. Pour into a 9" x 13" baking dish, cover with foil and bake for 35 minutes.

2. In a small bowl, combine cream cheese, garlic, thyme, and kale. Set aside.

3. Make crust: In a medium bowl, combine flour, salt, baking soda, and baking powder. Cut in butter using a pastry blender or fork. Whisk water and egg yolk together; add to flour mixture and stir just until dough forms.

4. Lightly dust a clean surface with flour and roll the dough into a circle that is roughly 18" in diameter.

5. Transfer the dough to a baking sheet lined with parchment paper. Spread cream cheese mixture into the center of dough, leaving about 3" of space from the edge.

6. Add vegetables to the center of the circle and fold the edges of the circle toward the center, overlapping the dough with each fold.

7. Using a whisk or fork, beat the egg white until frothy, and brush onto the crust.

8. Bake for 25 minutes, or until crust is golden brown.

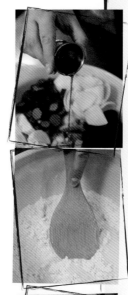

- **Prep Time:**
  45 minutes

- **Cook Time:**
  1 hour

- **Makes:**
  6 servings

- **Ingredients:**
  - 1 sweet potato, peeled and diced
  - 1 small beet, peeled and sliced
  - 1 parsnip, peeled, halved, and sliced
  - 1 onion, peeled and cut into 1 1/2" pieces
  - 3 small carrots, peeled and sliced
  - 12 Brussels sprouts, halved
  - 1/2 t salt
  - 1 T pumpkin seed oil
  - 1/2 cup (4 ozs) cream cheese, softened
  - 4 garlic cloves, peeled and minced
  - 2 sprigs thyme, minced
  - 2 cups kale, minced

Crust
  - 1 1/2 cups flour, plus more for dusting
  - 1/2 t salt
  - 1/4 t baking soda
  - 1/8 t baking powder
  - 3 T cold butter
  - 6 T cold water
  - 1 egg, separated

In this recipe

- CREAM CHEESE, see p. 61
  Also: Butter, p. 37

FARMSTYLE RECIPES
~ Dessert ~

Gluten Free

Flourless Chocolate Cake

- **Prep Time:**
  15 minutes

- **Cook Time:**
  28 minutes

- **Makes:**
  6 servings

1. Preheat oven to 375°F. Generously butter six 6-oz ramekins and dust with cocoa powder; tap to remove any excess powder.

2. In a small saucepan, melt butter and chocolate chips over low heat, stirring constantly. Once chocolate is melted, remove pan from heat.

3. In a small bowl, whisk eggs, sugar, buttermilk, and cocoa powder together. Pour in 1 1/4 cups melted chocolate and whisk to combine, reserving the remainder to drizzle over top.

4. Pour batter into prepared ramekins, place on cookie sheet, and bake for 28 minutes, or until a toothpick inserted comes out clean. Immediately invert cake onto plates; lift and remove ramekins (or you can leave in ramekins to serve).

5. Before serving, drizzle with remaining chocolate, reheating it if necessary.

Ingredients:

- 7 T butter, plus extra for buttering ramekins
- 1/4 cup cocoa powder, plus extra for dusting
- 2 cups semi-sweet chocolate chips, divided
- 4 eggs
- 1/3 cup sugar
- 1/4 cup buttermilk

Instead of using 6-oz ramekins, we used five 5-oz vintage gelatin molds filled to the top and then baked for 18–20 minutes.

In this recipe

BUTTERMILK, see p. 43
Also: Butter, p. 37

no
bake

Caramel Apple Cheesecake

1. Line the bottom and sides of a 9" springform pan with parchment paper, cutting one round and one long rectangle.

2. Make crust: In a small bowl, combine graham crackers, sugar, cinnamon, and melted butter. Press mixture into bottom of prepared springform pan and set aside.

3. Make filling: Peel, core, and slice apples into 1/4" rings, using a mandoline slicer (p. 163). In a large sauce pan, melt butter over medium heat, sprinkle in 2 T of brown sugar, add apple rings, and then sprinkle in remaining brown sugar over the apple rings. Cook for about 4 minutes on each side, or until golden brown. Remove from heat and set aside.

4. In a medium bowl, blend cream cheese, sugar, lemon juice, and vanilla.

5. In another medium bowl, whip cream until stiff and gently fold into cream cheese mixture.

6. Line the bottom and sides of the springform pan with apple rings and add filling, pressing filling against sides to prevent air pockets from forming around apples. Level the top and refrigerate for at least 4 hours before serving.

7. Right before serving, make the caramel sauce: combine butter, maple syrup, and brown sugar in a small saucepan. Bring to a simmer over medium heat, stirring constantly. Let caramel simmer for 2 minutes, then remove from heat and stir in vanilla and cream. Drizzle over cheesecake just before serving.

* **Prep Time:**
  1 hour plus
    4 hours chilling

* **Cook Time:**
  15 minutes

* **Makes:**
  one 9" cake

* **Ingredients:**

Crust
* 2 cups ground graham crackers
* 1 T sugar
* 1/2 t cinnamon
* 1/2 cup butter, melted

Filling
* 2 Granny Smith apples
* 4 T butter
* 4 T dark-brown sugar, divided
* 3 cups (24 ozs) cream cheese, softened
* 3/4 cup sugar
* 1 T lemon juice
* 2 t vanilla extract
* 2 cups cream

Caramel Sauce
* 3 T butter
* 2 T maple syrup
* 2 T dark-brown sugar
* 1/4 t vanilla extract
* 1 T cream

In this recipe

* CREAM CHEESE, see p. 61
  Also: Butter, p. 37

175

Don't toss your butter wrappers! They make the perfect wraps for caramels. Cut them in half lengthwise and use them in place of waxed paper.

Sea Salt Caramels
Omit the vanilla and walnuts in our traditional caramels recipe. In step 3, after caramel cools for 30 minutes, sprinkle 1 t coarse sea salt on top, then continue cooling.

Chocolate Caramels
In a double boiler, melt 8 ozs bittersweet chocolate. Cool for 2–3 minutes. After cutting caramels, dip each piece in the melted chocolate and remove with a fork, allowing excess chocolate to drain off. Place on a cooling rack with parchment paper underneath. If desired, sprinkle a pinch of sea salt on top. Allow to cool for 2 hours, then wrap.

176

Traditional Caramels

Ingredients:
- 1 cup cream
- 1 cup sugar
- 3/4 cup corn syrup
- 1/2 cup butter
- 1/2 t vanilla extract
- 1/2 cup chopped walnuts

1) Line an 8" x 8" baking dish with 2 sheets of crisscrossed parchment paper.

2) In a medium saucepan, combine cream, sugar, corn syrup, and butter. Gently stirring, bring mixture to a boil over medium heat.

3) Once mixture begins to boil, stop stirring and continue to boil until mixture reaches 245°F on a candy thermometer. Remove from heat; stir in vanilla and walnuts.

4) Immediately pour into prepared pan and allow to cool for at least 3 hours or overnight.

5) After caramel has cooled, remove from pan and cut into 4 equal lengths; cut each length into 10 equal pieces. To store, arrange in an airtight container in single layers between sheets of wax paper, or wrap individually parchment or wax paper.

- ⊙ **Prep Time:**
  15 minutes

- ⊙ **Cook Time:**
  20 minutes

- ⊙ **Setting Time:**
  3 hours

- ⊙ **Makes:**
  30 or 40 candies

chocolate caramels

Butterscotch Caramels

Ingredients:
- 1/4 cup butter
- 3/4 cup sugar
- 1/3 cup cream
- 1/4 cup honey
- 1/2 t salt
- 1/4 t cream of tartar
- 1 t vanilla extract

Special Equipment:
- Freshware 30-cavity Silicone Chocolate Jelly and Candy Mold (Amazon.com)
- candy thermometer

1) In a medium saucepan, combine butter, sugar, cream, honey, salt, and cream of tartar. Gently stirring, bring mixture to a boil over medium heat.

2) Once mixture begins to boil, stop stirring and continue to boil until mixture reaches 260°F on a candy thermometer. Remove from heat; stir in vanilla.

3) Place mold on a baking sheet for stability and evenly divide mixture between cavities. Cool for 3 hours. To store, wrap candies individually in parchment or wax paper.

1. In a medium bowl, combine ground graham crackers, 1/4 cup sugar, and butter. Press mixture into the bottom and up the sides of a 10" pie plate.

2. In a small saucepan, melt 3/4 cup chocolate chips over low heat, stirring constantly. Pour into pie plate, and spread over the bottom of the crust.

3. In a small bowl, combine cream cheese, remaining sugar, and vanilla; blend until smooth.

4. In another small bowl, whip the cream into soft peaks. Gently fold whipped cream into cream cheese mixture. Fold in remaining chocolate chips.

5. Pour filling into pie plate and top with marshmallows. Broil for 3–5 minutes, just until tops of marshmallows are golden brown.

6. Chill for about 4 hours, or until filling has set.

- **Prep Time:**
  35 minutes, plus
  4 hours cooling

- **Cook Time:**
  5–8 minutes

- **Makes:**
  one 10" pie

- **Ingredients:**
  - 2 1/2 cups ground graham crackers
  - 1/2 cup sugar, divided
  - 12 T butter, melted
  - 1 cup chocolate chips, divided
  - 1 cup (8 ozs) cream cheese, softened
  - 1 t vanilla extract
  - 1 cup cream
  - 1 1/2 cups homemade marshmallows using my ChillOver Powder (p. 183), cut into 1/2" squares

In this recipe

For a variation on s'mores,
put 2 cups (16 ozs) of cream cheese into a food processor and whip. With the processor running, add 1 1/4 cups sweetened condensed milk (p. 107) and 1/2 cup of lime juice (bottled or fresh-squeezed). Mix thoroughly. Spread the filling between graham crackers.

- BUTTER, see p. 37
Also: Cream Cheese, p. 61

I love this just-add-fruit-and-butter recipe for canning-jar gift-giving. Layer the ingredients in a canning jar, then copy the recipe below and place it in the top of the jar.

1. Preheat oven to 350°F.

2. Place peaches in an 8" x 8" baking dish. (Or use a 9" x 13" baking dish and double the ingredients for 12 servings.)

3. In a medium bowl, blend brown sugar and butter with pastry blender or fork. Stir in flour. Mix in oats until mixture is clumped together. Scatter over the peaches and sprinkle with walnuts.

4. Bake for 35 minutes (45 minutes if doubling the recipe).

5. Serve with Peaches & Cream Ice Cream (p. 193).

Prep Time:
15 minutes

Cook Time:
35 minutes

Makes:
6 servings

Ingredients:
- 4 cups sliced fresh or thawed frozen peaches
- 3/4 cups brown sugar
- 1/2 cup butter, cut in pieces
- 1/2 cup flour
- 1 1/2 cups old-fashioned oats (not instant)
- 1/2 cup walnuts, coarsely chopped

Quick tip

You can replace the peaches with apricots, huckleberries, blueberries, strawberries, apples, or a combination of fruits.

In this recipe

BUTTER, see p. 37

STRESSED
is
DESSERTS
spelled
backwards

182

⌒ Pastor's Wife's Pie ⌒

1. In a small bowl, combine ground graham crackers, sugar, and melted butter.

2. Press mixture into a 9" pie plate or cake pan, and place in the refrigerator.

3. For the blueberry filling, combine frozen blueberries, sugar, and lemon juice in a small saucepan. Bring to a boil over medium heat.

4. Once mixture is boiling, slowly sprinkle in the ChillOver Powder. Stir to combine and boil for an additional 3 minutes *exactly*! Remove from heat.

5. For the custard, combine milk and sugar in a medium saucepan. Over medium heat, heat the milk and sugar until steam begins to rise from milk. Place egg yolks in small bowl; whisk.

6. Once steam is rising from milk, remove 1/4 cup milk and stir into egg yolks, then pour the egg-yolk mixture back into the saucepan with the milk.

7. Continuing to heat the milk over medium heat, bring to a slow boil.

8. Once the mixture is boiling, slowly sprinkle in ChillOver Powder, and continue to boil for 3 minutes *exactly*! Remove from heat and once cool, add vanilla.

9. Once the blueberries and custard have cooled to room temperature, pour the blueberries into the bottom of the pie plate, and then pour the custard over the top of the blueberries. Refrigerate for 2 hours, or until custard has set.

- **Prep Time:**
  30 minutes, plus 2 hours cooling time

- **Cook Time:**
  25 minutes

- **Makes:**
  8 servings

- **Ingredients:**

  ### Graham Crust
  - 1 package ground graham crackers (about 1 1/4 cups)
  - 2 T sugar
  - 6 T butter, melted

  ### Blueberry Filling
  - 1 1/2 cups frozen blueberries
  - 1/4 cup sugar
  - 1 T lemon juice
  - 1/2 t ChillOver Powder

  ### Custard Filling
  - 2 cups milk
  - 1/4 cup sugar
  - 2 egg yolks
  - 3/4 t ChillOver Powder
  - 1 t vanilla extract

In the moo-d for a little therapeutic shopping?

Life-size street cow, Rio de Janeiro, Brazil CowParade, p. 364

In this recipe

This recipe calls for my ChillOver Powder (an alternative to gelatin), also used in my much-talked-about homemade marshmallow recipe, found here: RaisingJane. org/journal/19727.

- BUTTER, see p. 37

183

" Ice cream is happiness condensed. "
– Jessi Lane Adams

184

Express Ice Cream

This ice cream just sends me to the moon, it's so good—ice cream in seconds! I discovered it by accident when I poured some half-and-half on frozen raspberries. The milk didn't stay pooled up in the bottom of the bowl. Instead, all of it "ran to the aid" of the berries and dressed them from head to toe, completely covering them.

Prep Time: 1 minute
Makes: 1 cup

- 1/4 cup half-and-half
- 1 cup frozen raspberries or blueberries

1. Place berries in a medium bowl. Pour half-and-half over the top. Gently stir. Eat! (Or more properly, in written recipe style: Serve.)

Quick tips

DIY Half-and-Half
To make your own half-and-half, either mix 3 cups **whole milk** with 1 cup **cream** or 2 cups **cream** with 2 cups **skim milk** to make 1 quart. (Half-and-half won't whip into stiff peaks and it won't thicken a sauce like cream does.)

Short-order strawberry Ice Cream

This is a remarkably good, remarkably easy, short-order ice cream that doesn't require a complicated recipe or a hand-crank ice cream freezer. Plus, it's a good way to use up the berries you've grown and frozen or to avoid the expense and weird stuff in commercial ice cream. The flavor really is amazing.

Prep Time: 15 minutes, plus 1 hour chilling time
Makes: 1 qt

- 24 ozs frozen strawberries, sliced (approx. 5 cups sliced)
- 1/2 cup sugar
- 1 1/2 cups cream

1. If using whole frozen strawberries, remove from freezer and spread out on a tray until just soft enough to slice but not thawed, approx. 20 minutes.
2. In a blender, combine berries and sugar, stopping to stir several times, until berries are finely chopped.
3. Slowly add cream while blending, stopping to stir several times, until thick.
4. Pour mixture into a shallow pan (I used a 4-qt 15" x 10" x 2" glass baking dish) and freeze for about 1 hour, or until scoopable. (For later use, you can freeze solid, then remove from freezer and let mixture sit for about 15 minutes, until scoopable.) Store in freezer for up to one month in an airtight container. Note: For a red, white, and blue Independence Day theme, garnish with fresh blueberries and serve in white dinnerware.

Short-order Avocado Ice Cream

Prep Time: 15 minutes plus 4 hours chilling time
Makes: 1 qt

- 3 avocados, peeled and diced
- 1 1/2 cups half-and-half
- 1 cup powdered sugar
- 1 t lemon zest
- 1/2 cup lemon juice

1. Combine avocado, half-and-half, sugar, lemon zest, and lemon juice in a blender. Purée until completely smooth.
2. Pour mixture into a 2-qt baking dish.
3. Cover and freeze until firm, about 4 hours. (Can be transferred to an airtight container and kept in freezer for up to one month.)
4. Before serving, let stand at room temperature for 15 minutes. Use an ice-cream or watermelon scoop to serve. Top with fresh fruit or mango salsa.

Salted Caramel Ice Cream

Prep Time: 15 minutes, plus 8 hours chilling time
Cook Time: 15 minutes
Process Time: 30 minutes
Makes: 1 qt

- 1 1/4 cups sugar, divided
- 1 1/2 t lemon juice
- 1 1/2 cups milk
- 1 1/2 t salt
- 4 egg yolks, lightly beaten
- 1 3/4 cups half-and-half
- 2 t vanilla extract

1. In a large, heavy saucepan, combine 1 cup sugar and lemon juice. Cook over medium-high heat until sugar melts (do not stir; gently shake pan to encourage melting). It should take about 5 minutes for sugar to begin melting. Once sugar is melted, remove from heat.
2. Meanwhile, in a small saucepan, whisk together milk, salt, and remaining sugar. Cook over medium-high heat just until steam rises.
3. Slowly pour milk mixture into melted sugar (it will bubble and expand as you add milk), whisking constantly.
4. Whisk 1/2 cup of caramel mixture into egg yolks to temper, and pour back into pan. Cook over medium heat until thickened (mixture will coat the back of a spoon), whisking constantly. Remove from heat.
5. Whisk in half-and-half and vanilla. Refrigerate overnight.
6. Process mixture in an ice-cream maker according to manufacturer's instructions.

Pumpkin Ice Cream

Prep Time: 10 minutes, plus 8 hours chilling time
Cook Time: 10 minutes
Process Time: 25 minutes
Makes: 1 qt

- 1 1/2 cups milk
- 1 cup sugar
- 2 eggs
- 1 cup cream
- 1 cup fresh cooked or canned pumpkin
- 1/4 t cinnamon
- 1/2 t nutmeg

1. In a medium pan over medium heat, whisk together milk, sugar, and eggs. Cook until slightly thickened (about 10 minutes), stirring constantly. Remove from heat.
2. Whisk in remaining ingredients until well combined. Chill thoroughly.
3. Process mixture in an ice-cream maker according to manufacturer's instructions.

When I want to get my grandkids involved or have time for a bit of an arm workout, I prefer the Donvier 837409W 1-qt (hand-crank) Ice Cream Maker.

I love my Cuisinart ICE-21 (1 1/2-qt) Ice Cream Maker when I'm in a hurry. It's also great for frozen yogurt and sorbet and freezing milk for storage, p. 191.

Sweet 'n' spicy chocolate ice cream

It may seem counterintuitive to mix fire and ice, but this summer treat is nothing short of sensational!

Prep Time: 15 minutes, plus 8 hours chilling time
Cook Time: 10 minutes
Process Time: 15 minutes
Makes: 1 qt

- 2 cups cream, divided
- 1/4 cup cocoa powder
- 8 ozs bittersweet chocolate, chopped
- 6 egg yolks, lightly beaten
- 1 cup milk
- 1/2 cup sugar
- 1 t cinnamon
- 1/8 t salt
- 1/8 t cayenne
- 1 t vanilla extract

1. In a medium saucepan, whisk 1 cup cream and cocoa powder together. Bring to a simmer over medium heat; remove from heat and whisk in chocolate until melted.
2. In a medium bowl, whisk together egg yolks and milk. Whisk milk mixture into chocolate mixture.
3. Add sugar, cinnamon, salt, and cayenne. Cook over medium heat until thickened (mixture will coat the back of a spoon), whisking constantly. Remove from heat.
4. Whisk in vanilla and remaining cream. Refrigerate overnight.
5. Process mixture in an ice-cream maker according to manufacturer's instructions.

In this photo, my brother Kent (on the right) has the mumps—always a good excuse for soft, cold treats like homemade ice cream or one of my mother's occasional comfort foods, a gelatin dessert. Ice cream was a family affair. Because I was just the right weight but not big enough yet to crank the handle, it was my job to sit on top of the ice-cream maker to keep it from moving while my brothers and older sister took turns on the hand crank. The crank turned a paddle inside a canister surrounded by ice and rock salt. My mother stood by, ready to supervise if things got out of hand.

coffee can chocolate ice cream

Prep Time: 10 minutes, plus 8 hours chilling time
Cook Time: 10 minutes
Process Time: 25 minutes
Makes: 1 qt

- 4 egg yolks, lightly beaten
- 1 1/2 cups milk
- 1 cup sugar
- 1/3 cup cocoa powder
- 1 3/4 cups cream
- 1 t vanilla extract
- crushed ice
- rock salt

1. In a medium saucepan, whisk egg yolks and milk together. Add sugar and cook over medium heat, whisking constantly, until thickened (mixture will coat the back of a spoon); remove from heat.
2. Whisk in cocoa, then whisk in cream and vanilla. Refrigerate overnight.
3. Using two coffee cans that come with tight-fitting plastic lids, nest a small can inside a large can (we used a 12-oz can and a 31.5-oz can).
4. Place ice-cream mixture in the small can, put the lid on, and duct-tape shut.
5. Pack the large container with alternating layers of 1 1/2" crushed ice and 1/4" rock salt. Duct-tape the lid closed to prevent it from opening.
6. With two people, toss the can back and forth, shaking in between tosses (you may want to wear gloves, the can gets cold). Check the ice cream after 25 minutes. Continue tossing until it is the consistency of soft-serve ice cream.

Pistachio Ice Cream

Prep Time: 20 minutes, plus 8 hours chilling time
Cook Time: 15 minutes
Process Time: 25 minutes
Makes: 1 qt

- 1 3/4 cups unsalted shelled pistachios, divided
- 1 cup sugar, divided
- 2 cups milk
- 4 egg yolks, lightly beaten
- 1 3/4 cups cream
- 1/2 t almond extract

1. In a food processor, finely grind 1 cup pistachios with 1/4 cup sugar. Transfer to a medium saucepan. Stir in milk and bring to a simmer over medium-low heat. Simmer mixture for 8 minutes; remove from heat.
2. Strain mixture through a fine mesh sieve into a large bowl; discard pistachios.
3. Pour milk mixture back into saucepan; whisk in egg yolks and remaining sugar. Cook over medium heat until thickened (mixture will coat the back of a spoon); remove from heat.
4. Coarsely chop remaining pistachios. Stir pistachios, cream, and almond extract into custard. Refrigerate overnight.
5. Process mixture in an ice-cream maker according to manufacturer's instructions.

coconut Macaroons
w/ Pistachio Ice Cream (p. 189)

Prep Time: 15 minutes
Cook Time: 24 minutes, plus 10 minutes cooling time
Makes: 10 ice-cream sandwiches

- 3/4 cup sugar
- 2 1/2 cups unsweetened, shredded coconut
- 2 egg whites
- 1 t vanilla extract
- pinch salt

1. Preheat oven to 325°F with rack in middle of oven. Line two large baking sheets with parchment paper.
2. In a large bowl, mix together all ingredients.
3. Spread coconut mixture by tablespoons into 3" rounds, 1" apart, on baking sheets. Bake macaroons, one sheet at a time, until golden in spots and around edges, 10–12 minutes.
4. Cool on baking sheets until firm, about 10 minutes, then remove from parchment with a metal spatula and cool completely.

Quick Tip: Freezing Milk

If you've ever tried to freeze milk for future use, you've discovered it doesn't quite work. After it's thawed, it's congealed. For perfect consistency when thawed, put fresh milk into an ice-cream maker and churn until it's the consistency of soft-serve ice cream. Pour into a plastic freezer container and freeze. When you thaw it, you'll have milk again!

Decadent Triple Chocolate Cookies
w/ short-order Strawberry Ice Cream (p. 185)

Prep Time: 30 minutes
Cook Time: 32 minutes, plus 10 minutes cooling time
Makes: 8 ice-cream sandwiches

- 10 ozs bittersweet chocolate, chopped
- 1/2 cup plus 2 t flour
- 3 T unsweetened cocoa powder
- 1/4 t baking powder
- 1/4 t salt
- 5 T butter, softened
- 1 cup plus 1 T sugar
- 3 eggs
- 1 1/2 t vanilla extract
- 1 cup semisweet chocolate chips

1. Preheat oven to 350°F with rack in middle of oven. Line two large baking sheets with parchment paper.
2. In the top of a double boiler set over simmering water on medium heat, heat and stir chocolate until melted and smooth. Remove from heat; remove top of double boiler and cool for 5 minutes.
3. In a medium bowl, sift together flour, cocoa, baking powder, and salt.
4. In a large bowl, cream butter and sugar with an electric mixer until light and fluffy. Add eggs, one at a time, beating well after each addition. Continue to beat until mixture is light, pale, and creamy, about 5 minutes. Add melted chocolate and vanilla and beat just until blended. Blend in dry ingredients, then chocolate chips.
5. Using buttered hands, form the dough into 16 balls (about 1 3/4" in diameter), and arrange them 2" apart on baking sheets. Bake cookies, one sheet at a time, until tops are evenly cracked, but cookies are still firm to the touch, about 14–16 minutes.
6. Cool completely on baking sheets. Freeze cookies overnight. (Can be made up to three days ahead. Keep frozen.)

Ginger Snaps
w/ short-order Avocado Ice Cream (p. 187)

Prep Time: 25 minutes
Cook Time: 30 minutes, plus 10 minutes cooling time
Makes: 8 ice-cream sandwiches

- 1/2 cup butter, softened
- 1/2 cup sugar, plus additional for coating cookies
- 1/2 cup firmly packed brown sugar
- 1/3 cup molasses
- 1 egg
- 2 cups flour
- 2 1/2 t ground ginger
- 1/2 t ground cinnamon
- 1/4 t ground allspice
- 1 t baking soda
- 3/4 t salt

1. Preheat oven to 350°F with rack in middle of oven. Line two large baking sheets with parchment paper.
2. In a large bowl, cream butter, sugar, and brown sugar with an electric mixer until light and fluffy. Add molasses and egg and beat until smooth.
3. In a medium bowl, whisk together flour, spices, baking soda, and salt. Add the flour mixture to the butter mixture and stir until a soft dough forms.
4. Form the dough into 16 balls (about 1 3/4" in diameter), roll the balls in sugar, and arrange them 2" apart on baking sheets. Bake cookies, one sheet at a time, until crisp and cracked but still soft inside, about 13–15 minutes.
5. Cool on baking sheets for 5 minutes, then remove from parchment with a metal spatula and cool completely.

192

oatmeal cookies
w/ Peaches & Cream Ice Cream

Prep Time: 15 minutes
Cook Time: 24 minutes, plus 10 minutes
  cooling time
Makes: 8 ice-cream sandwiches

- 1/2 cup butter, softened
- 1/3 cup sugar
- 1/3 cup firmly packed brown sugar
- 1 egg
- 1/2 t vanilla extract
- 1 1/2 cups old-fashioned oats (not instant)
- 3/4 cup flour
- 1/2 t baking soda
- 1/2 t ground cinnamon
- 1/2 t salt

1. Preheat oven to 350°F with rack in middle of oven. Line two large baking sheets with parchment paper.
2. In a large bowl, cream butter, sugar, and brown sugar with an electric mixer until light and fluffy. Beat in egg and vanilla.
3. In a medium bowl, stir together oats, flour, baking soda, cinnamon, and salt.
4. Add the flour mixture to the butter mixture and stir until a soft dough forms.
5. Form the dough into 16 balls (about 1 1/4" in diameter), and arrange them 3" apart on baking sheets. Flatten to 2" rounds.
6. Bake cookies, one sheet at a time, about 10–12 minutes. Cool on baking sheets for 5 minutes, then remove from parchment with a metal spatula and cool completely.

Peaches & Cream Ice Cream
Use recipe for Short-order Strawberry Ice Cream (p. 185), substituting frozen peaches for strawberries and adding 1/2 t nutmeg.

meet Beau Vine at 3 months of age

meet Otis at 2 months of age

193

Let's Talk Cows

" I sort of fell asleep that day while milking that old cow; my head was nestled in her flank; I still can feel it now. "

– Otto Rosfeld

In This Chapter

• You Bought What?! ....p. 196

• All Tied Up.................................p. 202

• Inspiring Milkmaids....................p. 204

• Milking (hand & machine)...........p. 210

• Milking a Mini-cow.....................p. 220

• Housing ....p. 236

• Fencing....................................p. 246

• Feed...p. 254

• Hay/Straw Storage ....p. 266

• Cow-trough Gardening.................p. 268

• Sh@t Happens ....p. 272
  (manure management)

• Pest Control..............................p. 277

• Birth & Delivery ....p. 282

YOU BOUGHT WHAT?!

Talkin' 'Bout My Girl, My Girl

We've all heard stories about people who buy a vehicle from a seller who skirted around the issues of its problems like a pro. I'm sorry to say, buying a cow isn't any different. Those of us who are optimists are easy prey. But hoping for the best and making a quick decision based on the proverbial it'll-all-work-out attitude could put you in a bad moo-d when you find out that what you brought home isn't what you thought you bought.

Here's a post from my HeritageJersey.org chatroom:

"I got the cow (a short-legged Dexter). The cow calved. The milk came in. I marched, with high hopes, to the barn. I had a clean bucket, a jar of warm, soapy water, and a milk crate to sit upon. I fed the cow some grains, squatted down, cleaned the udder, and got to it. I got approximately enough milk for my morning coffee before we mutually gave up. Same story the next day. The biggest problem, though, was that I feel like my cow's teats are just unworkably small! I have experience milking goats, but not cows. I'm used to big handles I can wrap a whole hand around. I could get maybe three fingers around my cow's front quarters, and barely two around the rear. Is this to be expected for any of the smaller family cow breeds, or do I just have a girl without much of a build for dairy? Is this something that can be overcome with a machine-milking?"

Given my level of experience at this point, I could have gone with this woman to look at the cow before she bought it. More important, I would have asked her several questions en route about her expectations. Once we arrived, and after looking at the cow she was thinking about buying, I could have given her a thumbs up or a thumbs down, based on her answers to my questions. If all that lined up nicely, I would have then asked the owner about its tests, vaccinations, medical history, and what breed and size of cow it had mated with if it was pregnant.

My goal in writing this book, and this chapter in particular, as well as establishing a chatroom and "Marketplace" on HeritageJersey.org, is to provide some sort of TrueCar.com service for prospective cow buyers. In many ways, it's the same thing.

The questions that need to be asked first—and more important, answered—are:

How much milk do you want? Will you be milking by hand or by machine? Do you want a market for selling its calves or will those go into your freezer? Do you want the cow to look a certain way? Color preferences? Are you hoping to sell the extra milk?

My first milk cow happened easily enough. I lived on a working cattle ranch with another family that knew cows, and really, she was perfect in every way. Because of that experience, I knew I wanted a Jersey. But I needed to know more, so before I brought home my very own cow years later, I signed up for a one-day workshop put on by a man, now deceased, who had a small, raw milk dairy and also offered hands-on, how-to classes. What an eye opener! His learning center, The Udder Whey, helped dozens of wanna-be cow owners over the years. He also sold cows, so I was able to pick one, and he delivered her. She was already pregnant with her first calf. Perfect, right? When he said she'd been serviced by a Milking Shorthorn bull, I glossed right over that little detail. It'll all work out, right? Calf came. It was a girl. Perfect. I could sell her as a milk cow. I didn't want or need two at that time. Sadly, everyone who came to see her didn't like the way she "looked."

That was it!!!! It wasn't her udder, her teats, her size. **That's when I learned about the importance of presentation, in the same way people pick a car.** I picture myself in a rugged-looking Jeep, so that's what I own. I'm sure a Toyota Camry would get me around just as well, but that isn't what's in my mind's eye. I ended up giving the cow away. I wouldn't have had any problem selling a Jersey.

If what you want is a serious milker, you should look at the more common, well-known dairy breeds like Brown Swiss and Holstein-Friesian. If milk production isn't your main goal, you might want to check out a breed like Jersey, Ayrshire, Guernsey, or Milking Shorthorn—still good milkers, but not quite as much. If you're interested in more of a novelty breed (and this is where you need to know what you're getting into), check out breeds like Dexter, Dutch Belted, Normande, American Milking Devon, American Lineback, or miniature Jersey. **The smaller you go, the less milk you're going to get,** just like the woman on the previous page said regarding her Dexter. Most small teats can be successfully milked using a milking machine (p. 220) if they're too small for your hands. But, again, do your homework. There are many other breeds too numerous to mention. Go to TheDairySite.com/breeds/dairy for a more extensive list, complete with photos. Wikipedia has a wealth of information also.

Personal preference, coloring, and size are fun things to consider, but keep in mind requirements like availability and access to breeding if you're going to keep a line pure. My "Jeep" cow is a Jersey. But when it comes to my preference for size of Jersey cow, sometimes I like a two-door, sometimes not. Sometimes I drive with my top off (wow, that came out sounding wrong), and sometimes I like a more tame Jeep with heated seats. Will you find everything you dream of in one cow? Not likely, but you can get pretty close. It's all in the questions you ask and find answers to.

So you've done your homework and you know the breed you want. Where do you look? Well, I'm short on real answers. I could say "cattle auctions," but I don't know that for sure. And I've never been to one. **Auctions can be a place to find a milk cow that a large dairy no longer wants.** Is that a good thing or a bad thing? I know of one woman who bought what looked like a lovely cow from an auction, but the cow had been dosed with so many drugs in her tenure at a large dairy, she wasn't capable of getting pregnant again. On the other hand, it might be good news for you. She's already a trained milker with many years left, but the amount of milk she's giving has dropped below peak production. And that "less than" amount would be more than enough for you. I've oftened wondered if a milk-cow adoption service, similar to a "pound puppy" organization, would work. No doubt, **countless cows could use your love.**

We all know we're supposed to have a mechanic check out a used car before we buy it. We also know that getting a mechanical check on a vehicle is a pain in the patootie. A vet check can also be a challenge logistically. But **if you can get a vet check first, by all means, do so.**

The ideal cow for a beginner would be a cow pregnant with her second calf—due in six months. She'd be lactating, so you could watch her being milked and then bring her home to continue milking her yourself and get ready for her baby. (That might mean stopping at a rest stop to milk her on the way home.) **More important, she'd be a trained milker.**

Now here's advice that might seem discouraging at first, but once you dive in and think of it as a fishing expedition or a treasure hunt with clues along the way, I do know this: **YOUR cow is out there. Somewhere. She just is.** Start with **word-of-mouth.** Visit **dairy farms.** Ask your **local veterinarian** (great place to start). Check with **neighbors.** Drive around in the countryside and when you see dairy cows, **stop and inquire.** (You might want to bone up on some cow speak (p. 356) before embarking; cow owners tend to speak another language. **Look online.**

But. But. Online has its problems. As unpleasant as it is to bring this up, I must disclose that it took me years to get a miniature Jersey breeder on the East Coast to take down a completely made-up endorsement by me on his website. Unfortunately, there was a reason he attached his name to mine. He was able to take deposits from several unsuspecting people, even a group of nuns, who never received livestock. He also had a dog kennel that was shut down by the State of New York for animal cruelty. With regard to the deposits, he pleaded guilty to felony fraud and was sentenced to five years' probation, with one of the requirements being that he could not own and/or sell any animals, even though his two websites were still in existence the last time we checked and he's still answering his phone, ready to sell you an imaginary animal. After speaking with his probation officer several times, we came to the conclusion that this guy might be incorrigible. However you can pull it off, do a background check first.

Moving right along ...

Okay, so you think you found her! (And she's for sale by someone reputable.) **Now you have to get answers to the following questions:**

•••••••••••••••••• cow check list ••••••••••••••••••

Health Questions (backed up by records and verified by an ear tag or tattoo)

1. Did she get a vaccination for Bang's (brucellosis) before she was 12 months old? (Even though, it's still illegal not to get a test every year thereafter.)
2. Has she been checked for Bang's and TB every year? What was the date of her last test for both? (Preferably within the last month, for your purposes.)
3. Has she been checked for Q fever, BVD (bovine viral diarrhea), Johne's, and BLV (bovine leukosis virus)? When? If not, consider offering to pay for testing, p. 318.
4. If there are bulls in the herd, have they been tested for trich (bovine trichomoniasis), p. 307? When? (A cow can be infected with trich but she can't be tested.)
5. Any illnesses?
6. Who is the animal's vet? (If you're going to transport the animal across state lines, ask a vet what the requirements are for your state. To meet those requirements, the buyer usually offers to pay for the required tests. Results may take two weeks. The paperwork must travel with the animal in order to meet transportation regulations.)

General Questions

1. Ask for photos (including photos of the parents or at least the mother) and her current height.
2. How many pregnancies, if any? If she's older than 2 years of age, why hasn't she been bred? Artificial insemination or live cover (mounted by a bull)?
3. If she's currently giving milk, how much and how often? Ask if you can be there during a milking session. (It's ALWAYS best to meet a cow in person before buying.)
4. Is she halter-trained?
5. Any DNA testing ever done for things like horns, A1 or A2 milk (p. 359), and parentage? (It's inexpensive and easy to do, p. 319.) Always verify ear tags/tattoos against records.
6. Was she dehorned or is she genetically polled (born without horns)?
7. If she's a particular breed, is she registered with an organization? Ask to see a copy of the certificate.

Where was her height measurement taken? Ask to have her measured from the withers rather than her hook bone (hip area) because that point is lower than the top of her back (view size charts and measuring instructions at HeritageJersey.org/registry.aspx).

Transportation

Before any money exchanges hands, you need to know what you're going to do for transportation. I've hired truckers to bring animals from around the country. My longest haul was from Kansas. As can be expected, you get what you pay for. Cheap for me meant the trucker didn't communicate very well (his answering machine was often full), and the cow I'd purchased ended up being held at his residence for close to 30 days before he "came my way." That isn't what I agreed to but understandable given how little it was costing me. Gas alone for me to drive there would have been more that what he charged me. Consider this. If you're going to haul an animal by yourself and you have a trailer, add up the gas, your time away from work, food and hotel along the way and then compare that to what it would cost to hire a trucker who'll do a good job for you and your animal. It's usually about the same.

I enjoyed the customer service I received when I hired FolkensBros.com in Lester, Iowa (800-831-8553). Their employee who drove a bull and cow from Kansas to Idaho for me, called along the way with updates about water stops, etc. He was chatty and seemed to genuinely like my cows. I felt like they were in good hands.

Insurance

Did you know you can buy livestock mortality insurance on an animal that you purchase? Policies can cover the animal for as long as a year and cost anywhere from 6–8% of the purchase price of the animal. Before an animal I buy (usually paid in full up front) leaves the seller's premises, I have it insured for the trip at the very least. It's a straight forward, simple process. Try JamesFBessler.com (815-762-2641).

Contract

Most sellers will have a written contract ready. If not, you should consider working with an attorney to have one drawn up.

Price

In my experience, the price of a cow can be anywhere from $1,500 to $10,000. Sticker shock, right? For instance, if the cow you're looking at is a trained milker and has successfully birthed one calf already and is pregnant with another and the seller has a handle on all the paperwork to prove that she's had routine health tests, vaccinations, and a current certificate of health from a vet, you'll be paying more because you have less exposure on your end. If you're buying an animal from someone who can answer all the questions listed above (backed up with paperwork), they run a high-end operation and their asking price will reflect what they consider to be their investment to date.

Meet Miss Daisy at 1 1/2 years of age, progeny of a pedigreed line that was many times a winner at the Island Royals on the Isle of Jersey.

FIRST PREMIUM

PALOUSE

201

ALL TIED UP

Hitchin' Rail Knot

● ●

① Rope is licking the palm of your left hand.

② Go under the rope that's connected to your cow, making the number 4.

③ Check your watch on your left hand (rotate wrist).

④ Put the loop in your right hand down through the loop in your left hand.

⑤ Pull through.

⑥ Tighten against rail.

⑦ Put loose end through loop in left hand.

⑧ Pull it through.

⑨ Pull against rail.

⑩ Cinch 'er up!

202

Hitchin' Post Knot

Take 2 wraps around post and tighten.

Follow the more detailed directions for Hitchin' Rail Knot, keeping the rope taught against the post.

Rope Twist Storage

1. To store a 10' lead rope (all neat and tidy), bend the rope about 14" down from the brass latch and start winding the end along the loop created.

3. Cinch 'er up!

(For cows, I use a Weaver Poly Lead Rope 5/8" x 10', Amazon.com. Weaver also makes three different sizes of halters. For my calves, I buy their smallest size and punch a few extra holes in the strap.)

2. When you get near the end of the loop, thread the end of the rope through it and pull.

Inspiring Milkmaids

✑ Jenny Padgett ✑

If you've ever wondered how you could possibly fit a milk cow into your life, much less your backyard, it's high time you met Jenny Padgett.

Jenny's cozy house isn't bounded by acres of green. In fact, it's nestled snugly into a nice, quiet neighborhood in Manti, Utah (population 3,276). Her yard is just shy of an acre, and a tidy quarter of it belongs to Mona, Jenny's Jersey milk cow.

Jenny spotted an online ad for Mona nearly eight years ago, and she knew it was her calling. "I bought her as a 'springer heifer,' pregnant with her first calf," Jenny remembers. "I paid $1,500."

The decision to bring a cow into her life (and yard) wasn't a whim. Jenny had raised dairy goats before and knew that keeping a cow would be a serious commitment, not to mention that she was one busy momma already. Jenny ran a daycare in her home and had seven kids of her own. "One is a grown foster son; the others I either gave birth to or adopted. They range in age from 35 down to 15."

But Mona was welcomed into the family with open arms, and she has been a labor of love ever since. "I can't imagine my life without Mona!" Jenny croons. "She was my dream for a very long time. Fortunately, my neighbors and the city council have been great about it."

So, what's the payoff? Sure, Mona is gorgeous—have you seen those eyelashes?—but isn't she a lot of work?

"She *is* a lot of work, but it's worth it to me. It's the kind of work I enjoy. It's wonderful to have enough milk and cream to feed my family and then have extra to experiment with to make cheeses, yogurt, and ice cream."

Mona provides up to seven gallons of milk per day. That means lots of fresh butter, mozzarella, and ricotta at Jenny's house. "I have two hand-cranked butter churns, and I freeze extra butter for when Mona is dry."

Jenny regularly barters extra milk for hay and grain, but she has also traded it for haircuts, fruit, corn, honey, and once for some tasty tamales.

So, let's get down to the nitty-gritty. What exactly does a milk cow require in terms of equipment and time? "You do need to be set up," Jenny explains. "Cows need higher and sturdier fences than say, sheep, and they eat a portion of a bale of hay a day."

A milking barn is a must, but Jenny will tell you that big and fancy aren't required amenities. "Mine is a little 10' x 12' wooden shed that is barn-shaped. My oldest son built it for me about 10 years ago. Inside, I have a wood stanchion. Mona loves to stand in her stanchion to be brushed and petted all over. It helps a cow to be less jumpy if they're used to being touched. Mona has a very sweet personality and is calm and easy to milk."

Jenny uses an electric milking machine. She also milks by hand on occasion. She stores fresh milk in gallon glass jars in the fridge until the cream rises. Then, after skimming the cream into quart jars, she transfers the milk into quart and 1/2-gallon milk bottles for family and friends.

"I love having a milk cow right outside my back door."

Jenny stresses that a cow must be milked routinely. "It doesn't have to be 6 a.m. and 6 p.m. milkings (mine certainly aren't), but within 10–12 hours apart, for sure. Any upset in the routine really throws them for a loop, and they can develop mastitis. I like a routine too, so it works for me."

Jenny stops milking Mona for 40–60 days before she calves to allow her milk-producing tissue to regenerate. Her method for getting Mona pregnant every year has been artificial insemination (AI) so that Mona will bear a calf and continue producing milk.

"I love having a milk cow right outside my back door. Mona is a big part of our family, and I have never regretted bringing her home."

Heather Laudie

Heather Laudie had never milked a cow until she brought home Lola, a gentle-eyed Jersey, eight years ago. "Kinda hard to believe it now when I think about it," Heather admits. "If I had really known all the hard work I was in for, I might have run screaming through the pasture!" Lucky for Lola, Heather and her family stuck with farming and have fallen madly in love with living off the land.

I first met Heather in 2009, when I featured her fledgling farm in my magazine. She had recently relocated to rural Missouri from Puerto Rico with her husband and five kids (baby number six arrived in 2010!). Although living in a tropical paradise had its perks (think fresh seafood and exotic fruits), the Laudie family longed for the comforts of their Midwestern homeland. Heather told me that milk, which most of us take for granted, was a rare commodity on the island. While ultra-pasteurized boxed milk was available, fresh milk was frequently spoiled due to power outages in the sultry southern climate. With dreams of cultivating their own farm, as Heather's great-grandmother had done three generations earlier, the Laudies headed back to the States and settled on 12 acres of fruitful farmland now known as Sagecroft Farms.

Today, Sagecroft Farms is bustling with happy Berkshire pigs, sheep, chickens, Muscovy ducks, and beef cows. But Heather seems to hold a special place in her heart for her herd of dairy darlings that has grown to include Gladys, Lucy, Coco, Florence, Ida, Bell, and "moo-dy" Mable. When Lola was the only milk cow on the farm, Heather hand-milked her every day and got about five gallons of milk and five quarts of cream. Today, she uses a milking machine to help manage more cows efficiently.

"I flip the switch for the vacuum pump, and the swish and tick of the milker is like a gentle slow dance," Heather muses. "I sit next to the cow that is being milked with my head in her flank, listening to her breathing. I talk to the cows about anything and everything—they are thoughtful listeners. I have really come to love my time in the barn. It centers me and gives me solace and peace from my very hectic life."

After each day's milking, Heather can expect to have about five gallons of milk and five quarts of cream from each cow. "What do we do with all that milk and cream, you ask? To start, we skim the cream and make butter. It takes me about a half-hour to make 2 1/2 pounds of rich, beautiful butter," explains Heather. "I use the skim milk to make cheese. I love making cheese, or I guess what I really like is eating the cheese! We sell some cheese, but most of it gets used by us. Of course, we also drink lots of milk. With six kids, we can go through a gallon a day."

Heather says that many people think she's "a bit off her rocker" for going through so much trouble when she could simply go to the market and purchase dairy products to her heart's content. "Well, that is true," she tells naysayers, "But I cannot get milk that isn't full of growth hormones and other things that I don't want to feed my precious children. I agree that having a milk cow is a lot of work, but it is well worth it."

It has also been rewarding to sell some of the farm's Animal Welfare Approved and Certified Naturally Grown dairy products, natural meat, eggs, and gourmet jams via a CSA (Community Supported Agriculture) and the local farmers' market. Heather loves knowing that her hard work is also helping to feed her community as healthily as she does her own family.

"I am amazed when I think of how this all started with Lola. All the fear and questions have faded with time," Heather reflects. "Once I enter the barn, I fall into a rhythm. I have done this so many times that my body seems to know what to do even if my brain is deep in thought. I am so thankful for the opportunity to care for these gentle, loving animals. I get so much more than milk from them."

~❧ Amy Hetrick ❧~

"When I was little, I had to empty my pockets before I was allowed in the house because I might have had something like a baby bunny tucked inside," said Amy Hetrick, an avid lover of animals. When Amy was working toward her degree in Plant Biology at Washington State University in Pullman, Washington, she lived in a small apartment. Even so, she had a pound-rescue dog, a cat, and two chickens.

"In the evenings, I'd hike to a field above my apartment," recalls Amy, who originally came here from Pennsylvania. "Carrying a ball in her mouth, the dog would lead. The cat would follow her. And the two chickens would follow them. Trix and I played fetch, the cat sniffed around, and the chickens scratched for bugs. Then we'd all head down the hill again." She smiles as she reminisces, "My neighbor across the street started calling me Noah."

Since then, she's settled into an 1890s house she's renovating herself in the small town of Albion (population 600), seven miles from Pullman. No doubt handy with tools (she even rebuilt the engine on her Jeep), she's obviously passionate about animals and has turned her double city lot, right smack-dab in the middle of town, into a haven for a hodgepodge of critters.

"I called the city to ask if I'd be able to have a goat. The answer was yes. So I brought home Gretel." With a neighbor's blessing, Amy enlarged her fenced yard to include part of his city lot. Then she turned the back of her garage into a "barn" that includes a fold-down stanchion for milking and a customized "doggy" door that gave Gretel all-day access to a larger pen.

Since then, animals have arrived by ones and twos and threes and more. She's added more goats, ducks, additional chickens, and a pair of curling feathered, flightless Sebastopols as watch geese. Six Angora rabbits live next to two pound-rescue bunnies in specially built hutches. And a sheep (half wild and half domestic) shares space with Gretel and the other goats. And if that doesn't sound like a full farm, she borrows an empty city lot directly across from the post office for a Jersey cow named Brie, in addition to a herd of Highlands and two more Jerseys that she keeps outside of town. "With her sweet-sounding cowbell chiming away all day, everyone in town knows and loves Brie."

Her farmette—where every animal earns its keep—allows Amy to work full-time taking care of the greenhouses at WSU's Institute of Biological Chemistry. "I did my undergraduate studies in Biology, my master's in Plant Science, and am working toward my PhD in Plant Science," she says. "Originally, I wanted to be a vet. But one day, I taught a science class for a professor and loved it. Now, I've decided that if I teach botany, I can have my own animals instead of going around at all hours of the night taking care of everybody else's animals.

And so she does. She built the chickens a proper coop with an attached run. The ducks live next door with shelter and a wading pool for swimming. All the outside animals, and some of the inside ones, take daily exercise in the yard. The goats, sheep, and cow keep the grass mowed. And a hive of bees stays busy pollinating plants and making honey. The only animals that don't live in town with Amy are two head of Scottish Highland cattle and two more Jersey cows—Brie's mother and her most recent calf, a heifer named Cheddar, Brie's sister. "The city might draw the line at me bringing my Highlands into town. Amy says with a grin. "So they live out of town on a friend's land. My goal is to breed my Highlands and raise an oxen team someday."

"I like having fresh eggs and milk. I like knowing where my food comes from. I like composting and putting good manure into my garden soil. I like having the fiber from the rabbits that I'm learning to spin into yarn on a replica of an old treadle-type spinning wheel." But at the end of every day, when Amy comes home to see that everybody gets fed and petted, it's the companionship that is most important. "They're family," she says.

MILKING

For many years, I milked by hand. I liked it for several reasons—the rhythmic motion; the sound of the milk hitting the pail; my head resting gently on the flank of a sweet, gentle cow—all of these things are calming and comforting to me. It's a therapeutic break from my busy life. However, once I added more cows to my family, the time it took to milk was taking up too much of my day, so I researched milking machines and took the plunge. I'm glad I did.

When my milking machine arrived, I put it all together and braced myself for several days of getting my cows used to it. As I was getting Maizy ready for the first time, I gave her a bit more alfalfa pellets to distract her and turned on the pump. It isn't quiet, but not horribly loud, either. Maizy looked over at the pump and then went right back to her treat. No reaction at all! When I attached the "claw" to her teats, she didn't even look up. None of my cows were bothered by my new machine. I make no promise that all cows will react like mine did, but I was pleasantly surprised by how calm mine were when I introduced them to my "replacement."

After doing some research on small milking machines, I settled on a NuPulse Bucket Milker from HambyDairySupply.com. I picked the NuPulse because I can milk more than one cow at a time if I choose. And in addition to the inflations that suction the milk from my mid-size to full-size cows (inflations are black rubber-tube thingies that massage the teats), I was able to also order more lightweight outer shells for my miniature cows. My machine pumps smooth and steady, sucking and squeezing the milk gently from the udder in a fraction of the time it took me to milk by hand. Maizy, my full-size Jersey, produces about 4 gallons from her once-a-day milking, and the machine milked her dry in about five minutes. I was done with milking and clean-up in less time than I spent just *getting* the milk out of her teats before when I milked by hand. For more details on my machine, see p. 225.

210

Pre-Cleanup

When it comes to milking cows, it's all about cleanliness whether you milk by hand or machine. Keeping your milking area—and your cows—clean is the best way to protect your milk from contamination. Here's how I get my girls ready for milking.

To help keep the milking parlor clean, I like to clean the cows outdoors before I bring them inside to milk them. I made a cow-cleaning and foot-washing station directly outside my milking parlor using four 4' x 6' black rubber stall mats and an antique head gate.

Before milking, each cow is locked into the head gate and given a snack of organic alfalfa pellets (p. 259) to nibble on while she's being cleaned.

First, she gets a thorough brushing, head to tail and everywhere in between (including her udder), to remove straw, loose hair, and dirt.

Then, I spray the dirt and mud off each foot with a nozzle attached to a hose attached to a frost-free hydrant. In the winter, I have to drain the hose after each use.

Once a week, I trim the hair around each teat with an Oster A5 single-speed clipper, using an Oster Cryogen-X Blade size 40 (sold separately, both available on Amazon.com). Keeping the hair around each teat clipped short helps with cleanliness.

After her outside cleaning, I bring her into my milking parlor (p. 238). It's amazing how quickly a cow learns the routine of milking. With a little work and consistency, your cow will get used to standing for cleaning and then enter the milking parlor and walk right into the stanchion. The first few times, you'll have to lead her where you want her to go.

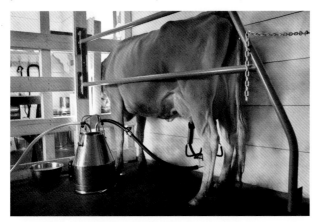

The best way I've found to train my girls is to reward them with small amounts of organic alfalfa pellets.

I feed about 1 1/2 lbs (approx. 6 cups) to each cow (depending on the size of the cow) during cleaning and milking. For easy measuring, I use a 3-quart feed scoop that has measuring marks on it. Alfalfa pellets give them a nourishing treat and help distract them while I'm milking.

Even though my girls are, for the most part, well-behaved, I like to use a milking hobble (HobbleMan.com). It's a piece of webbing with loops at each end. In my setup, I hook one loop to her rear lower leg and the other to the back of the stanchion. (If you don't have a milking sidebar like I do that fastens to the wall with a chain, you can use it to hobble her rear legs together.) Then I pull and tighten the strap so that she can't rest her weight on her leg, but can still use it for stability. Because stanchion setups and cows come in so many different sizes, I've easily customized some of my hobbles using a heavy-duty sewing machine. If you can't buy exactly what you need, think "make do!"

After her head is secured in the stanchion, I clean her udder and teats. Making sure you get them clean is the most important part of milking. You'll be washing off dirt, hair—and, yes, poo—from her udder and teats.

Feeding Grain

The grass-fed movement is most certainly a good thing for many different reasons. Because the diet of cows in large dairies and feedlots is often 50–90% "grain" that isn't really grain, but instead a mixture of genetically engineered corn, sorghum, soy, and by-products from other industries, grain ended up getting a bad rap. Corn, sorghum, and soy are very-high-energy feeds that are low in fiber. When cows are fed predominantly high-energy feed without enough fiber, they have a high risk of ulcers in the rumen, which leads to infections, which leads to antibiotics, on and on. Feeding antibiotics throws off the ruminal microbial ecosystem even more. When the rumen cannot digest properly, a high amount of yeast is passed on to the intestines. The yeast feeds and consequently increases the amount of E. coli bacteria that is normally kept in check. The cows end up being a breeding ground for E. coli. Even though I feed my cattle alfalfa pellets, I have on occasion mixed all-purpose livestock and dairy pellets in with their alfalfa pellets. I used an organic pellet composed of wheat, corn, peas, vitamins, and minerals. I mixed this with organic alfalfa pellets and gave it to my girls ONLY as a treat, not a food source. So if you think of "grain" as a treat and not as a food source or even a food supplement, it can be part of your milking protocol. If you're not convinced, then go with just the alfalfa pellets (my chickens love them in the winter soaked in milk when greens are scarce). Both are available organically grown (important so that you know they're non-GMO) at ModestoMilling.com.

My first method for cleaning the udder and teats is definitely old-fashioned. In fact, it's outdated in certain circles, but I think it's more accessible psychologically, so I included it, along with several other options that have more modern-day dairy science behind them. I figure it's all about options, right? There's one thing I know for sure—you want a backyard milk cow because you have a mind of your own!!!

First, I fill a 6-quart, stainless-steel bowl (bowls are easier to keep clean than buckets) with water (warm if you can, because that will help your cow let down her milk) and one tiny squirt of organic, liquid Castille soap (MountainRoseHerbs.com).

Then I put on a pair of rubber gloves. This is to protect the cow from what might be on my hands and protect my hands from what might be on the cow and to keep my hands cleaner for the job ahead. Sanitation. Sanitation. Sanitation.

There's a reason for sanitation. Milk is an excellent medium for microbial growth. Around the turn of the century, milk became recognized as a source of disease. For example, between 1912 and 1937, some 65,000 people in England and Wales died of tuberculosis contracted from consuming milk. (The State of Idaho requires that my cows be tested annually for TB.) But milk doesn't need to be on anyone's danger list because it's so easy now to make it safe. And if you're not the one doing the milking, make sure you check in occasionally on the person who is and pay close attention to his/her attention to cleanliness. Don't just hope for the best. Make sure you're getting the best. Remember, no shortcuts when it comes to cow cleanliness.

I use a sponge (Scotch-Brite makes a scrub sponge version from recycled and plant-based fibers) because it holds the amount of water I need for squeezing cleansing water onto the base of her udder and teats as it drips back down into my bowl. I don't use the scrub side on her and I use a new sponge every day. After its one-time use as an udder wash sponge, it goes into my washing machine and then into the dryer or it gets sun-dried on my clothesline before being used for a million different cleaning jobs around the farm—floors, water tanks, etc.

ouch!

This teat has a scabby boo-boo because I put my girl out to pasture in some tall grass that cut her teats. I disinfected them with iodine twice a day and then softened them with shea butter (MountainRoseHerbs.com). I continued to milk her (she'd be in a world of hurt otherwise), but I can't imagine it felt good to have them milked. I discarded her milk until her teats were healed.

213

For an alternative to cleaning the udder with water, you can buy disposable Teat Wipes (HambyDairySupply.com). Essentially "wet wipes" for cows, they come in a 5-gallon bucket with a dispensing hole in the top and instructions to wipe and massage each teat for 15 seconds, one wipe per teat.

Or, you can clean the base of her udder and teats using the iodine–based antiseptic teat dip solution you're going to dip her teats into just before you milk her. I know it's weird, but it works. Simply fill a spray bottle with the iodine solution and spritz the base of her udder and teats while you spread it around, using a disposable shop towel, one per teat. (Shop towels are stronger than regular paper towels.)

Now, after making sure the udder isn't dripping any water or iodine, "strip" each teat into a cup. A proper strip cup (HambyDairySupply.com) has a plastic screen for easy identification of clots of abnormal milk, but because my girls have never had a case of mastitis, I use mine without the screen. Stripping means to milk out several squirts of milk from each teat that you discard after inspecting it. This cleans out the teat ducts and allows fresh, sterile milk to enter the teats.

Then, I do the California Mastitis Test or CMT (p. 215), HambyDairySupply.com. This test lets me know if my cows are starting to get mastitis even before they show any signs. I do this test every day, using the instructions at right. My vigilance has paid off, because my girls have never yet had a case of mastitis.

Next, I dip each teat in a fresh batch of iodine–based antiseptic teat dip solution using a dip cup (HambyDairySupply.com), and wait at least 30 seconds while I go back to the sink to rinse out the cup (it doesn't hurt to have 2 teat cups on hand—they're cheap) and take off my rubber "wash gloves" and hang them to dry until the next milking. Sorry, you can't get away with mixing your own iodine solution by mixing iodine with tap water because it can deactivate the iodine's antiseptic properties. Commercial teat dips include things like glycerin to help keep the skin soft and additives to stabilize the iodine so it stays effective as an antiseptic. Commercial iodine-based teat dips (HambyDairySupply.com) are allowed for use on organic dairies by the USDA National Organic Program.

If her teats aren't dry by the time I come back, I dry them with 4 different single–service paper towels, avoiding contact with my hands. A good industrial-style, wall-mount, paper-towel holder with a single-handed trigger is a handy thing to have nearby.

Now it's time to milk!

California Mastitis Test (CMT)

1. After cleaning and stripping the teats but before dipping them in iodine, squirt 6–8 squirts of milk from each teat into a corresponding CMT cup. One teat per cup.

2. Tilt tray to the side and pour out milk until the milk is level with the raised outside circle in each cup.

3. Now, tilt the tray back up slightly and add enough activation solution (make sure you shake it first—this is important!!!!!) to each cup until the milk touches the inside circle in each cup. (The kit comes with directions.)

4. Level it and swirl. Look for coagulation of milk in any of the four cups.

If you see the milk starting to coagulate in any of the cups, then mastitis is starting to form in that corresponding quarter of the udder. (Not only does your cow have four teats, her udder is divided into four distinct quarters.) I do this test every time before I milk. Because I take such good care of my girls and feed them only organic feed and make sure they have clean bedding and daily exercise, I've never yet had a case of clinical mastitis that required antibiotics. I have had slight coagulation a few times. When that happens, I give my girls vitamin C powder (Wholistic Ester-C from TheWholisticPet.com under Health Care Supplements) in their alfalfa treat and within a couple of days, the slight coagulation disappears. This is why I check every day, so I can ward off any infections. If you have a cow that won't eat her alfalfa treat with vitamin C powder added, mix a bit of molasses in also and she should gobble it up. If that doesn't work, put the vitamin C powder and molasses mix into a 50 ml drench syringe (HambyDairySupply.com) and empty the syringe onto the back of her tongue through the side of her mouth.

Hand Milking

Once I'm done with the pre-cleaning of the cow and her udder (p. 211), I wash and dry my hands (think surgically clean!) and I put on a pair of nitrile gloves. (I find the gloves not only keep everything cleaner—hands harbor a plethora of different bacteria—but they make it easier for me to grip the teat.) Then I take a seat and get into position. A 5-gallon bucket turned upside-down works just fine for a stool. I milk two teats (two quarters in dairy jargon) at a time—the two on the side closest to me—and then I milk the other two teats either by moving around to my cow's other side or by staying in the same place and reaching past the first two teats. Some beginners find it easier to milk just one teat at a time until they get the hang of it. Also, if you lean into your cow with your head, you'll be able to feel (sense?) her muscles tightening before she actually moves, enabling you to grab the bucket should she decide to lift or move a foot and spill your hard-earned treasure. Once she settles again, you can proceed. You should consider hobbling her rear legs so you're not crying over spilled milk (p. 212).

When hand milking, the object is to pinch off the back flow of milk from the teat back into the udder at about the same time you begin squeezing the milk trapped in the teat down and out through the teat duct.

First, position the teat where it attaches to the udder into the crook of your thumb and forefinger.

Next, grip the teat with your thumb and forefinger in order to pinch off back flow going from the teat back up and into the udder.

In the same motion that you're using to close off any back flow, squeeze the milk trapped in the teat down and out of the teat using your other fingers. Depending on the length of the teats, your ring and little fingers might not serve any function at all other than to stay out of the way of the stream of milk squirting into your bucket.

Finally, open your hand to let the teat fill up with milk again and continue, pulling down gently. Repeat. Did I say repeat? Repeat MANY times.

Be patient with yourself. It'll take a while to get a rhythm down. Go slowly at first. Take your time. Don't look at your watch. Just go with the flow! If you're getting a strong, steady stream of milk each time, then you're probably getting it right. As you do it more, you'll figure out your own particular motion and what works best for you. Everyone seems to do it a little differently. For the comfort and health of your cow's udder, it's important not to pull or squeeze too hard (that can damage the tissues in the teats) and to keep an even, steady pace.

When I first started milking, it would take me a full hour to milk my cow dry. After half an hour, my hands were tired. But within a couple of weeks, my hands got stronger and faster and I was down to 45 minutes. It speeds things up if you can get a helper to milk the other side at the same time. That's what good friends are for! Or spouses. Or children.

216

~ Machine Milking ~

While there are different types of milking machines to choose from, they all operate under the same principle— vacuum pressure sucks the milk out of the teat. Here's my milking protocol using a NuPulse milking machine (the basics will be pretty much the same for other brands of machines).

Clean your cow (p. 211).

Make sure the hose that leads to the milking claw is clamped shut, then turn on the pump and wait for it to reach the right pressure (or follow the instructions that come with the machine you've chosen).

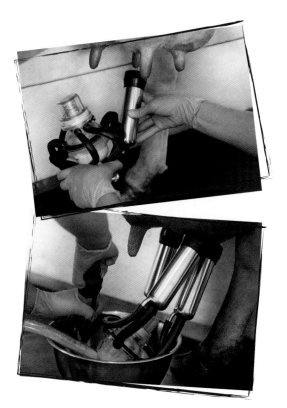

Wash and dry your hands and put on a pair of nitrile gloves. If you have big hands (I don't), take the claw in one hand and hold it so that all four hoses going to the inflations (the rubber thingies inside each metal tube) are pinched off. Open the clamp on the main milk hose to start the suction to the claw, and one by one, unpinch the hoses and put an inflation on each of the four teats.

If you have small hands like I do, this is where another 6-quart, stainless-steel bowl comes in (not the bowl you used to clean her udder and teats). My bowl method also comes in handy for milking cows that are short and lower to the ground like my mid-size Jerseys. I nestle the claw into the bowl with each inflation plugged using the red stoppers that came with my machine. (See p. 220 for how to milk a mini-cow.)

If you have all four inflations sucking air when you open up the main valve, you'll be sucking hair and other debris into your milk tank. Not a good idea! Using my nitrile-gloved (AKA clean!) hands, I make sure the hose to each inflation is pinched off while I pull out its red stopper and drop it into the bowl. In other words, I'm putting them on one at a time while the other inflations rest in the clean bowl and not on the ground. I also like using the red stoppers because I can take an inflation off and leave the others still sucking, should a particular teat run dry before the others. This will happen if you're letting a calf nurse on your cow.

More on Milking Machines ...

Even though I bought a 7-gallon milk bucket for my NuPulse milker, they also offer a 3-gallon. My machine without milk weighs 28 lbs. A gallon of milk weighs around 8 lbs. If you're not producing more than 3 gallons of milk in one milking, you should buy the 3-gallon bucket so it isn't as heavy. (Keep in mind, if your cow ever produced more than 3 gallons and it backed up into the machine, you'd have a problem on your hands.) So if you add up 28 lbs and the weight of the milk, you have a bit of poundage to haul around. My milking parlor is a good jaunt from where I process my milk, so I haul my machine on a dolly that I customized with a strap and a bottom plate that's a tad wider than it was originally. As it turns out, my milk dolly has been put to use in a dozen different ways around the farm. I also use it to haul around my 50-lb sacks of organic alfalfa pellets.

It can damage teat tissue for a dry teat to continue to be sucked for too long. I can tell if a teat has gone dry with my NuPulse because the four tubes going into the mixing chamber are see-through. To remove an inflation, simply pinch off the small black hose going directly to it and gently remove it from the teat. Once removed, put the red stopper in while the others continue to extract milk.

Now back to the big-hand method! One by one, attach an inflation to each teat. When you attach the inflations, make sure to keep the hose to each inflation pinched off until the teat is aligned in the opening, about a half-inch down into it. Then, unkink the hose and the teat will suck down into the inflation. Again, the reason you want to keep the hose pinched off until the moment it's in position to suck the teat down into the inflation—rather than bring an already sucking inflation to the teat—is because the air will suck in dust particles and hair (think of them as powerful mini vacuum cleaners).

After all four inflations are on her teats, let the machine do the work. How long it takes depends on the cow and how much milk she's producing. I can get as much as 3 gallons in 3–5 minutes.

When there's no more milk coming into the see-through chamber, she's done!

Secure the claw with one hand and set the metal clamp closed on the main hose using your other hand. Once the suction is clamped off, the claw and the inflations will easily drop off into your hand. Bring the claw to the milking machine at the same time you're coiling the hose. Hang it on the hook on the side of the milk tank.

Turn off the pump.

Give all four teats a post-milking iodine dip with fresh iodine, not the same batch of iodine you used for the pre-dip. You've discarded that. You do a post-dip because there will be a slight capillary action in each teat that will cause it to uptake a smidgen of protective iodine before she heads out into the manure scene again.

Now, let her teats air dry. It's good for her to stand for a bit after milking so the wax-like seal of the teat orifice seals back up. Post-dipping has been proven to dramatically reduce udder infections. Teat dips are allowed under organic standards, and I highly recommend them. They have glycerin added to condition the teats and the iodine is stable and has a long shelf life.

Give your girl a loving pat. Tell her you love her and send her on her way back outside. Then, away you go to process the milk. You'll come back to clean the area where you've milked after you've processed the milk and cleaned the milking machine. It's important to cool the milk immediately and clean the machine so that you don't end up with a deposit of fats and proteins on the various parts of the machine.

4 months later, momma & baby

meet Etta Jane at 2 years of age, almost 7 months pregnant

BABY ON BOARD!

Dairy Queen

⌘ Milking a Mini-cow ⌘

Just when you thought you had a handle on milking a cow, along comes a teensy, tiny mini-cow. With teats smaller than a goat's and barely enough space between the floor and her udder for the claw of a milking machine, mini-cows can be a unique challenge. I tried everything I could think of before ending up with a setup that I think will work universally for all mini-cows.

For perspective, here's my milking machine on my full-size Jersey (3–4 gallons once/day, 53" tall at the withers).

Here it is on my mid-size Jersey (1 1/2–2 gallons once/day, 46" tall at the withers).

And here it is on my mini-Jersey (1–2 quarts once/day, 39" tall at the withers).

During the last trimester of Etta Jane's pregnancy (her first), I brought her into my milking parlor every day for training. I locked her into the stanchion and fed her alfalfa pellets and then handled her udder so she'd get used to the idea. In theory, that's supposed to work, but let's just say this—Etta Jane behaved like a Radio City Rockette when it came time to actually milk her.

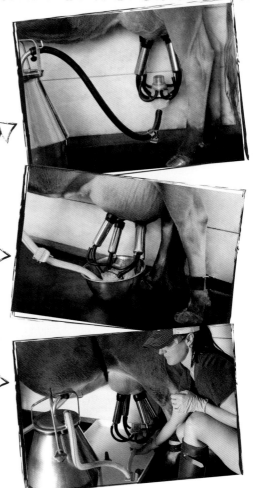

The first thing I do (or in this case, my daughter does) is put on a pair of "attractive" safety glasses. Seriously. When you're "down there" and tail hairs pepper your face, protective eyewear is mighty nice.

Once I have her head locked into the head gate on the stanchion, I fasten the side rail to the wall.

Then I tie a "flank rope" around her, using a rope with a slip knot for quick release. (In the photo, my daughter is using a lead rope, p. 203.) Remember to be calm and patient even though your cow isn't. My little Etta Jane was so scared, her legs trembled and she emptied her bowels about five times per session during her first week of training. Tie a loop in one end of the rope. Drape the untied end across her back and down her other side. Feed it through the loop, leaving it loose enough to slip it down in front of her hip bones and udder. Pull it tight. It should be tight enough to stop the kicking, but loose enough that she won't act like she's going to fall over. You should be able to get a couple of fingers under the rope.

Next, I hobble Etta Jane's outside back leg to the side rail, and pull it slightly back so she can still put weight on it for stability.

Then, using a much shorter hobble, I hobble her two back legs together. I had to do this because her unhobbled leg still wanted to shift and pull the milking claw off.

I had Hobbleman.net customize their "cow cuff links" for me per my specifications. Based on your setup, you can have them lengthen or shorten the middle connecting strap. I also have them put four extra holes in each cuff they make for me because my mini's legs are thinner. Ask for Connie at 989-386-2910.

Next, I prepped her udder per my instructions on p. 211.

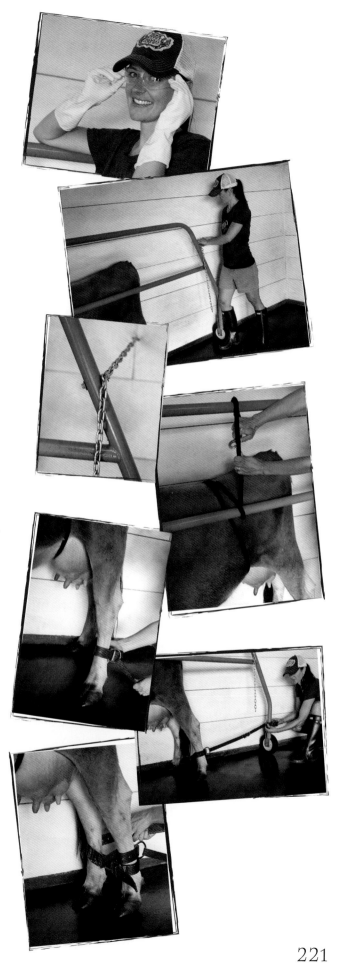

Ooops! Etta Jane gave my daughter a treasure! Truly. There are farmers in other cultures who catch their cow's "blessed nuggets" in ornate pots for giving life back to the soil—no manure, no crops. I've always said that if I had a choice between a pile of manure and a pile of money, I'd choose manure. Pure gold, that stuff.

An unexpected cleanup ensues, using a shovel, a small hoe, some water, and a quick swipe with a mop.

Now prep her udder as detailed on p. 213.

Here's the tricky part. Because the milking claw is only slightly more than an inch off the ground (once she's more comfortable being milked, I'll try getting her to put her back legs up on a piece of wood), I had to come up with a system where one hand takes out the red stoppers and the other hand holds the claw on by exerting slight pressure upward. With my bigger cows, once the inflations/shells are suctioned onto a teat, they stay. But with my mini, her teats are so small, the suction isn't all that great. It suctions enough to extract milk, but not enough to stay on reliably. It almost does, but more often than not, she'll shift and one will drop off and then the whole thing loses suction and the other three drop off.

That's where a white fiberglass tray I just happened to have came in handy. (I can't use a bowl like I do with my mid-size cows because I don't have enough clearance.) A quick spritz from my 200 ppm bleach spray bottle and I'm ready!

I wash and dry my hands and put on a pair of nitrile gloves. With the claw lying on the tray (the 2" sides keep the inflations/shells from straying over the edges—I tried to use a cookie sheet, but the sides weren't high enough), I pull one red stopper out and put an inflation/shell on the back right teat. From then on, I keep my right hand under the claw (exerting slight pressure upward) and with my left hand, take the other three stoppers out, one at a time, and allow the inflations/shells to suction onto the rest of the teats.

Once all four inflations/shells are on, I get in a comfortable position while still holding the claw and watch the claw fill with milk and pump into the nearby tank.

Once I no longer see milk coming into the claw, I reach with my left hand and close the valve on the tube. All four shells drop onto the clean tray (with a little guidance from my right hand).

Standing, I lift the claw into the air after I've re-opened the valve to make sure all the milk from the claw goes into the tank and then close the valve again and hang the claw on the side of the tank. I unplug the machine.

I pick up the stoppers and remove the tray.

I dip her teats in iodine, and in reverse order, remove her constraints, all the while whispering sweet nothings in her ear.

Quick tip

Moisturizing Milk Mask
Mix 2 T honey with 2 t milk and apply to face and neck area. Leave on for 10 minutes; rinse well with warm water.

Butters' Buttermilk Hair Conditioner
This deep conditioner hydrates and strengthens your hair, boosts manageability, and helps prevent dandruff. Mix 1/2 cup buttermilk with 1 cup plain yogurt, 1 egg yolk, and 2 T honey. Apply to hair and scalp. Leave on for 30 minutes, then rinse with warm water. Shampoo and style as usual.

Cleopatra's Milk Bath
Cleopatra, said to be the greatest beauty in history, was famous for bathing in honey and milk to keep her skin soft. The lactic acid in the milk is a type of alpha-hydroxy acid, and it naturally dissolves the bonds that hold onto dead skin cells. Mix 2 cups fresh milk or buttermilk with 1 cup honey and a few drops of your favorite essential oil. Pour mixture into tub as bath is running. Relax and soak for about 20 minutes. Exfoliate with a loofah sponge.

Milk-based body care products are available ready-made, DairyFace.com, p. 378.

Etta Jane really calms down when I talk to her. It goes something like this: "Aren't you a pretty girl, Etta Jane, love of my life, sweet, sweet ..." You get the idea. Over time, **I know Etta Jane will eventually get used to being milked**—just like her mother, who's a pro—and I won't have to constrain her so much. **And then off to process the milk I go.**

Side note:

You might be thinking, "Why can't I use a milking machine designed for goats on my mini-cow—they're about the same size?" Here's why. Goats have only two teats. (I think nature got it backwards because a goat can have four kids, but a cow almost always has only one calf.) Also, the teat orifice on a goat is much smaller than on a cow. Consequently, the tubing that carries the milk can't carry the rush of milk a cow can give, even a mini. The milk can flood back up and out the top of the inflations/shells.

That said, I did end up buying four shells designed for use on goats that I paired with the four cow inflations (MZ-10057-4 NuPulse Super) that came with my NuPulse milking machine. (I did try almost every kind of inflation presently sold, including triangle-shaped inflations. I even tried cutting the tubes shorter.) My NuPulse milking machine was clearly built to last because it was originally designed for large dairies. That means the stainless-steel shells are heavy and will stand up to lots of wear and tear. All four shells that came with my machine weighed close to 3 pounds. The goat shells I replaced them with weigh just under 2 pounds.

When it was all said and done, I ended up preferring the setup for my mini-cow (goat shells paired with cow inflations) for ALL my cows because it's lighter, and I think easier, on their teats. This was verified when I realized that when I strained their milk right after milking, it was always a tad foamy. I thought that was normal, but as it turns out, the suctioning was compromised somewhat because of the sheer weight of the shells. So for milking all my cows, I bought four shells designed for goats from HambyDairySupply.com, NuPulse L (light) 505-MZ207LL as opposed to the NuPulse H (heavy) shells that came with my NuPulse milking machine.

⌒⌒ Strain. Thermize. Bottle. Cool ⌒⌒

As I explained on p. 15, I don't think the concept of heat-treating milk is the culprit that has compromised the quality of modern-day milk. I think it's homogenization and things like ultra-or high-heat pasteurization, routine antibiotics, growth hormones, GMO-tainted feed, etc.

So for me, processing milk is a four–step process: Strain. Thermize. Bottle. Cool.

Strain:

I strain the milk while I pour it into the inside container of the pasteurizer (which is set to 150°F so that the milk is thermized, not pasteurized). The strainer is a wide, stainless-steel funnel called a "milk funnel" with a center ring that holds a disposable milk filter that catches anything that may have fallen into the milk, available at BobWhiteSystems.com. When hand–milking, straining is even more important for catching any hairs, straw, or particles that might have fallen into the bucket. The first time I strained the milk from the milk machine, I was pleased to find absolutely nothing on the pad. Not so when I milk by hand. Even with a thorough pre-cleaning of my cow, I usually have a hair or two or little flakes of debris that have somehow found their way into my milk bucket. Using a milking machine keeps the milk much cleaner.

226

Thermize:

I use the Kleen-Flo Pasteurizer (p. 30) to heat-treat my milk. It's a 2-gallon, stainless-steel, electric double boiler that you set at a desired temperature and plug in. When it's done, a buzzer goes off and you unplug it. If you set it at 150°F, you'll be thermizing the milk, not pasteurizing it (p. 17). It takes about 15–20 minutes to reach 150°F. Not a problem. I use the time to clean the milking machine, and that takes about 20 minutes. The directions that come with the Kleen-Flo have you cooling the milk after you've heated it by running cold water into the outer canister. This seemed to take forever, so I don't recommend it. But because the hot water level goes slightly above the inside container, you'll need to ladle a bit of it off before taking off the lid of the inside canister to get to where the milk is.

Bottle:

I use a wide-mouth, stainless-steel ladle and a funnel to get the milk into 1/2-gallon canning jars. I cap each bottle with a white plastic storage lid made by Ball because they don't rust and are easier to clean.

Cool:

Our state requires that fresh milk be brought down to a temperature of 40°F within two hours. (Your fridge should always be at 36°F). Putting bottles of milk (even if they haven't been thermized) into your refrigerator won't get the milk down to temperature fast enough. Milk that is cooled quickly and then kept at 36°F will keep much longer than improperly chilled milk, plus it's safer—bacteria grows rapidly in warm milk, doubling in count every 20 minutes.

When I embarked on choosing a method to get my fresh milk down to a temperature of 40°F within two hours, I thought I had several options, but as it turns out, I ended up discovering that only one method really works. However, I did try them all—saline slush kept in your freezer (the salt settles out and gets messy); antifreeze slush kept in the freezer (toxic substance to have around food, and besides, it has a chemical odor); alcohol slush (the alcohol evaporates and is expensive to buy and replace); a stainless-steel wort chiller used by home brewers (unless your tap water is 40°F or less {unlikely}, this won't work, plus it's time-consuming to clean the chiller in between batches); a Rapi-Kool cold paddle used by restaurants (this is like a giant frozen popsicle encased in plastic—requires lots of stirring and not very sanitary because you have to keep the milk in a tall, open container in your fridge); putting bottles of milk into the freezer for two hours (this didn't even work with fresh-from-the-cow milk that was only 100°F to start with—after two hours, the freezer only brought it down to 49°F, so it definitely won't work for thermized milk.)

And finally, an ice bath (this worked, but it required some fine-tuning—see next page).

> An average micro dairy farm of four pasture-grazing and relaxed cows can easily produce 20 gallons of milk a day—enough to supply 60 average families. Many Vermont raw-milk producers sell their farm-fresh milk between $6–8 per gallon. To average, if micro dairy farmers can sell milk at $7, they can turn a profit of $3.60 per gallon. Approximately half of this revenue would go towards production costs, while the other half could make an estimated $20,000 annual income. (All dairies selling products must follow the regulations of the state they are in.)
>
> – BobWhiteSystems.com

Here's a tried-and-true method that works every time, anytime, anywhere. But first let me say this: I've learned more about the principles of heat exchange and the properties of ice than I thought a milkmaid would ever need to know!

An ice-water bath is ideal, especially if you use an insulated ice chest. (Less wasted energy. Why use something like a galvanized tub and transfer your hard-earned cooling energy out into the room?) As each ice cube melts, it immediately changes the temperature of the water surrounding it, and the chilled water, in turn, cools the milk in the bottles (you do have to jiggle your jugs ☺—milk bottles—every half-hour or so to circulate the milk in the bottles and bring the inner hot milk out closer to the bottles' edges.) But that's a lot of ice cubes every day, right? In order for that to work (even for milk that isn't heat-treated), I ended up buying bags of ice in town. That's not very sustainable, plus bags of ice cost money. So, I thought, frozen water packs! But as store-bought ice packs melt, you end up with an ice mass surrounded by water that can't circulate and, in fact, acts as insulation so the ice isn't chilling the water surrounding the bottles enough. In other words, ice packs weren't getting my milk down to 40°F in two hours. Hmmmm. That's when I decided to toss three dozen 16.9-ounce containers of bottled water into my freezer. I bought the cheapest bottled water I could find because that meant the plastic was thin and flimsy to allow for them to bulge when they were frozen without me having to open each one and pour out some of the contents.

I put six 1/2-gallon bottles of thermized milk (150°F) into an 80-quart Rubbermaid ice chest and then surrounded the bottles of milk with frozen bottles of water (about two dozen). Next, I filled the ice chest with cold water until the water level was up to the shoulders of each bottle of milk, and then I shut the lid. After two hours, my milk was at 50°F. More head-scratching, but I felt like I was getting close. After my next milking, I made sure I twirled the bottles of milk every half hour. I also took out half the bottles of frozen water and added a new batch that were fully frozen. The result? 48°F. Close, but not quite. Okay, I thought, how about circulating the water with an aquarium pump? The first pump I tried wasn't powerful enough, so I bought a more powerful aquarium pump and it worked!!!! Success.

So to recap, start with an ice chest that matches the number of milk bottles you need to chill. My 80-quart ice chest chills six 1/2-gallon bottles of milk. Ice chests come in all sizes from 25-quart on up to 150-quart.

Buy three dozen 16.9–ounce bottles of water and put them in your freezer.

Purchase a Hydor Koralia Circulation and Wave Pump with a flow rate of 425 gph. For an ice chest larger than 80-quart, you'll probably need two of them or one 750–850 gph. Both types can be found online at Amazon.com.

And remember to jiggle your jugs every half hour. You're way cool now! Whether it's milk fresh from the cow (100°F) or thermized (150°F) milk that you're trying to bring to a temperature of 40°F in two hours, this method works every time and requires less fussing than anything else. Just remember to put your bottles of water back into the freezer so you can re-use them.

Now that you've cooled your milk, the bottles go into your refrigerator. Here's a new saying for you: "Never trust a refrigerator." It's wise to invest in a secondary thermometer that hangs on a shelf so that you can monitor the temperature of your fridge easily. It should at all times be 36°F. Any warmer, and your milk won't keep as long.

I've also used a "spring cooler" that I made out of a large plastic storage tub, but this only works for me during the winter. Why only the winter? My well water is pumped into a 3,000-gallon, above-ground storage tank that is housed in an insulated building that doesn't let the water in the tank freeze, but does keep our potable water at a temperature between 32°F and 40°F during the winter. Water straight from my well in my geographic location averages 55°F. Depending on where you live, well water can be anywhere from 37–77°F. What a range, right? A spring cooler might work for you, even in the summer, but first you have to get out your thermometer and check the temperature of your well water. Years ago, when I lived on a remote ranch without electricity, we cooled and then stored our fresh milk in a small, insulated house built over a bubbling spring (obviously, our artesian well water was closer to the low end of 37°F). To recreate an old-fashioned "spring cooler" at my farm (remember, it only works during the winter for me), I drilled 3/8" holes in a plastic tub level with the shoulders of my bottles, then I fill it with water from a garden hose attached to a frost-free hydrant. Once the tub fills to the holes, I turn the water down to a tiny trickle and put the bottles of milk in the tub, held in place using old-fashioned wire baskets. The overflow runs down a ditch behind the tub and through a culvert and then into a creek on my property. The cold water circulating around the bottles cools my heat-treated milk down to 40°F within two hours. Perfect!

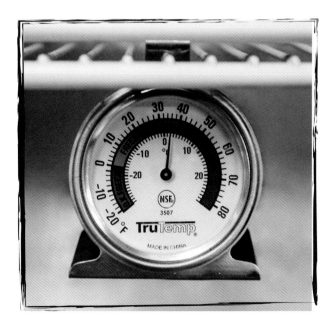

Just to be sure—get your milk tested.

Once you get your milking routine down, it's a good idea to send off a milk sample to Udder Health Systems (UdderHealth. com) for quality testing. Think of it as a correspondence course you've just completed and now you're going to be graded on your cleanliness performance. Udder Health of Idaho (you can ship milk to them from anywhere, but you should check with your state to find out if there's someone closer to you) tests milk for three things: **Coliform**, **Somatic Cell Count (SCC)**, and **Standard Plate Count (SPC)**. The Coliform test is a total count of Coliform-type bacteria, including possible *E. Coli* bacteria. The SCC is a count of the somatic cells present in a milk sample. Somatic cells are produced in the udder of a cow. When there's an infection in the udder, the number of somatic cells in a sample goes up (all milk naturally contains some somatic cells). The SPC is a count of all other bacteria. When I failed my first test, I passed the Coliform test and the SCC, but the SPC (all other bacteria) count was high, so I was pretty sure the contamination happened somewhere in the processing of the milk and not because my cow had an infection or I'd failed to clean her udder and teats well enough. I went through each part of my milking protocol, looking for anything that could be contaminating the milk with non-Coliform bacteria— things like dirty hands or equipment or bottles that weren't getting cleaned well enough.

To sell raw milk in the State of Idaho under the State of Idaho Small Herd Exemption (dairy laws vary from state to state —you can see our regulations on p. 336), we are required to have our milk tested monthly and have a Coliform count of less than 25, a SCC of less than 500,000, and a SPC count of less than 15,000 mg/l. (Idaho foots the bill on this by sending our local veterinary dairy inspector here once per month to collect a sample that he sends off for testing.) The milk must also test negative for any drugs that are restricted by the state in milk production. At the time of the collection, the temperature of the milk sample must be at or below 40˚F (36˚F is ideal). Udder Health Systems will send you a test kit in an insulated box with an ice pack and information on returning it to them by either FedEx or UPS next day air delivery.

Udder Health Systems, INC.
Milk Quality Testing
901 N. Lincoln
Jerome, ID 83338
(208) 644-9381
UdderHealth.com

Post-Cleanup

The only down side to the milking machine is the fact that it needs to be sanitized after each use. You can buy a "washing system," but even then, you'll need to take everything apart once a week to clean it more thoroughly. (I did buy the washing system for my machine, but decided it wasn't saving me any time.) Besides, the State of Idaho prefers that I take my milking machine apart and wash all its parts every day. Not a problem. I've gotten into the routine and like knowing all its nooks and crannies. My machine isn't keeping any nasty secrets from me!

Our state inspector discussed bacterial contamination with me. He pointed out that my milking machine and all its various tubes and parts, after being cleaned every day, needed to be allowed to dry completely in a sanitary place. He said, "Standing water is your enemy." I also purchased a variety of different cleaning brushes for my particular machine, in addition to a cleaning cable for cleaning inside the hoses. I put hooks (called a Giant Spring Grip) on the wall so the hoses can hang vertically, allowing them to dry completely, because a loop traps moisture.

I resurrected an old portable dishwasher from my basement to use as my "sanitary place." After rinsing everything in warm 100°F water in my sink (the temperature of fresh milk)—not hot water yet because that might cause the milk fats to melt and coat things, and not cold water because that might turn the milk fats into butter, and we all know about butter's ability to coat things—I start cleaning everything with liquid soap and water as hot as my gloved hands can stand. As I'm thoroughly washing all the machine parts using all the different brushes designed specifically for the parts of my machine and a clean, new sponge each day, I give them one final, warm-water rinse and then place the parts in the dishwasher, including the cleaning brushes (all but the milk tank that goes upside-down on a clean dish drainer and the hoses that hang on the wall).

Quick tip

There's a tricky procedure on my NuPulse that was threatening to break my thumbs. The instructions say to pull the inflation through the stainless-steel outer shell past the ridge, but getting that pushed back through for cleaning wasn't exactly a picnic. I've found that it isn't necessary to pull them all the way through, and the machine still works like a charm. And I have happy thumbs again.

When I'm done, I run the dishwasher without soap (just warm water), but I have the heat cycle turned OFF so that the rubber parts of the machine don't get warped from the heat. After the dishwasher is done, I crack the door open so everything inside dries. All the machine parts, even the special cleaning brushes, stay in the dishwasher (my sanitary place) until I'm ready to assemble them again (using gloved hands). The gloves actually make it easier to grip the hoses when I'm putting the machine back together again. (My favorite gloves for this are Playtex Living Drip-Catch Cuff because they grip the best.)

Our state inspector also suggested that we spray or wipe down our counters, etc. with a 200 ppm (parts per million) bleach solution (p. 234). By following all these steps (and always keeping our milking parlor sparkly clean), we've passed our state test every time since our first failed attempts.

Quick Tips for Post-Cleanup

1. There's a gasket on the lid of my pasteurizer (used to thermize milk in my case) that I remove daily for cleaning. If you attempt to put it back in place when it's dry, it will try to pop back off continually as you're stretching it to fit around the edges. It goes on first try and stays on if you stretch it into place while running hot water over it.

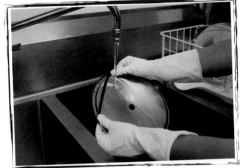

2. Make sure you get into the habit of spritzing (with your 200 ppm bleach solution) and then wiping dry the inside of the canister on your vacuum pump.

3. It's also good to sanitize the long stretch of air hose that goes from your vacuum pump to your milk tank. To do this, I spritz some of my 200 ppm bleach solution into one end while I have the hose coiled. Then I slowly twirl it until the solution comes out the other end. Then I hang the hose in a giant spring grip (p. 231) near the ceiling of my milking parlor (using a small step stool to reach that high) to drain and dry overnight.

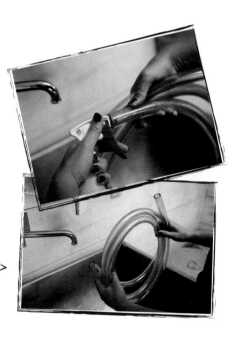

4. ## Liquid Dishwashing Soaps

I diligently tried a variety of all my favorite "green" liquid dishwashing soaps, but they either made the equipment too slippery to handle or rinsing off the soap afterward took too long. I ended up preferring the liquid soap designed specifically for cleaning milking machines because it removes the milk deposits so effectively. (Your machine will get dingy-looking and increasingly difficult to clean over time if you're not removing these deposits.) It suds up nicely, rinses away quickly, has no odor, and doesn't make the parts of my machine slippery to handle. It's concentrated, so a little goes a long way. Liquipfan is available at HambyDairySupply.com. Its Material Safety Data Sheet can be found on the red download button right below the order button. I added a handy-dandy, one-gallon-bottle dispensing pump from Amazon.com. Depending on the quality of your water, you still might end up over time with a film known as milk stone on the stainless-steel components of your milking machine. If that happens, you can "acid rinse" them using Citrophos, also available at HambyDairySupply.com. I've never had to acid-rinse my milking machine.

What's a sanitary milkmaid to do?

Even though you can find information on the Web about "natural" sanitizing using hydrogen peroxide, vinegar, and even isopropyl alcohol, a diluted bleach solution is still the most effective germ killer. (In the chart at right, note that **both hydrogen peroxide and vinegar need to be heated to 130°F**, a difficult task in a milking parlor.)

Chlorine Bleach

When cleaning your dairy surfaces and equipment, remember this mantra: Clean, rinse, sanitize. First, wash and rinse all surfaces. (Both dirt and detergents deactivate chlorine, and the ammonia in urine can cause noxious fumes.) Then, sanitize with a bleach solution of 200 ppm (1 scant t to 1 qt water). Perfect for a spray bottle! Allow the solution to sit on the surface for at least a minute to give the bleach time to work. (At this concentration, the bleach won't harm stainless steel surfaces.) Diluted bleach also breaks down quickly (primarily into table salt and oxygen) in the environment. Never combine it with ammonia, cleaners, or any acid (like vinegar), as this can cause toxic gases.

Choose "regular" bleach instead of "concentrated" with no added soaps or fragrances. Sodium hypochlorite of the concentration of 5.25% to 6% should be the only active ingredient in the bleach. (Note: In the endless quest to market "bigger, better," the only bleach I could find in my local supermarket was either "concentrated," with 8.25% hypochlorite, or fragranced. Since I haven't found any reliable sources of conversion for the 200 ppm mixture I need, I simply add slightly less of the concentrated bleach.)

Did you know ...

Bleach has a shelf life? Bleach decomposes with heat, and only remains highly effective in its original container for about 6 months. Clorox adds more hypochlorite (the active ingredient in bleach) to batches made in the summer months to maintain a 6% hypochlorite level, the disinfection standard set by the EPA. Since it takes 1–2 months from manufacture to store, be sure to replace your bottle every 4–5 months and store it at room temperature. Also, diluted solutions (like in your handy-dandy spray bottle) need to be stored in a dark place (under the counter) and refreshed weekly.

Hydrogen Peroxide (See chart at right.)

Vinegar (See chart at right.)

While Isopropyl Alcohol does have antimicrobial properties, the FDA has not approved any sterilant or high-level disinfectant with alcohol as the main active ingredient. Alcohols aren't recommended for sterilizing because they lack sporicidal action and cannot penetrate protein-rich materials. They also evaporate rapidly, making extended exposure times difficult. Alcohols kill bacteria by destroying the proteins and enzymes within their cells. A 70% alcohol solution kills germs better than 90+% solutions because the more diluted alcohol can penetrate cells more effectively. (In this case, "more" isn't better.)

Iodine has been broadly used for prevention of infection and treatment of wounds since its discovery in 1811. Because molecular iodine can be toxic to tissues, formulas that dilute it with carriers were developed. Povidone-iodine (PVP-I) has been the universally preferred iodine antiseptic since 1955 and is available in solutions, creams, ointments, teat dips, and scrubs, but doesn't work for sanitizing equipment.

Sanitizers for Dairy Surfaces & Equipment

Item	Concentration	Temperature	Contact Time	*Listeria Monocytogenes*	*E. Coli*	*Salmonella*
Chlorine Bleach (6%)	1 scant t to 1 qt water	Room Temperature (77°F)	1 minute	✓	✓	✓
Hydrogen Peroxide (3%)	Undiluted	130°F	1 minute	✓	✓	✓
Hydrogen Peroxide (3%)	Undiluted	Room Temperature (77°F)	10 minutes		✓	✓
Distilled White Vinegar (5%)	Undiluted	130°F	1 minute	✓	✓	✓
Distilled White Vinegar (5%)	Undiluted	Room Temperature (77°F)	10 minutes			✓

✓ means that the product was effective at reducing the presence of the pathogen with more than 99.999% reduction.

Points to remember when using chlorine bleach:

- Diluted chlorine bleach is a **very effective sanitizer.** The amount needed is very small, and no chlorine residue will be left behind using a concentration of 1 scant t of chlorine bleach to 1 qt of water.

- Chlorine reacts quickly and becomes inactive quickly. Detergents and dirt deactivate chlorine; surfaces must be cleaned first to ensure sanitation.

- Chlorine solutions need to be made at least weekly and must be stored in a dark place.

- Don't use chlorine with added fragrance—this isn't food-safe.

Thanks to Ohio State University for helping with this information.

HOUSING

What is it about old barns? They speak to us, but what is it they're saying? You mustn't forget, they say. Don't forget your roots, the barn dances, the fiddler's reel, do-si-do, jumping from the haymow, the sighs of contented animals bedding down for the night, the shafts of morning light, the corncrib, the silo. It's no wonder we long for an era when barns were bigger than houses and the size of an outbuilding wasn't about the number of cars it held.

Over the course of many years, I've ended up with a hodge-podge of sheds and shelters fashioned from one of those historic barns (our own) that took a deep breath one day, exhaled, and caved in. The good news? We were left with a bounty of weathered tin and stout wooden beams, planks, flooring, and hardware. Talk about patina! I wonder if my cows know their home décor could be a dreamer's pin on Pinterest?

It took me years to upgrade my hay and straw storage from the use of a neighbor's barn in conjunction with on-site bales sitting on a tarp-covered pallet, to this. Meet Myrtle, the grain truck I once drove when hauling our wheat to-market-to-market. I could probably get her running again, but like *Mike Mulligan and His Steam Shovel*, she seems more than pleased to call it a day and hit the hay.

Not to be thought of as blueprints (you'll want to come up with your own plans), the following pages show the floor plans for our milking parlor and feed bunker, as well as the layouts from two of my smaller pastures that have animal shelters (backyard possibilities). Take from them what you will and then get out your hammer.

Milking Parlor

We whitewashed the inside of our milking parlor with old-fashioned milk paint, p. 370. For flooring, we put down 6" of compacted gravel covered in 3/4"-thick, black, rubber stall mats that come in 4' x 6' sheets. (I special ordered mine from our local feed store.) Because I mop the inside floor on a daily basis after milking, I purchased smooth stall mats for the inside floor. For the outside flooring, I bought non-slip stall mats. The rough surface of the non-slip mats wreaks havoc on your mop. Ultimately, I'd love to replace the mats with a concrete floor that has a drain in the middle. A girl can dream, can't she?

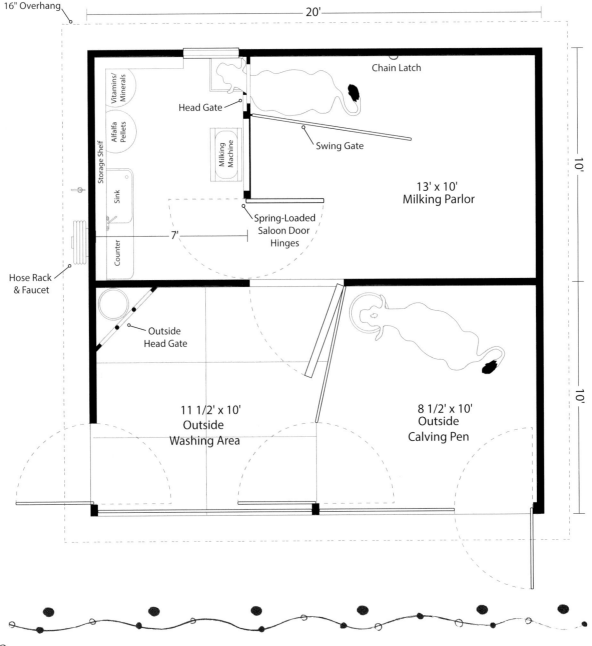

Milking Parlor Tips

• I keep a Eureka AirExcel Compact NLS Canister Vacuum (Amazon.com) handy for clean-up. It's small, has good suction, and comes with a HEPA filter and easy-empty dust cup.

• For daily mopping, I like the Quickie HomePro Premium Wet Mop (Amazon.com) because it's lightweight and a new mop head installs easily. Rather than deal with squeezing it out and trying to keep a mop bucket clean (you are dealing with poo, you know), here's how I mop the inside of my parlor. After I've sprayed off the feet of my cows outside the parlor (p. 211), I also hose my boots off, even the bottoms (the reason I like high-top, waterproof boots, p. 377). After I've processed the day's milk, I come back to clean. Starting in the outside washing area, mop in hand, I lay the mop head on the black mat that was recently hosed off, and spray the mop, even in the winter. I step all over the mop to "wring" it out and then go back inside to mop. After doing this several times, I've never bent over once or touched the poo-ey mop with my hands. Makes quick work of mopping. Before I hang the mop inside to dry, I squirt it with water one last time after adding a bit of soap, and then step on it while twisting the handle with my hands. Clean and primed with soap for tomorrow! (Plus, my boots end up squeaky clean.) If it's winter, I drain the hose before I leave. Has anyone figured out how to house-train a cow yet?

• For hot water, I plugged in a 4-gallon, simple-to-install, Bosch Ariston GL4S Point-of-Use Electric Mini Tank Water Heater, Amazon.com.

• For fly control, I hung an Insecta Kill 30 Watt Commercial UV Lighted Bug Zapper (GlobalIndustrial.com) on the wall.

Feed Bunker

Designed to feed 15 cows, my feed bunker also has storage for hay and straw.
I love this kind of setup for feeding. Everyone and everything is protected from bad weather, but it's still light and airy and easy to keep clean.

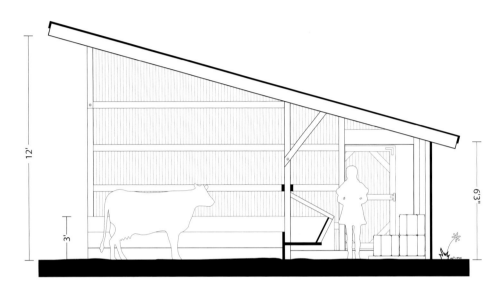

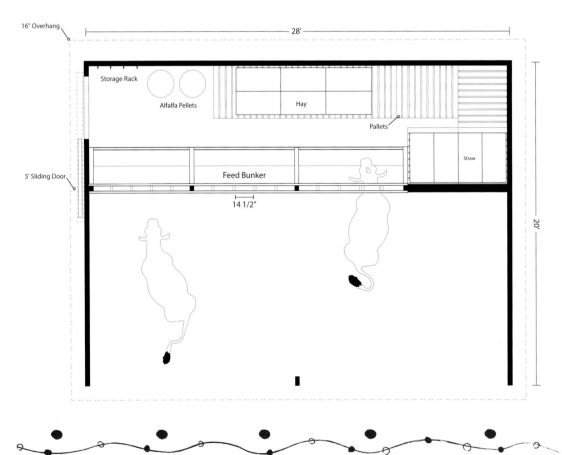

Score!!!! Because of a fire at one of our local cedar mills, their stockpile of wood chips smelled like smoke. They didn't think their customers who buy chips in plastic bags for their yards would be okay with the smell, so I got several semi-truck loads for free!!!!! All I had to do was cover the trucker's wages for the day it took him to bring a pile so big it will provide us with chips for years to come. Wood chips are great for mud control.

241

Backyard Possibilities

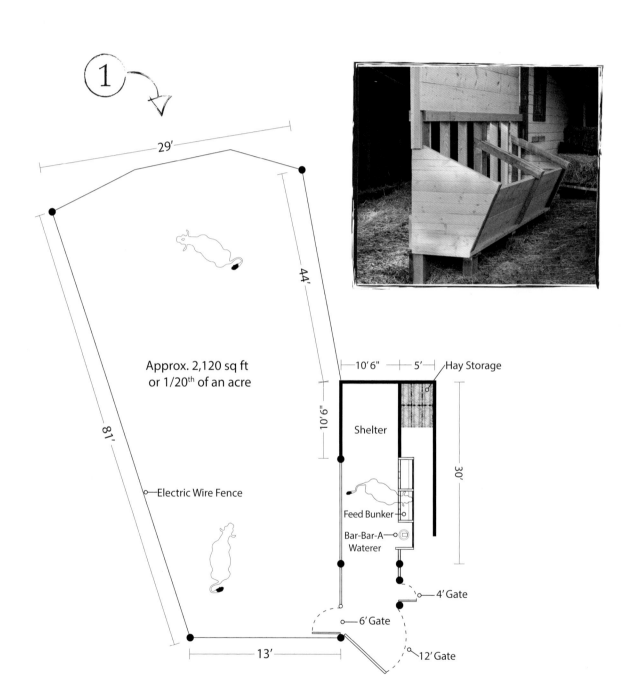

①

29'

44'

81'

Approx. 2,120 sq ft
or 1/20th of an acre

Electric Wire Fence

10' 6" — 5' — Hay Storage

10' 6"

Shelter

30'

Feed Bunker

Bar-Bar-A
Waterer

4' Gate

6' Gate

12' Gate

13'

Note: drawing not to scale

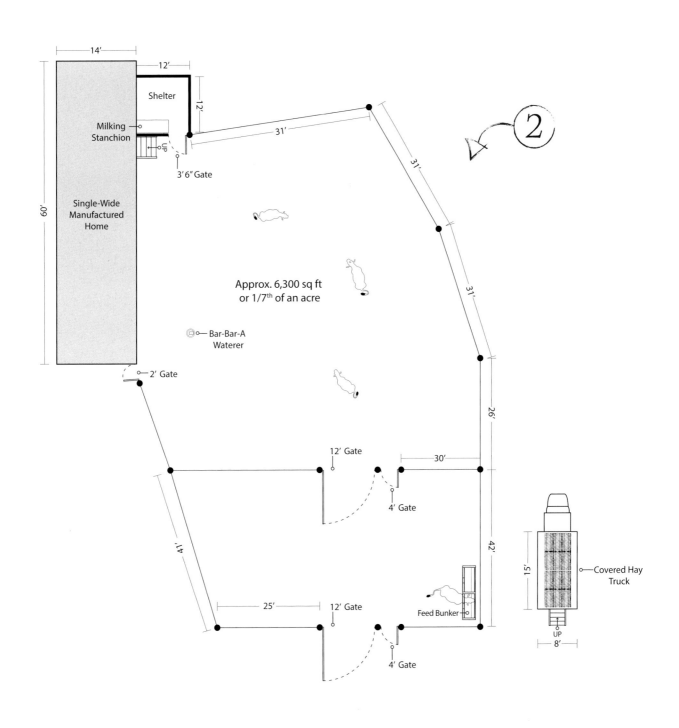

14'

12'

Shelter

12'

Milking
Stanchion

UP

3' 6" Gate

60'

Single-Wide
Manufactured
Home

31'

31'

31'

26'

Approx. 6,300 sq ft
or 1/7th of an acre

Bar-Bar-A
Waterer

2' Gate

12' Gate

30'

41'

4' Gate

42'

Covered Hay
Truck

15'

25'

12' Gate

Feed Bunker

4' Gate

UP

8'

Note: drawing not to scale

Stanchion how to

Supply List:

Wood — approx. $100:

2	6' 4x4s
2	4' 4x4s
2	7' 4x6s
2	6' 4x6s
2	7' 4" 2x6s
14	28" 2x6s
2	31" 2x6s
2	28" 2x6s
2	5' 2x4s

Wood for your feeder box will depend on the height you make your head gate.
I used:

2	19 1/4" 2x6s	side piece
2	19 1/4" 2x8s	side piece
1	31 1/4" 2x6s	front piece
1	31 1/4" 2x8s	front piece
5	31 1/4" 1x4s	bottom of feeder box

Hardware — approx. $75:

16	3/8" x 10" hex-head bolts
36	3/8" washers
16	3/8" nuts
16	3/8" x 7" carriage bolts
16	3/8" washers
16	3/8" nuts
56	3 1/2" wood screws
2	1/2" x 8" hex-head bolts
4	1/2" washers
2	1/2" bolts
4	1/2" x 1" pieces galvanized pipe

Directions:

1. Place one 6' 4x6 piece of lumber on top of one 7' 4x6 piece with the 4" side on flat ground. Align the top piece and bottom piece to one side—this will be the front of your stanchion. A step will be created where the pieces aren't aligned. You will need to make two stacks of 4x6 pieces.

Note: The width of your stanchion should be adjusted to fit your milk cow. I measured the width of my cow and then added 6" on each side to give her some room to move without falling off the stanchion. That measurement is the width of the floor. Subtract the size of the 4x4 vertical posts from each side of the floor to get the width that the base of 4x6s should be apart.

2. Bolt the 4x4 pieces vertically on the outside corners of the 6' 4x6s. The two 6' 4x4 pieces will be placed at the front (where your base pieces are aligned); the two 4'

Removable wooden blocks to secure her head once she's in.

4x4 pieces with be placed in the rear. The rear 4x4 posts should align to the top 2x6 base piece. Use two 3/8" x 10" hex-head bolts with washers on each side to secure the boards.

3. To create the floor on my stanchion, I screwed 28" 2x6 pieces into the top of the base with 3 1/2" wood screws. I like to use self-drilling wood screws with square-drive heads. These save you time because you don't have to drill guide holes and the start heads don't strip out as easily as Phillips heads do. Use a hand-held jigsaw to notch out the vertical 4x4s at each corner. (Remember that board sizes aren't exact. A 4x4 measures approx. 3 1/2" x 3 1/2".)

4. Place the 7' 4" 2x6 pieces on the outsides of the vertical 4x4 posts. Connect them 4' above the ground and even with the rear 4x4 of the stanchion. The 2x6 will extend past the front 4x4s, making the sides of the feeder box. Use two carriage bolts at each connection. Place the bolts so that the smooth head of the carriage bolt is on the inside of the stanchion. That way, your cow won't scratch her side on the protruding bolt end.

5. Attach two 31" 2x6 pieces to both sides of the front vertical posts approx. 12"–16" above the floor. These are the bottom braces for your head gate—their placement will determine the bottom of your head gate and support the feeder box. Adjust this height to fit your cow. I placed mine 12" above the floor.

6. To make the head catch of the head gate, bolt two 5' 2x4s between the two 2x6s you just placed. You will need to measure the width of your cow's neck to see how far apart the 2x4s need to be. To allow the boards to move, attach them with two 1/2" x 8" hex-head bolts with a 1" piece of pipe on each side of the 2x4 as a spacer.

7. Bolt the two 28" 2x6 pieces to the top of the front vertical 4x4s. These are the top braces of the head gate and should not attach to the 2x4 pieces so they'll move freely. I use different size wooden blocks to keep the boards of the head gate closed around the necks of my cows.

8. Create a feeder box on the front of the stanchion. The size of the boards will depend on the height that you set the bottom of the head gate. I made mine 30" x 24" x 14". I like to have the sides high so my cow can't turn her head out of the box while she is eating, scattering her precious alfalfa pellets on the ground.

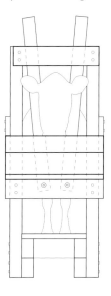

Lastly, I used a hacksaw to cut off all the ends of the bolts that were too long and rubbed linseed oil over all the wood to help protect it. I also used ground or earth anchors to secure the stanchion so it can't tip over.

optional suggestion:

You can cut a black rubber mat to fit the floor of the stanchion to help with cleanup. If she gives you a "surprise," you can hose it off and it won't be as slick as wet wood. Just make sure you screw the mat to the wood so it doesn't slide.

FENCING

There are lots of different types of fencing: wood, barbed wire, smooth wire, New Zealand wire, electric fencing, etc. Wood is beautiful, but very expensive for a large area. Composite wood isn't as expensive, but it's still spendy. Barbed wire is good for cattle if you have lots of land to fence—it's reasonably easy to put up and maintain, but if animals ever get tangled in it, they can get cut up. Animals can push through smooth wire easily. New Zealand wire (a type of woven wire) can be expensive for a big area.

I couldn't decide what I wanted, so I started looking at fences whenever I was out driving. One of our neighbors has a small herd of beef cows that have calves every spring and his fences are beautiful, made from four lines of electric rope wire. It seemed to do a good job of keeping the cows and calves in the pasture. I decided electric fencing would work best for me.

There are three main types of electric fencing: high-tensile wire, and synthetic tape or rope. High-tensile wire has the longest life span, but it's very hard for animals to see. If an animal breaks through, it can cut them more easily than tape or rope. Electric tape is by far the most visible and comes in a variety of thicknesses, most commonly, 1/2" to 1 1/2", but in areas that get lots of wind, rope holds up better than tape, so I chose rope.

While I was doing research on what type of fence I wanted, I found Premier1 (Premier1Supplies.com), an animal-supply company based in Washington, Iowa. They have all their merchandise online and many items have free shipping.

246

I called them at 800-282-6631 and was able to talk to someone who became our personal consultant. She was very knowledgeable and walked us through exactly what we would need. Premier1 runs sheep on their company property, and tests all of their products before selling them.

I ended up buying most of my electric rope, insulators, and accessories from them. I could have bought our metal posts from them too, but that was something I could get locally.

Premier1 sells three types of electric rope fencing. I chose EnduraSoft rope—it has a 25-year life span and is soft to the touch, which makes it much nicer to install.

You have to use insulators to connect the rope to both the wood and metal posts so the electricity won't short out by running into the ground instead of along the fence. There are hundreds of different types of insulators.

I knew I wanted to use wood corner posts and metal T-posts for the longer stretches (called line posts because they stand all in a row). I needed screw-in insulators for the wood posts (Premier TuffRings) and clip-on insulators for the T-posts (Premier Combo Insulators).

Once I decided where my fence line would run, I had to get measurements for how much fencing I would need. While it's possible to pace out a field by walking it, you won't get a very accurate number. I rented a measuring wheel from a construction rental store in town for $10 a day.

All you have to do is walk the perimeter of the pasture, pushing it along like a bicycle wheel. (When measuring a section, always round up—it's good to have leftover supplies for repairs later.)

When you have a good measurement for the perimeter of your pasture, multiply that by how many lines of rope you are using. I chose five lines, so that meant 25,000' of rope, or just under five miles. I would also need rope connectors to tie off the rope at one end of the fence or to connect one end to another end of rope. You can buy the spiral connectors that Premier1 offers. I've also used Gallagher connectors.

If you do use Premier1 spiral connectors, make sure you put a little bit of electrical tape around the ends of your rope so it doesn't unravel.

You'll also need P-springs to help keep the ropes nice and tight. I also decided to use Rope Tensioners that allow you to tighten the fence without having to take a line down and re-stretch it.

I broke the fence–building process down into three stages.
Stage 1: build wood corner posts and plan gates
    (gates will always be attached to wood posts)
Stage 2: set T-posts
Stage 3: install electric rope lines

Any type of fence must be pulled tight so it stays up between posts. When there's a turn in the fence line, you have to build a supported wooden corner or the force of the tension on the fence will pull the post down. While there are other ways to build corner posts, I chose to do H–brace corner posts.

I also decided not to do 90° corner posts, but instead use two 45° corner posts linked together, resulting in less tension on the corners than 90° turns. This also makes it easier to move a truck or tractor around the corners when mowing or spreading manure.

I used 8' wood posts and wanted a 5' high fence, so we needed to sink the posts 3' into the ground (about the minimum amount for good, strong posts). I have a tractor with an auger attachment for digging holes. Or you can use a hand–operated posthole digger.

I started on one of the end posts first so I could measure off of it. (My wood corner posts are 8' apart.) My first corner post was also going to have a gate (more about that later).

When filling the holes, the first foot of the hole is the most important. You have to get a good firm base or the post will move over time. Because we have a lot of rain in the spring, the ground was plenty moist, so I had to fill some of the holes with a mixture of gravel and dirt first and then fill with dirt.

Find a heavy metal pole with a blunt end to pack down the dirt and gravel while you add it.

While you pack and fill the hole, use a small level to make sure the post remains vertical. You'll want to "check for plumb" on each side of the post to get an accurate read. The sides of posts can be uneven, so it's best to inspect each post to make sure you're putting the level on the flattest part.

Once your first post is sunk, measure the hole for your second post. Put that post in. Before you start to fill the hole, measure the distance between the two posts to make sure they're still about 8' apart. It's okay to be a little less than 8', but not more than 8' because I used 8' 4x4s for the horizontal piece in the H-braces.

Measure about 4" down from the top of one of the wood posts. Placing a level on the top of the 4x4, hold the 4x4 at the 4" mark and move the post up or down slightly to make it level, then mark the post on both sides for cutting the notches.

Using a 3/8" drill bit, cut a guide hole where you'll put a 12" nail. Drilling on the flat, notched side will keep the drill bit from moving as much as it would on a rounded post. Once you have drilled through the post, set the 4x4 and use the hole you just drilled as a guide to drill a hole in the 4x4.

Drive a 12" nail through the wood post into the 4x4 to set the H–brace. Use a large framing hammer or a small sledge hammer to drive the nails. To keep the fence from shifting, use diagonal-wire braces on the wood H-braces.

To create a wire cross-brace, cut a piece of 12.5-gauge wire that is long enough to wrap around the TOP of one post and around the BOTTOM of the other post. Secure both sides with fencing staples.

Twist the ends together. Using a 12" nail, twist the two strands together in the middle until the cross-brace pulls tight. Repeat the process the other way to make an X with the wires between the two H-brace posts.

We installed two 8' metal utility gates on one corner of the fence that we could use to get tractors or trailers through.

You can also use electric gates with "safe handles." However, electric gates must be unlatched and taken down each time you want to go in or out of the field, and with five lines of fencing, that takes much longer than metal gates. But if the electric gate isn't going to be used much, it's less expensive—electric gates cost about $20 each; metal gates can cost anywhere from $80–$200 each.

Once all the corner posts and gates are built, you can move on to the line posts (T-posts). If your posts are placed in as straight a line as possible, they will be under less pressure and the fence will hold up better.

To get a nice, straight line, stretch twine between the corner posts. For our fence, I placed the line posts a maximum of 30' apart, with a wood post every 8 T-posts.

To make measuring easier, I took twine and measured out 30', then tied a knot. I looped the end of the twine to one line post, then stretched out the twine to the knot to know where to drive the next line post.

To drive in a T-post, you need a post driver—a hollow steel pipe with a closed top and two steel handles welded to the sides. You put the driver over the T-post, lift the driver up off the end of the post, and then slam it down over and over again, forcing the post into the ground. We used 8' T-posts and drove them in 3'.

You might have to position the posts closer than 30' if your terrain isn't flat within that 30'. Ups and downs between posts might leave large gaps under your bottom wire or put the bottom wire on the ground.

etta Jane at 5 months of age

250

Once all the line posts have been driven, you'll need to put insulators on the posts. I used five lines of rope fencing, at 12" intervals from the ground. To figure out what heights will work best for you, put the first line halfway up the leg of your smallest animal and the top line above the shoulders of your largest animal, then fill in between with lines about 12" apart. You might want to install an on/off switch on the bottom line so you can turn it off in the winter if it gets buried in snow.

To make measuring quick, tape the measurements on a piece of dowel and then place the dowel next to each post as you put the insulators on.

When all the insulators are installed, it's time to attach the rope by rolling it out and clipping it to the insulators. To help keep the rope tight, attach a P-spring and a Rope Tensioner every 1,000'.

The final step is to attach the fence to the electric energizer. There are many different power levels for energizers, depending on what you are trying to keep in or out and how long your fence is. It's important to get the right size for your needs and that's where a fencing consultant like Premier1 comes in handy. You don't want to over- or under-energize your fence.

One of the best inventions since the paper clip is a removable fence and/or gate panel, known as a "corral panel." Once I discovered these luggable (and in my mind, huggable) farmgirl helpers, I wondered where I'd been. I don't have any problem moving these around by myself when I need containment for an animal or want to coax a cow into my trailer (although a second pair of hands is mighty nice). Did I tell you yet how much I love mine? You can check them out at BehlenCountry.com. (I pick mine up at my local feed store.) I've tried the different-size gauges and prefer the heavy-duty category—otherwise, a big cow can bend a panel. When I need a quick fence repair, I also like a lightweight "feedlot panel" that comes 8' or 16' L x 50" H. You can view the concept at TractorSupply.com. I also like (no, *love*) a single-handed gate latch (right) for my permanent gates so my other hand can hang onto an animal or a bucket of feed (Farmex 2-Way Lockable Gate Latch, Amazon.com).

calf shelter
made
from pallets

bull
shelter

milking
parlor

removable
panels & gate

squeeze
chute

chicken run

hay & cow
shelter

removable
panels

removable
gate

feed
bunker

removable panels
waiting to be
used to funnel
cows into trailer or
squeeze chute

FEED

meet Eliza Belle
at 1 month of age

254

There's one thing you should know in order to qualify for milkmaid status, and that's the difference between hay and straw. Hay provides protein. An animal can live on it. Straw is lighter in weight than hay. It's merely the stalk of the plant from a crop like barley or wheat. Cows love to bed down in straw. (If it has some stray seed heads in it, they'll gobble them up.)

Finding good hay is a regular topic of conversation wherever clutches of cow owners gather for coffee. However, sources tend to be closely held, similar to how a person guards the location of their favorite huckleberry patch or fishing hole. If you're new to needing hay, think of it as a treasure hunt that can be as thrilling as a tour of garage sales. Get out and start talking to your neighbors about hay, ask around, scour ads. "Hey, know of a good place where I can get some good hay?" (Specify cows. Their needs can be different from those of other animals.) You'll find some. It's out there. If not, here's a grower who will ship organic hay to most points north, south, east, and west (that might include you, just ask!): IdahoBeef.com. Or try the HayExchange.com. The main thing is, don't wait until the last minute. Get your hay lined up way in advance of when you'll need it.

As you can see from the photo above, we grew our own hay for several years. It was brome (grass) hay. But then my herd of cattle grew and I needed the ground to permanently pasture them.

Prior to that, we'd struck up a relationship with a neighbor who was providing us with the straw we needed to mulch our gardens and for cow bedding. We didn't have enough room to store straw at the time, so pallets, tarps, and ropes worked for a few bales for a few years, and he was willing to keep most of it in his barn and allow us to come and get a truckful when needed, on the honor system (love the working concept of neighborliness in a rural community). But more recently, we converted our old truck "Myrtle" into the cattle-ac of hay sheds.

When our neighbor offered us an upgrade to hay, I knew I'd be signing up—handy because I can check it out during its growing and harvesting stages. As it turns out, he grows it and bales it and then we haul what we'll need for the coming year off his fields and into a large machine shed we've freed up at my son's house, now officially a hay shed (sold the machinery). It's an all-hands-on-deck week when it's time to bring in *his* hay in order for us to call it *our* hay. As it turns out, *our* crew stuck around to help him bring in *his* hay (that would remain *his* hay.) Again, the neighborliness thing.

Depending on the weather, some years, hay crops are better than others. Perfect hay has to be cut at the perfect moment, before it's too mature but only when there's a window of several days without the prediction of rain. Once it's cut, it lies in the field in something called windrows that are allowed to dry out in the sun by turning them, mechanically, at least once.

It's a drag when it rains on your hay parade. Once it's dry (hopefully without ever getting rained on), it's baled and taken off the field. Should it rain on any part of the process, you might have hay that grew to be too mature (because it was raining and couldn't be cut); or once it was cut, it rained, and the hay needed to be turned and dried several times; or once it was baled, it rained on the bales and they had to be turned and dried. All of this results in hay that is more yellow (sun-bleached and somewhat less nutritious) than hay "in a good year," or worse, it has to be tossed because it molds. Does the weather generally cooperate? Rarely. (If you ever need a moment of pure happiness because it did rain, look up a short clip of "Gene Kelly singing in the rain" or "Gene Kelly tap dancing on roller skates" on YouTube.com.)

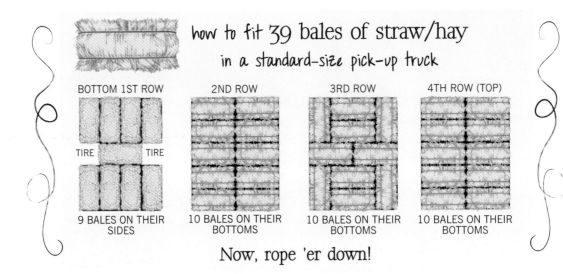

how to fit 39 bales of straw/hay
in a standard-size pick-up truck

BOTTOM 1ST ROW	2ND ROW	3RD ROW	4TH ROW (TOP)
TIRE TIRE			
9 BALES ON THEIR SIDES	10 BALES ON THEIR BOTTOMS	10 BALES ON THEIR BOTTOMS	10 BALES ON THEIR BOTTOMS

Now, rope 'er down!

Hay

Besides pasture (not a possibility for me in the winter), good-quality hay is the next best thing. For most backyard milk cow owners, hay is the only option year-round. (That and letting the cow regularly mow and fertilize their lawns.)

The most common types of hay are: grass, alfalfa (or other legumes such as first-bloom clover and birdsfoot trefoil), and mixed (grass/alfalfa.) Common grass hays include timothy, brome, Bermuda, orchard grass, and bluegrass (similar to your lawn). Alfalfa hay (a perennial plant) is talked about in terms of first cutting (highest quality), second, third, and sometimes fourth cuttings (can be more stem-y, hence more fiber).

Similar to shopping for a car, shopping for hay requires some tire kicking. Here are some things to watch for:

- buy from a reputable grower
- be a responsible buyer (let go of the notion that the grower should be willing to take less than what it costs to produce it)
- even if it was advertised as "no rain," open a bale (your choice) and smell for mold because it can cause an abortion in a pregnant cow (white, chalky dust or a musty, sour smell is a deal breaker)
- brown or black coloration means it got too hot and caramelized (deal breaker)
- look for weeds
- if buying alfalfa or alfalfa/grass mix, the alfalfa leaves shouldn't shatter out when you handle it
- green color isn't always an indication of quality, but it's something to look for

The best way to know if it's good? Ask the grower if they've tested its quality by paying for a forage test; if not, do one yourself. Contact your local extension office to see if they have the "forage sampler tool" or "hay probe" needed to collect a hay sample, or you can buy one at BestHarvestStore.com. It's a device that consists of a long tube with a cutting edge on one end and a shank on the other that can be fastened to an electric drill or hand brace. (A "grab sample" won't pull enough of a cross-section.)

Your extension agent should also be able to tell you where to get a sample tested locally and how to interpret it. For more information, try ForageTesting.org. Even if you don't do a test before you buy hay, you might want to do so after you buy it (making sure you pull a sample from several different bales), so you can determine what minerals your animals might need in a supplement. What's in your hay is a function of what's in the ground it was grown on, and that can vary from place to place.

Legume hay can have twice the protein and three times the calcium, etc. of grass hay. I feed my girls (and guys) a grass/alfalfa-mix hay. Here's why. A dairy cow needs the highest quality hay (more nutrients per pound), but I can't possibly keep alfalfa hay just for them and additionally, grass/alfalfa mix for my bulls, growing cows, young bulls, and steers. I want to be able to grab just one kind of hay and feed it to everyone. So what I do for my "girls" that are producing milk or pregnant is to supplement their diets with organic alfalfa pellets. (It's also a great training tool.) My bulls, steers, and young calves don't need as much protein or calcium (they aren't producing milk), so the grass/alfalfa hay mix I give them is adequate.

I buy around 22 tons (2,000 lbs/ton) of hay per year for feeding from October to March. (These dates aren't rigid. Sometimes I'm feeding hay to a new mom in August or I've run out of grass in early July in some of my pastures.) Each standard bale weighs roughly 50 lbs (bales come in all shapes and sizes). I pay $125 per ton, for a total of $2,750 per year for 11–13 animals—close to $250 per animal.

To figure out how much hay you'll need, here's some handy math. Based on feeding a daily ration of 2% of a cow's body weight, you come up with a number and go from there (dividing it in half for feeding them twice per day). To figure out how much a dairy cow weighs, you can use something called a Dairy Cow Weigh Tape, Amazon.com.

For my mature bulls, I make sure that whenever I take one to the vet, I have it walk onto their scale for a current weight reading. Waistline readings aren't a big hit with my guys.

Speaking of bullish waistlines, it's easy to over-feed a bull (they LOVE food), but it isn't wise. They can get too much fat around their testicles that might hinder their fertility. Keep in mind when figuring how much hay they'll need, you'll be feeding your cattle more hay should the weather turn unusually cold. They'll need it in order to generate more body heat.

Actually, I'm going to say it's easy to over-feed all makes and models at any time of the year. Cattle love to eat. Take the time to be exacting. Weigh a handful (called a flake or a section) of your hay. Do your daily feeding knowing how much of a portion of a bale of hay to serve them.

If you have a larger, more aggressive animal that's eating more than its fair share, tie her or him up to eat its portion, making it wait for the others to finish before you untie it. (A couple of my cows push and shove like it's Black Friday.)

Pregnant cows are the exception. Midway through a cow's pregnancy, you'll want to increase the amount of hay she gets, not by leaps and bounds, just more. After she gives birth, you'll want to give her as much as she can eat for a month or so while she adjusts to producing milk. There aren't any hard and fast rules or percentages I can give you. Use your intuition.

Straw

Good, dry, lightweight straw is my preferred material for bedding. That's because when laden with manure from "picking" it daily (think chambermaid), it decomposes well in my gardens. Pine shavings, hulls, etc., not so well. In fact, the poo-ey pine shavings we harvested from my chicken coop one year lasted forever in my garden soil in the spot where I put it. Its resins actually turned the plants in that spot yellow for a couple of years.

Alfalfa Pellets

Love 'em. Even more so, I love the company that makes them. No, I'm *downright grateful and beholden* to the folks at Modesto Milling (ModestoMilling.com) who, against all odds, source non-GMO, organic alfalfa and turn it into easily-handled pellets for my animals.

What more can I say? And in the larger scheme of things, it's important for me to support organic alfalfa producers, lest my only choice down the road becomes genetically-tampered-with GMO alfalfa.

Water

You should never provide water for your cows that you wouldn't drink yourself. Seriously, I'm a fanatic about it. No stale and slimy water for me. But my well water (that I've had tested for purity and is free and clear of anything bad) wants to befriend red algae, green algae, and black algae for me to scrub out routinely. I've had some luck keeping goldfish in an animal stock tank in the summer to eat the algae, but still, the algae kept the upper hand.

However, there is relief from algae in the winter; it's a fair-weather friend to water. To keep the water in a galvanized tank from freezing in the winter, you can install a "Farm Innovators Traditional Submergible De-Icer" in the bottom, Horse.com.

In my "watering hole" evolution, I moved up from plastic buckets in the beginning (actually pretty easy to keep clean but have to be filled constantly), to galvanized stock tanks, to a nifty insulated Behlen Cattle Waterer that's hooked permanently into an underground water line that is in turn hooked up to electricity so it doesn't freeze in the winter. It's definitely a step up from a galvanized tank, but in the summer, its full-time job is growing green algae. Also, birds like to splat in it while bathing.

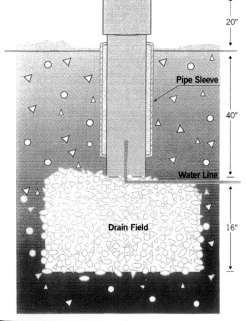

When I saw a neighbor's Bar-Bar-A Horse & Cattle Drinker, I knew what I wanted for my 60th birthday. Over time, as I've replaced all my troughs with a Bar-Bar-A, I knew I'd finally arrived. It's insulated but doesn't require electricity. A small bowl fills with fresh water when a cow pushes its mouth down on a stainless steel paddle. As soon as a cow isn't pushing on the paddle, the water drains back into the ground, so it never freezes. And because of its design, cattle keep it licked shiny clean. It's the cat's me*cow*. And it's not *too* much of an ordeal to install one. They aren't cheap, but when I think of the amount of time and water I've frittered away keeping my cows' water fresh and clean, I'm in like Flynn, HorseDrinker.com. The man who invented it is a genius.

• It doesn't come with the required outer sleeve, so we purchased a 9' length of 18" diameter black plastic culvert and cut it into three even lengths for three waterers.

Just one little caveat: it took my bulls forever to get the hang of it. Seriously, we were in tears from laughing so hard.

260

My girls walked right up, "Hmmm, what's this? Oh, water. When you push on it, you get water." My guys, even after watching the girls do it for days, seemed to ... forget? (Or some such thing. Maybe they're preoccupied with ... politics at work?) If you have a guy who doesn't get it right away, go out twice per day and show him how it works by pushing the paddle down. He'll come over and drink like there's no tomorrow. I pulled in the driveway one night to find one of my young bulls in the garden where he shouldn't be, trying to get water from a garden hose. On that day, I hadn't given him his afternoon lesson, thinking it was high time he followed the lead of the girl he was living with. As I was putting him away, I wondered how in the world he'd gotten out. Soon enough, I could see that it was easier for him to push through and tear down an electric fence (an electrifying experience, for sure) than it was to push a paddle with his nose. The next day, he finally, permanently, figured it out. Maybe shock treatment is the answer. When Karina went out to snap a photo of our Bar-Bar-A for you, he (Beau Vine) walked right up to demonstrate how it's done, ever so proudly posing for the photo. Own it, Beau Vine! You worked long and hard to get here.

Vitamins and Minerals

Trying to figure out what supplements your cow needs can be as confounding as coming up with a word that starts with X. I'm talking about that entire *wall* of different salt/mineral/vitamin licks in a feed store. Selenium in this one, more copper in that one, protein in the one over here. Fortunately for me, Michael Wicks (WicksLivestock.com), from the northeast corner of Nebraska, tackled all those same questions and made himself available for mine. And yours. His XYZs of animal supplements are fairly straightforward and easy to understand. And buy. His formulas come with instructions. I purchase his Certified Organic Hi-Phos Dairy Premix (2000), but he has others that might work better in your locale or setup. Different areas of the country, based on what's naturally available in your soil, require different vitamins and minerals. When I give them to my cattle, I err on the side of caution. I do the same thing with supplements for myself. More isn't necessarily a good thing.

And in the summer when fly season hits, I incorporate a bit of something Wicks calls Salt Sidekick that adds more sulfur, iodine, and alfalfa meal to the diet of my cattle. Flies aren't as attracted to a cow that eats sulfur. (Did you know that's the reason we're told to eat plenty of garlic in the summer? Mosquitoes don't like sulfur either, and garlic has sulfur in it and so do onions—the reason you cry when you cut up an onion.)

But the easiest thing for me to do in order to make sure each animal is getting its fair share of vitamins and minerals (and not too much—I'm a worrywart) was to invent a recipe for cow cookies (p. 265) that includes some of their supplements, kind of like a cow's chewable vitamin pill. (Not to appear too far gone on my cows, but I call them cow pookies, you know, cookies for my pookie pooh moo friends.)

Salt

There's some salt in the Dairy Premix I give my animals, but even so, I put self-serve salt "rocks" in their feeders. ModestoMilling.com sells "rocks" of salt called Redmond Rock, 7–10 lbs each, that my cows prefer over all else I've tried. These rocks also last longer than the kind of salt blocks you typically see in a feed store.

Apple Cider Vinegar

Many of us know about the benefits of apple cider vinegar when it comes to human health. But did you know that cows are capable of benefiting from it also? I installed several Little Giant 16" fence feeders (Amazon.com), supported by a stout piece of wood beneath each one, in various places around my farm that are covered by a roof. I keep the feeders about half-full of straight-up, organic, "live," apple cider vinegar. My cows lap it up in small amounts, kind of like sipping fine wine, and I've noticed that when it freezes in the winter (vinegar freezes at around 28°F), there will be lick marks in a depression in the middle.

What does vinegar do for your cows? I've tried various things over the years, including garlic, and you know what? Every time I send in a stool sample, my animals are free and clear of parasites. Think of all the chemicals I've avoided. Conventional protocol for parasites is a regular dose of a systemic chemical concoction that you pour on their backs. No thanks! But just to make sure I'm on the right track, I gather a stool sample from my cows once per year and send it off to be tested (p. 281). Parasites aren't anything to mess around with.

Diatomaceous Earth (DE)

Oh, and also diatomaceous earth (DE) to guard against parasites. It's a well–known treatment for pets, including dogs, cats, and chickens (even humans). You'll see that I list DE in my cow cookie recipe (p. 265). But make sure it's food-grade. And make sure you don't breathe any of it—it makes a very fine dust that isn't a good thing for your lungs. I buy mine from ModestoMilling.com.

Kelp

My cattle are offered organic kelp on a self-serve, free-choice basis because it's so full of good-for-you trace minerals. Because it has a salty flavor, they take a few licks every day. Available from ModestoMilling.com.

Sodium Bicarbonate

If you're new to the health benefits of sodium bicarbonate, you might be wondering about this particular supplement. I offer it to my cattle on a self-serve, free-choice basis and they do in fact nibble on it, not as readily as the kelp, but I like knowing they're getting a little bit of intestinal buffer on a routine basis. A component of the natural mineral natron, its versatile qualities for both cooking, household use, and as a proven medical agent became more wide-spread in the mid-1800s when Dr. Austin Church began to sell the compound that we're familiar with today as baking soda. It has a slightly salty taste. Restoring and maintaining pH balance is good for not only humans, but also cattle. Available from ModestoMilling.com.

• And don't forget the healing power of Vitamin C (p. 215) whenever they get the sniffles or a cough.

Cautionary Note: DO NOT offer free-choice apple cider vinegar and sodium bicarbonate to your cattle at the same time. Remember what happened when your mother gave you baking soda and vinegar to play with? It turned into a bubbly volcano. I offer both supplements to my cattle on a free-choice ROTATIONAL basis only.

Kelp

Sodium Bicarbonate

• Here's how much four mid-size cattle ate in eight days.

During an early-morning expedition with my camera in 2004, I shot this photo, thinking a local, innovative farmer had gotten creative in a field adjacent to the Veterinary School at Washington State University. As it turns out, "she" was part of a traveling "Makin' Hay" exhibit funded by the Alturas Foundation (AlturasFoundation.org), featuring the work of the amazing artist Tom Otterness (TomOtterness.net), an American sculptor whose works adorn parks, plazas, subway stations, libraries, courthouses, and museums.

Cow Cookies

You can get a cow to do most anything you want when you have these in your pocket as a reward for good behavior.

Prep Time: 20 minutes
Drying Time: 8–12 hours
Makes: 32

- 2 cups organic thick oats
- 1 cup organic alfalfa pellets, p. 259
- 2 cups water
- 1/4 cup organic molasses
- 1 cup organic vitamins/minerals, p. 261
- 1 cup organic diatomaceous earth (DE), p. 263
- 1/4 cup Salt Sidekick (add only in the summer during fly season), p. 261

Note: My full-size Jerseys (both bulls and cows) get two cookies per day, my smaller cattle get anywhere from half a cookie to one cookie per day, depending on their size. The recipe increases easily for a bigger batch.

1. In a large bowl, combine alfalfa pellets and water. Let sit 30 minutes.

2. In a food processor, pulse the oats into flour.

3. Mix molasses into the alfalfa pellets. Add oats from the food processor. Mix thoroughly. Add the rest of the dry ingredients, being careful to stir it gently so as not to create dust from the DE; blend thoroughly.

4. Using wet hands, form into balls and then smash between both hands to form 2" patties; place on the tray of a food dehydrator. (If it doesn't form balls, add water by the teaspoon if necessary.)

5. Dry for 8–12 hours on medium heat or until dry throughout.

- fair price paid to farmers
- green cut; fields not burned
- hand harvested; sustainably grown; produced by small farmers in Paraguay
- sugar mill energy self-sufficient; crushed cone generates electricity

Cautionary Note:

In non-organic crops, there's an herbicide used for control of broadleaf weeds, especially thistle, that's an absolute no-no when it comes to hay or straw. Make sure you ask if **Clopyralid** (3,6-dichloro-2-pyridinecarboxylic acid), most commonly called **Curtail**, was used in any stage of its growth.

Why? Clopyralid is known for its ability to persist in dead plants and compost, and has accumulated to phytotoxic levels in finished compost in a few highly publicized cases. This first came to light in my area because, during 2000 and 2001, a cattle research facility at a nearby university offered free compost to local gardeners that had residues of clopyralid in it, resulting in plant deformity. Word quickly spread to other local and state governments, and in 2002, DowAgro, the manufacturer of clopyralid, deregistered it for use on domestic lawns in the U.S. (it's banned entirely in several U.S. states), but it's still found in brand names used for agriculture in the U.S. that include **Stinger, Transline, Reclaim, Curtail, Confront, Clopyr AG, Lontrel, Millennium Ultra, Millenium Ultra Plus,** and **Redeem**.

Make sure you ask. I've seen the havoc it wreaked on our town's community garden. It is particularly damaging to peas, tomatoes, and sunflowers and can render potatoes, lettuce, and spinach inedible. It must not have been used on the grain crop (that was eventually baled into straw) or the hay crop that you are thinking about bringing home and composting.

Hay/Straw Storage

Hay/straw shed

I have a neighbor who is endlessly handy with a hammer and tremendously prone to improvising. Her pallet barn caught my fancy—so much so that I built my own for less than $200 total. She used two store-bought carports (canopies) positioned back-to-back, then took the zippered entries that came with the canopies and used them for another storage project. For her entry, she built a faux front/façade using scrounged items. I followed her lead, but used only one canopy for a smaller "hay/straw shed." I also had to put guylines on mine because we get a lot more wind than she does (she's in a protected draw).

For the interior walls, I picked up a couple truckloads of free pallets from my local building supply store (check your local building supply store or home center to locate some in your locale). Then I got out my hammer and put on my thinking cap. (Why let a perfectly good pallet go to waste?) Now it's your turn! Given all the variables in terrain and materials, I can't give you exact plans. But here's what worked for me.

You'll Need:

- a portable carport (Sometimes listed as a "canopy," carports are available at most home centers. I bought a Steel-Frame 10' x 20' Canopy, but models are constantly changing as well as what they're called. Just make sure you buy a good quality carport—read online reviews!)

- four 10' 2x6 lumber for carport frame footings
- ten 1/2" rebar pins, about 2' long, to pin footings to the ground
- sixteen 5/16" x 1 1/2" lag bolts to secure carport feet to wooden 2x6 footing
- six 3" x 18" screw-type earth anchors
- 100' 1/4" braided nylon rope for guylines
- 13 pallets
- five 10' 2x4 lumber to cap the pallets on interior walls
- 1 lb 3" deck screws to fasten lumber
- 2 rolls metal plumber's tape
- 1/4 lb 1 1/2" truss-head screws to attach plumber's tape to walls and wood framing
- eight 8' 2x4 lumber to frame in the end wall with a door and windows
- salvaged door, windows, metal siding/roofing

• Our local building supply store gives pallets away for free year-round.

• Since having a cow means daily animal chores, heavy snows aren't a problem. It's easy enough to tap the roof from the inside using the broom end of a push broom to knock the snow off the roof.

266

Instructions:

1. Set up the portable carport on level ground in a wind-sheltered location. Place the 2x6s under the frame feet (two on each long side and one on each short end) to provide a larger surface to bolt the carport frame to and to anchor it to the ground more securely.

2. Bore ten 1/2" holes through the 2x6 lumber (three holes on each side; two on each end) and drive the 2'-long rebar pins into the ground through the holes. This prevents lateral shifting of the structure in strong winds.

3. Secure carport feet to wooden footing with lag bolts.

4. Plant the six screw-type earth anchors several feet away from the exterior of the structure. Securely attach guylines from the anchors to the carport frame at locations high on the walls.

5. Interior walls are made by standing similar-sized pallets together, then capping them with 2x4s. Our 20'-long x 10'-wide structure required 13 pallets laid lengthwise (5 for each long side and 3 for the back end), capped by 10' 2x4s, using 3" deck screws.

6. The free-standing pallet "wall" can then be fixed to the carport frame at the top and bottom with flexible metal plumber's tape wrapped around the tubular legs of the carport and secured to the pallets with 1 1/2" truss-head screws.

7. Instead of using the fabric end wall with its zippered entry, I constructed a simple frame matching the dimensions of the open space. A salvaged door, windows, and galvanized siding (from an old barn that collapsed) were fitted and fastened with screws. This entire end wall is anchored to the ground with a couple of rebar pins and secured to the carport frame using the marvelous, flexible, and utilitarian plumber's tape and screws.

• Your carport kit should come with nifty elastic ties that hold the "canvas" in place, allowing for some give when the wind blows. (It's not true canvas, but plasticized somehow.)

• I drilled holes through the 2x6 plates for hammering the rebar pins into the ground. If you're in a high wind area, you'll also want to stake your canopy down using "earth anchors" and some rope.

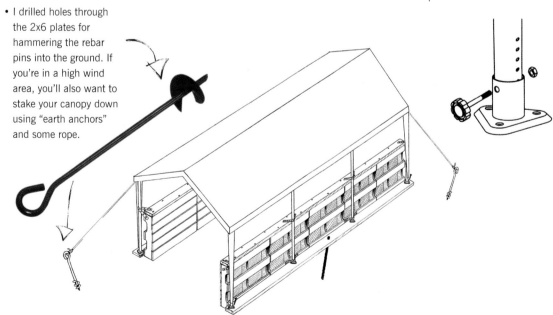

267

Cow-trough Gardening

In my lower three–acre garden, I have a troublesome wet spot. By the time it dries out enough for us to get in and cultivate it in the late spring, it's already full of weeds, so I knew I needed to come up with some sort of raised–bed system. I thought about wooden beds, but that isn't very permanent—been there, done that. They rot within a few years and then you have a mess to dismantle. I pondered concrete or cinderblock beds, but that takes up a lot of room, not to mention disruption of the soil in order to pour proper concrete footings so they don't heave and shift around when the ground does its freeze-thaw thing.

I was filling a trough (aka stock tank) with water one day when the idea hit me—trough gardening! I've experimented with almost every kind of container garden over the years, but the File Box Vegetable Garden featured in my magazine in 2008 has been by far the most successful of all my attempts. Because the bottom layer is a water reservoir, the roots don't end up compacted and the soil doesn't really need to drain. The concept is a cross between a hydroponic garden and a soil garden.

For my trough idea, I researched the possible toxicity and endurance of the plastic plumbing parts I would need: PVC and polypropylene. I didn't want to use a metal screen because of the rust that would ensue and the fact that I wanted my beds to last "forever." I wanted to be able to fill the bottom reservoir easily and I wanted to make a soil mix that wouldn't easily compact. After I did all my homework, I was so convinced my idea would be fabulous, I special-ordered 40 2' x 2' x 6' galvanized, round-end stock tanks from my local feed store, plus a 2' high, 6' diameter round one for an herb garden.

Here's the funny part: I remember once reading about Martha Stewart's favorite garden tool. It was a dainty little handheld hoe, and I thought at the time, wow, I use *big* shovels, sharp *killer* hoes, and *life-threatening* machete-type tools to garden—nothing dainty. Well, guess what? I can garden now without bending over and I use dainty little tools to weed and plant. And I've finally outsmarted the rabbits that love to nibble on all my veggies and chew holes in my hoses. (Seriously, they do that.)

First, I put down a felt weed barrier. Because I wanted something more long-lasting than the variety sold in garden stores, I went with heavyweight, nonwoven, black geotextile (used in roadway construction projects) that comes in a 15' x 300' roll, item #Propex 801, GeoTextile.com, 800-445-7732 to find a dealer near you. On top of that, I put down straw or wood chips to protect the felt from UV damage. (This is important!) It's proven to be a fantastic way to build weed-free pathways in quite a few places around my farm. Water and air get through. In fact, I've found an earthworm paradise under my fabric. (The fabric isn't impregnated with weird toxic products.)

1. Even though the tanks are galvanized, they'll rust more quickly than you'd like if you put them on a surface that stays constantly wet. If you need to put something under the troughs to level them, think gravel—the smoother or more round the gravel, the better. (There are an increasing number of new-fangled poly stock tanks on the market that might be better because they can't rust. However, I haven't tried them.)

2. Your stainless-steel tank (Behlen is a common brand) will come with one drain hole on its side with a new-fangled—in my estimation, cheap—plastic drain plug that I replaced with a sturdy old-fashioned galvanized plumbing setup. To build a better one, buy two 1" galv. locknuts, one 3/4" galv. plug, and one 1" x 3/4" galv. bushing. Use good butyl caulking to seat it and then wrap some plumber's Teflon tape around the threads of the plug before you screw it in and then tighten it with a crescent wrench. Voila! The problem with the plastic plugs the tanks come with is that when you try to take them out in the fall, the whole thing turns, making it so you have to somehow (did you hear me cursing the first year?) go down into the soil (past the plastic screen) to secure the locknut on the inside of the tank.

Keep the drain plug in until late fall, when you'll take it out to prevent rain water from filling up the lower water reservoir and then freezing and possibly buckling the bottom of the tank.

3. Now, you'll need to drill one 1/2" hole 4 1/2" up from the bottom on the end where you plan to put your filler pipe.

(continued)

filler pipe

1/2" hole

(continued from p. 269)

4. You'll need something to hold up the "screen" that will allow the water from the reservoir to wick upwards into the soil to keep it wet and free of compaction. I used 4" diameter rigid PVC perforated sewer drain pipe cut into 4" lengths. These stand vertically on the tank bottom to support the "screen" that will be the soil floor.

Note: In the beginning of your growing season, you'll need to gently water from the top until the plant roots figure out how to seek the water in the bottom of your trough and the wicking process gets established. Once the plants sprout, you can mulch with straw or grass clippings but make sure you don't use too much or end up incorporating it into the soil at the end of the season. You don't want to use up your precious nitrogen with plant matter that is being decomposed.

5. The screen is 3/16" thick rigid polypropylene with 3/16" diameter holes on 5/16" staggered centers. The material comes shipped in 4' x 8' sheets just like plywood. I purchased mine from Ametco.com, 800-321-7042, item #19,18731218748 (this same material can be obtained from other sources in smaller sizes, but at a higher cost). To cut the screen the exact size of my troughs, I used a jigsaw. My troughs arrived nested two together, so one was slightly smaller than the other. They were both roughly 24" deep, but one measured 22" x 67" and the other was 24" x 69". Both ends were semicircular. It's best to make a template out of cardboard. Once the oval shape was transferred from my cardboard template, I cut the screen with the jigsaw, including a 1 1/2" hole cut on one end close to the edge to allow for placement of the filler pipe— photo in step 3.

6. To make sure your water wicks up into the soil body quickly and efficiently, you need to add five "soil legs" by cutting five 4 1/4"-wide holes in your plastic perforated bottom. Into the holes, insert a piece of 4" tubing that is 6" in length in which you've drilled a couple dozen 1/4" holes. Line each of these with some of the black felt you bought for weed control. Eventually, you'll fill them with soil.

7. The 24" filler pipe (1 1/2" PVC) allows you to stick a hose down into it to fill the reservoir in the bottom of the trough. You fill it until water starts to come out the 1/2" hole that you drilled in Step 3. In order for the filler pipe to quickly drain into the bottom of the trough, cut the bottom end at a 45° angle. You'll add water routinely up to the level of the drain hole. You will be amazed at how little water you use in contrast to the amount of food you'll be growing.

Trough Soil Mix

Each tank will take about 16 cubic feet of soil mix (approximately five wheelbarrow loads). My recipe was one-third #2 vermiculite (asbestos-free), one-third peat moss, and one-third good, rich soil (screened if necessary). I mixed all three in a wheelbarrow and then shoveled it into each trough. Once the troughs are filled with such rich, aerated, good soil, all I have to do at the end of the season is pull out the dead plants, put some manure compost on top, pull out the drain plug on the side near the bottom, and let them rest until the spring, when I plant them again. (Some years, I put fall-planted garlic in them.) I can also feed my trough gardens during the growing season with a filtered, mild manure tea or liquid seaweed fertilizer by pouring it down the filler pipe.

271

Sh@t
Happens

Manure

Manure and me, we go way back. Picture this. On a quiet street in Ogden, Utah, modest homes line both sides. It's autumn, late '50s, early '60s. At the home known for the greenest of lawns, a 1953 red Chevy pickup backs onto the perfectly manicured front lawn of the Butters home that sits on slightly more than a quarter acre lot and their children begin the annual task of **shoveling truckload after truckload of pungent cow manure gleaned from their uncle's dairy onto the front lawn and large garden in the backyard.**

Every year, I tell you. Without fail. "Ewwwww," my friends would say. **But guess who had the greenest grass and the biggest, best–est produce from their garden and monster fruit from their trees?**

Now that everyone "feeds" their lawns with tidy granules of chemical "fertilizer" (never, ever as good as manure), I appreciate even more the wisdom of my father, who was an outspoken disciple of Robert Rodale's *Organic Gardening* magazine. **My father mounded manure around our fruit trees; he had us dig it into my mother's flower beds;** he pushed wheelbarrows full of what he called cowplops down the street to mound around our neighbor's trees. (Over time, they all welcomed it because their trees would be so much healthier the next spring.) An avid fisherman, he even buried the heads of the fish he brought home around his prize-winning roses. It's no wonder I would grow up to be a manure aficionado, an *entre-manure*, with a dozen-plus manure-making "units" of my own. Gold, I tell you, pure gold.

272

An adult dairy cow produces as much as 100 pounds of urine and cowplops every day. That's 18 tons per year. Add to this the straw used for bedding, and you have yourself a goldmine of nutrients—a composter's dream come true. You see, cows do this awesome thing. They take the grasses we don't easily digest and turn them into nutrients for us, for use in our kitchens and for growing food. When you factor in the bone-building, protein-rich milk and cheese products they give us, cows completely earn their keep and then some. (The love and companionship they give you also keeps you from spending any money on mood pills or sessions with a therapist.)

What to do with all that golden good stuff? If your cow is pastured, she'll spread it around by herself. I had a visitor who said, "You must pick your pastures." I replied, "No, my bovine friends are masters of dispersal." (My visitor assumed I was pushing a wheelbarrow around every day "picking" up mounds of cowplops.)

A fresh plop dries quickly. If you go back to that same plop a few days later, you'll see hoof prints in it. In other words, the cattle are already breaking it up, not to mention the insects and birds that have been feeding on it. It's a fundamental law of grassland ecosystems—

I like an old-fashioned hayfork with sharp points for pitching hay. It's also a great manure "picking" tool.

poo one day, gone tomorrow. Besides keeping soil fertile for plants, manure improves soil structure in a big way, in a way that chemical fertilizers can't.

I always knew my bovine team of Jerseys was destined for greatness. But I didn't know they'd be the solution to Planet Earth's demise. (I see a blockbuster movie in the making—Planet of the Cows.)

fresh with hoof print

2 days later—dispersal already happening

hayfork picking tool

273

How many essays have I written where I've made my case for the use of protein harvested from local deer, elk, and moose rather than from soybeans and oats grown in the Midwest— where the land has been tilled, sprayed, and eroded—in order for a trucker to deliver granola and soymilk to our doorsteps? I've reasoned further, Aren't bucolic, perennial pastures growing high-end protein better than the constant turning of soil?

But first, a little background. Like I said, my father loved the philosophies of Robert Rodale. I was drawn to what a guy named Allan Savory had to say. He became a hero of mine when, in my 30s, I started calling myself an environmentalist. Now that I'm an older, more seasoned, less strident environmentalist with things like a dairy and a farm business to manage (and books to write and a magazine to produce), I haven't caught even a glimpse of him in the last 10–15 years. Now I know why. He's been busy figuring out a way to reverse climate change.

Calling all cows!

In the 1950s, Allan Savory was a young research biologist and game ranger in eastern Africa. He was passionate about wildlife and came to vilify the livestock that seemed to run roughshod over the native habitat. A world away and decades later, I followed suit. While working as a wilderness ranger in the Uinta Mountains of Utah, I learned to blame herds of sheep that grazed their way across public land for the environmental degradation I saw. The solution was clear: get rid of the sheep and restore the wilderness. Savory saw it that way, too. But as he developed a growing and persistent concern for the state of the world's wild grasslands, he resorted to desperate measures. Watching the lush African landscapes that he loved shrivel into barren deserts and native people being driven to starvation, he deduced that overgrazing was the problem.

Overgrazing by livestock had initiated the growing global problem of desertification (and consequently climate change), he reasoned, but wild game animals were now contributing to the crisis as well. Something had to be done. He conducted extensive studies. He gathered data. He came to some difficult conclusions.

In 2012, a newspaper headline said, "This man shot 40,000 elephants before he figured out that herds of cows can save the planet."

This statement, albeit sensationalistic, is true. Despite his love for elephants, Savory recommended that the government of Zimbabwe drastically cull large herds in order to revive a dying ecosystem. Thousands and thousands of elephants were culled. Imagine his shock when the effort made no real improvement in the health of the grasslands. "This was the saddest and gravest mistake of my life," he has confessed.

Yet, it was a mistake that awakened this visionary man to the true solution for his ailing homeland, and, ultimately, an ailing planet. There's a lot of science behind his premise, but the basic equation is simple: Desertification is rapidly claiming the lion's share of the earth's land and is fueling climate change faster than the burning of fossil fuels. The tan areas of this map show how extensive desertification is.

The solution, which Allan Savory has discovered through a lifetime of hard-earned lessons, is ... grazing.

Savory has joined forces with a team of revolutionaries to establish The Savory Institute, a groundbreaking effort that taps into the way large herds of wild herbivores naturally interact with—and benefit—the land. "I have a message for you that offers more hope that you can imagine," he said.

NASA

Looking to the past, once again, is the key to preserving the future. Historically, vast herds of herbivores such as buffalo, caribou, and wildebeest moved like tides across the grasslands of the earth. They grazed, pooped, peed, drooled, and trampled the ground as they went—but the result wasn't destructive. Instead, the intensive and unique disturbance caused by these herds was nature's tool for keeping the soil and vegetation healthy and ALIVE.

As human populations have grown, wild herds have dwindled while till-plant-spray agriculture practices have swept the planet (including most of North America and its heartland—go back and check the map), and the soil has become increasingly sterile and well, dry. The domino effect is devastating:

- deserts are claiming grasslands at an alarming rate across most of the Earth's land surface;
- people are losing their livelihoods;
- and all the while, our climate is changing in ways we never imagined possible.

I've seen it here in Idaho, and I'm guessing you've seen it where you live, too. So you can see why, to me, Allan Savory looks a lot like a knight in shining armor. The Savory Institute has been busy introducing his concept of Holistic Management to countries around the world and the Institute offers video footage that is living proof he's on the right track this time.

top: Photo courtesy of NASA, middle: Photo by Harvey Barrison via Wikimedia Commonsbottom: Photo of Tibetan desert by Bernt Rostad via Wikimedia Commons

How? By helping people create strategies to purposely manage domestic livestock to mimic and restore the natural cycle of herd disturbance, decay, and revitalization of grasslands. And the best part for me? Now I have living proof that my love of cows can save the world! If you want to know more, I highly recommend watching Allan Savory's 22-minute presentation on Ted.com. Grab a cup of tea and settle in.

A few last things about manure. If you have very little "pasture" or perhaps only a small backyard, you'll need to "pick your pasture," just like my visitor said. In addition, you'll also have what you glean from your routine cleaning of the cowshed to put somewhere. Because you probably already compost your grass clippings, leaves, and kitchen waste, get ready for the next level of soil-building. The addition of manure to your compost is going to speed the process up dramatically. You'll see the difference the next time you turn and aerate your compost, whether it's in a proper compost bin or in a pile out back. (Turning compost allows oxygen to get to the bacteria and microorganisms that will turn your "waste" into soil.)

• I caught Maizy napping with her udder and teats in a fresh pile of goo-poo. This is why a dairymaid's mantra is sanitize, sanitize, sanitize.

With as many cows as I have now, my manure pile is big enough for me to turn it regularly with a tractor. I let my chickens do some of it for me. When I add soiled bedding to my main manure pile, they always come running, especially once I've unearthed new treasures (earthworms) by turning it with a tractor.

But that hasn't always been the case. When I had only one milk cow, my three-compartment compost bin that I built from pallets worked like a charm. Make sure you locate your compost away from where there's likely to be runoff and away from household wells, waterways, and low spots. Let's keep our streams clean! Managing a compost pile isn't rocket science. If you're in a climate where your compost gets soggy from too much rain, cover it with a tarp. If you're in a warm climate and it seems to get too dry, add some water. It should have enough moisture that a fistful when squeezed holds together somewhat but without excess water wringing out of the "damp sponge" you hold in your hand. The internal heat that is generated will kill parasites and weed seeds and make your dark, rich compost ready again for your gardens and yes, lawn! Although I have to confess, the stuff my father had us apply to our lawn was, well, fairly fresh (and pungent) cow manure. Just ask one of our neighbors.

276

PEST CONTROL

Repeat after me: "Be gone you pesky pestiferous pests!" You know, flies that bite, mosquitoes that nibble, and the even peskier hornets. Mice? Total, complete drag. I really do hate meeses. To pieces. And then there are the unmentionables, the ultimate pesky pests, internal parasites. Oh, the pestiferous peskiness of them all.

Simple, upfront preventive measures are your best defense for pest control. And yes, I know, they play an important role in our ecosystem. Short of moving into a hotel room, pests are a way of life. If you create a routine approach and stick with it (how many times did your dentist tell you to floss your teeth before you finally turned it into a habit?), you won't end up one day finding yourself scanning real estate ads as you dream of condo living.

Flies

Pa's cow doesn't give as much milk as Ma's cow. (You've *herd* of Ma'sCow, Idaho, where I live, right? This is what happens when you live there. On a farm. At the end of a dirt road. In Moscow with Ma's cow.)

What do you call a cow covered in biting flies? Moo-dy.

Whatever happened to Grandpa's cow that ran off? No one ever herd.

Why shocking your cows to get them to behave doesn't work? They've herd it all.

Joking aside, cows + flies aren't anyone's idea of a good laugh. But neither are the chemicals commonly sold to repel them. Anyone can walk into a feed store and walk back out with a concoction of powerful chemicals notorious for killing insects. If you follow the application directions, making note that it's harmful to insects, fish, mammals (including you), and absolutely dead-on-arrival for your kitty cats, you can proceed to administer them to your cow based on body weight. What you just dosed them with will enter their systems through their skin "systemically" and set out to kill annoying critters that like to nibble and bite (including internal parasites). But soon, you'll discover it doesn't always last the number of days required before it can be reapplied (for safety reasons). In some cases, and with some cows, it might last less than X number of *hours* rather than the X number of *days* stated on the label. I'm of the opinion, why bother with the toxins in the first place?

The first thing I do every winter in preparation for the upcoming fly season is go to Spalding-Labs.com and order routine shipments of fly predators, the first shipment arriving in April. These *really* work. Not so much for biting flies, but definitely they work like a charm on annoying "house" flies. Everyone who has tried fly predators swears by their effectiveness.

For biting flies, I use a non-toxic homemade fly spray that I dispense from a backpack sprayer every day for the four to eight weeks (in my locale) that biting flies are the worst. It takes me about 15 minutes to spray 12 head of cattle. I do it either while they're eating or I spray my cows one by one when I bring them in to prep them for milking.

For a few days' supply, I fill my sprayer with water to the 1-gallon mark. To that, I add 2 cups organic distilled white vinegar, 2 T "green" dish soap (necessary surfactant), and 1 T citronella essential oil. I put the sprayer on, do a happy dance to shake things up, and then I spray my bovine friends—first along their backs and their behinds, then down their legs and under their bellies. When I need a change from the smell of the citronella oil, I switch to tea tree or eucalyptus oil, or my favorite: lavender. Essential oils are available organically grown from MountainRoseHerbs.com. If you have only one cow, you can use a small, hand-held sprayer that has a built-in mechanism for putting the liquid under pressure. Using the kind of sprayer you use to wash windows is time-consuming. And hard on your hands.

My recipe does a good job deterring the big bomber "horse" flies. It does an "okay" job on biting flies— deterring more than half of them, known by many different names: barn flies, deer flies, stable flies ... insanity, lunacy, madness. Buggy? I also noted that even though some flies still landed on my cows, the actual bites were reduced. Shimmy and shake well before every application. In my milking parlor (and also my chicken coop), I installed a commercial, UV-lighted bug zapper, p. 239. Old-fashioned fly paper also works, but it has to be replaced regularly and it's messier. Who hasn't had the thumbtack fail as the strip of sticky goo fell back onto your head? Is that where the term "slap*strip* comedy" came from?

However, hands down, the most important thing you can do for your cows to deter pests (both internal and external) is to make sure they're getting a dose of iodine and sulfur in their mineral supplement and a daily dose of organic apple cider vinegar. Sulfur directly repels intestinal worms and biting insects because critters don't like how it makes the animal taste. (Sulfur is the main ingredient in pure garlic.) Iodine functions as an immune tonic and parasite resistance fighter. And apple cider vinegar can prevent most forms of internal and external parasites. All of this is covered in detail in my FEED chapter, p. 254. I might add that I haven't yet detected an off-flavor in their milk due to the supplements they take.

I always love the first day after a heavy frost in the fall when the flies have taken a serious hit. It's a scene that brings me great contentment—cows "lowing" peacefully in the sun, eyes closed, cuds being chewed. When my cow, Chocolate, was pregnant with her first calf many years ago, she let me join her (well, not so much for the cud-chewing part), using her belly for a pillow. Udder tranquility.

278

Hornets

Don't just curse hornets, wasps, yellow jackets, black jackets, bull wasps, or whatever else you're accustomed to calling them. Instead, you're going to "help" them monitor their populations. What we think of as hornets, wasps, etc. are insects that aren't officially bees, but neither are they ants. Genetically, they "land" somewhere in between the two—an ant with wings. And a stinger. Rest assured, however, the vast majority of them are not pollinators. Generally, bees can sting you only once (and die because of it), while a hornet can sting you multiple times (and live to brag about it).

Hornets like to congregate around the edges of water troughs, similar to how they're attracted to an open soda can. And just like us, when a cow is stung by a hornet, it ends up with a swollen eye, lip, or nose. When that happens to me or a cow buddy, I turn to nature's perfect remedy, plantain, a widespread "weed" that is as overlooked as often as it is underfoot (check your driveway). It will soothe a fresh sting on you or your cow within minutes. Simply pluck a leaf, chew it into a mash (don't worry, it's edible), rub it on the sting area, and relish the relief.

A strategically placed reusable catcher can fill up in a few days at my farm. When full, I put it in a bucket of water for a few minutes, dump the remains, and then load it again with attractant. For that, I use a small ball of raw hamburger or a piece of raw meat.

Disposable traps already loaded with an attractant are also available. Just add water and hang. One trap can hold as many as 3,000 hornets. It's wise to plan ahead for hornet outbreaks. When our outbreak hit in late August one year, our local hardware store ran out of traps. How do I know this? They'd had so many people coming in to buy a trap—to no avail—they posted on a sign on their front door, "We are OUT of hornet traps! Try back next Tuesday."

Or you can make your own by cutting the neck off a large water bottle. Trace a mark around the bottle. Using a sharp knife (while wearing gloves), cut the top off, making sure your cut stays true. Make four small holes on four sides of the bottle near the top as well as four matching holes around the funnel you've just created (I use a small 1/8" paper punch). Put a 2" plug of raw meat in the bottom. Use two sets of holes to fashion a handle and the other two to further secure the funnel to the top of the bottle. Now, add 1 cup of warm water. Once the meat ripens, the hornets will crawl down the funnel, unable to get back out.

But be careful when you're handling this type of trap. Make sure the top is secure and you've plugged the opening with something like a cotton ball before you take it down full of angry hornets. I fill it with water and wait an hour or so before I take it down, dispose of the contents, and then recharge it with another plug of raw meat.

Should you find one of those familiar gray paper nests somewhere (I get them in the rafters of my hay barn), put on some protective gear (I use my beekeeping mask and gloves), and hit it with a stream of non–toxic spray. I buy a brand called EcoSMART Wasp & Hornet Killer, Amazon.com. After stunning them with a stream of spray, I come back a few minutes later and knock the nest down with a pitchfork handle, and carefully (still with my anti-sting gear on), dispose of it. Sometimes, hornets come back to the same spot to build another nest so I keep a bottle on hand for newcomers. It's a million times easier to check regularly and spray the nests when they're just getting started rather than having to deal with a large nest full of angry hornets.

Or vacuum them up. I have a skylight in my milking parlor where they like to congregate—short order job for the hose of my vacuum, p. 239.

Rodents

Gnawing rodents (mainly mice and rats, rarely chipmunks or squirrels), in my mind, are a force to be reckoned with when trying to keep animal feed free of fecal contamination. Mouse droppings and urine are notorious for spreading disease. Not only that, but I lost an entire field of clover one winter to burrowing mice dining on yummy clover roots buried beneath the snow. I've lost more young fruit trees than I care to admit to mice and rabbits that nibbled the bark off when the snow was deep. (Once a tree loses its bark in a continuous circle around its trunk, referred to as "girdling," it will die.) One year, they came close to decimating my raspberry patch. Same thing. They nibbled on the outer bark of the canes during the winter. But over time, I've outsmarted them. Mice happen, but with a plan, you can keep their numbers at bay. Barn cats? Not at my farm. I've avoided outdoor cats because I love and value my songbirds too much. So for me, it's all about traps. And checking traps. And setting traps. Regularly. That's the key, regularity. Once their numbers peak or even start to peak, you feel like you're starring in an Alfred Hitchcock movie.

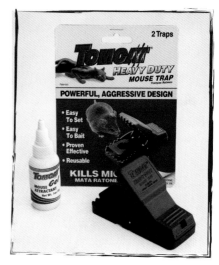

• I like the "heavy duty" version of the Tomcat mousetrap. And rather than mess around with something like peanut butter to bait it, I use their attractant gel (sold separately), Amazon.com.

Is there a better mousetrap? No doubt. I've probably brought at least one of all of them home at one point or another. Goo traps, mouse mazes, poisonous pellets, buckets of water with a peanut-butter-loaded plank perched atop the bucket that dumps the critter into the drink and then springs back up for the next mouse. I've even "caught" a mouse when it got stuck during the night in the honey jar on my table. Ewww, right? All that and more, but you know what I've come back around to? The old-fashioned wooden mousetrap (actually a plastic version that's a little less messy). Here's why.

Poison is poison, and we all know that if it's eaten by the wrong animal, it's bad news. I do put some out in places indoors that I don't frequent much in the winter, like my barn library. It's mouse proof (for the most part), so I'm not going to go there to check a trap regularly, but just in case, I've bought myself a little time with the poison (an outbreak of offspring happens fast). If I see that the poison has been getting nibbled on, then it's time for a mousetrap and more regular visits to monitor things—it gets added to our "rodent patrol" routine.

But to have poisonous grain or pellets anywhere near an animal that might eat it is dangerous. In fact, in my 2,000 square-foot, on-site dried-foods facility, the health department told us it's prohibited. Traps. We check traps. And because of our vigilance, the number of mice outside in our gardens and orchards hasn't gotten out of control in years.

Mites, Lice, Ringworm, Parasites ... Oh My!

I won't lie. I'm a work in progress when it comes to the internal/external parasites and the contagious skin disorders of cattle. "Parasites" are listed as a category on our HeritageJersey.org chatroom because that's what it takes to control them—a village, a community of caring, sharing, constantly experimenting cow lovers. I will say this. My cows have never had a case of mites, lice, or ringworm, and, I might add, not even a case of mastitis, p. 215. I've had a horse and a dog come down with ringworm (caused by a fungus, not a worm), but none of my cattle. And so far, even though I'm not using chemical wormers, when I've sent stool samples in to check for parasites, the counts come back very low (and in some of my animals, "no parasites detected"), low enough for my vet to say, "Whatever you're doing, keep doing it." What am I doing? Nutrition. In short, summer grazing, local hay, organic alfalfa pellets, organic dairy minerals, something called salt sidekick, organic "live" apple cider vinegar, diatomaceous earth, kelp, and sodium bicarbonate (p. 262). Routine chemical treatment with wormers isn't as beneficial as it might seem because this can allow for resistant parasites to gain an even stronger foothold. Also, it doesn't allow your cow to build up her own natural resistance to parasites. Plus, it's toxic stuff!!! If you do decide to go the chemical route, use only when absolutely necessary. Work with your vet to send off a stool sample first. A sample can be easily collected from a cow's rectum using an obstetrical sleeve/glove, Amazon.com, or watch your cow until she drops a plop and grab a handful. Put the sample (about 1/2 cup) in a properly identified, tightly sealed, plastic jar wrapped in padding, and send it off for examination to Washington Animal Disease Diagnostic Laboratory (WADDL) in Pullman, Washington (unless you can find a closer lab). If you go to their website (WSU.edu) and search for DIAGNOSTIC LAB, then FORMS, then GENERAL WADDL ACCESSION FORM, you'll find the form you need to fill out to send with the sample. Or call for instructions, 509-335-9696. Your sample will need to get there as quickly as possible. It's wise to ship it 2nd Day Air.

For details on my natural parasite prevention strategy, see my FEED section, p. 254. To keep up on the latest (and perhaps the greatest yet) ideas for what does and doesn't work, go to HeritageJersey.org and join in on the conversation.

BIRTH & DELIVERY

A cow's reproductive cycle is similar to a human's cycle. Cows go into estrus every 17–24 days, with the average being 21 days. Her pregnancy takes 9 1/2 months, with the average being 283 days. Once she gives birth, she'll produce milk, just like a woman. So if you want a cow to give you milk, she needs to get pregnant and have a calf.

Let's say you're going to have the same milk cow for many years. Planned parenthood goes something like this:

Your cow is either AI'd (artificially inseminated) or "covered" by a live bull (p. 300). After 30 days, you mail off a blood sample (taken from under her tail, p. 298), and for $2.50, you get a pregnancy "yay" or "nay" e-mail later the following day. Using my chart on p. 299, you write her delivery date on your calendar based on the day you know she got pregnant.

Within a couple of days after she gives birth, you start milking her. This is where opinions vary. You can either take all her milk and bottle-feed the calf (using some of the milk you extracted, or store-bought, powdered "calf starter" that you rehydrate each time) or let the calf continue to suckle and be happy taking what the calf doesn't drink. I'm in the latter camp.

Two months later (give or take a week depending on her renewed cycle), you'll get her pregnant again and then continue to milk her for 7 1/2 more months (she'll have two months left in her pregnancy). Soon after her seventh month, you'll start taking less and less milk. Then, both you and she will take a break—two months off until she has her calf. (You will have weaned her last calf two months into this pregnancy when the calf was 4 months of age.) She'll put all her energies into the latter stages of her pregnancy, and you'll make sure she's getting proper nutrition and plenty of love. She isn't nursing and she isn't giving you milk for two months during every pregnancy. If you want a year-round supply of milk, you'll need two cows in order to schedule their pregnancies so their two months' time off to rest isn't at the same time.

That's it! Breed cow. Have calf. Milk cow. Breed cow. Once you get the schedule down, you can do things like plan a vacation or pick the time of year you want a calf to be born. Late spring calves are good—the summer heat hasn't hit yet, and if they're born in the winter, keeping them warm takes some effort. I've had calves born in every season of the year, and you know what? I don't mind a winter calf because I have room for one cow and a calf in the bay outside my milking parlor or inside the parlor, should the weather get really nasty and cold. It's kind of a cozy time for everyone. That said, a new calf wants to run and kick up its heels within a week after being born (adorable beyond description), and deep snow makes that difficult. Exercise and movement for a new calf are important. Not just for all the reasons you'd think, but because it helps their developing bowels adjust to life outside the womb. (You don't want to be giving your calf an enema, right?) The birthing schedule you come up with should take your weather into consideration. When I have a new calf born in the winter, I consider it the perfect time to get it used to walking beside me with a halter and lead rope. A long daily walk down a snowy, plowed road or a jog around the neighborhood (just like walking your dog, p. 293) keeps things moo-ving in the bowel department and gives you precious time for bonding. I'm a big fan of walking a cow, especially cows in the later stages of their pregnancies. It's good for them and you—again, bonding time.

• Early Labor (2–6 hours): contractions begin; Active Labor (1/2–2 hours): water sac breaks and dark-yellow fluid rushes from vulva or water sac comes out intact ahead of calf or right after calf; Final Stage (1/2–12 hours): placenta (afterbirth) is shed.

Do you need to attend to the birth? Ideally, yes. Do you need a plan if anything goes wrong? Yes. Just like a human birth, home births can be a good thing, but it's wise to have a backup plan and a doctor on call (more about that in my Vet Care chapter). When I lived on a remote cattle ranch many years ago, I assisted in a human birth, alongside a trained midwife. We were four hours away from help via a dirt road and it was the dead of winter, but the woman wanted to be at home to deliver her baby. Understandable, but she ended up tearing horribly, so we had to load her and the baby into a Jeep and drive the four hours on treacherous roads to a clinic where she could get stitched up. I was pregnant with my first child at the time. After that experience, I checked into a motel room across from a small country hospital when it was my time. With the advent of birthing centers and the willingness of doctors to work with midwives and doulas, it's now possible to enjoy the best of both worlds. Cow births aren't any different. If your goal is to be able to assist a cow in trouble during birth, make sure you have all the necessary knowledge and tools on hand. You owe it to your cow not to make your decision to "go it alone" based on some kind of John Wayne frontier attitude. The goal is a healthy calf and mom, not bragging rights. It's a good thing to hope for the best, but it's your responsibility to have a plan for the worst. When money's been tight, I haven't met a vet yet who wasn't willing to work with me to come up with a payment plan when I've broached the topic ahead of time and explained my situation.

I snapped these photos several years ago when my cow Chocolate was in labor. You can see that it's very early spring. The snow has only recently melted; her pasture hasn't started to green up yet. My daughter, pregnant with her first child, was able to witness the birth with me. I could tell Chocolate was ready because she was rocking back and forth and the area surrounding her vulva was more swollen than it had been the day before.

On a side note, notice the darkened color of Chocolate's face and then take a look at her on p. 282. Even fawn-colored Jerseys tend to darken when their winter coats come in, returning to their lighter color the following spring/summer once they lose their winter coats. A good reason to give them a good brushing every day! Some Jerseys are permanently dark around their eyes and muzzle. Chocolate's baby, Molasses, was part Milking Shorthorn, hence the mottled coloring of her coat.

This is a photo of the area surrounding the vulva of one of my mini-cows several hours before delivery.

Here's what the area surrounding her vulva looks like normally.

285

Statistically speaking, it's rare for there to be complications, and a normal cow birth happens rather quickly. Nevertheless, I'm always relieved the moment I see two hooves followed by a tiny nose coming out at the same time. That means my vet isn't on high alert anymore. Once your cow shows signs of labor, things should progress within an hour; if not, call your vet and give her an update to see if she thinks she should head your way. The actual delivery part is under an hour. Most are within 10–20 minutes. If you want to watch videos of what pulling a misaligned calf entails, try YouTube and search for things like "difficult cow birth" or "pulling a stuck calf."

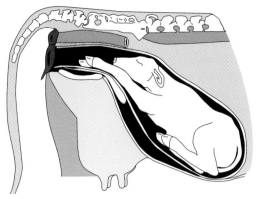

• Normal position of a calf

Now that your bundle of joy is safely out, step back and proceed to disinfect your hands (p. 216) while you observe what momma does next. Sometimes, a first-time mother doesn't figure it out in time, and that's where you come in. If the mother doesn't start nuzzling and licking around the calf's face and nose immediately to help it start to breathe, you're it. A calf should start breathing within 30–60 seconds after birth. Usually, it will do so on its own accord without momma's help or yours. If it doesn't start breathing, you need to attend to its nose and nostrils with your disinfected fingers in case there's amniotic fluid blocking them, and in general, gently jostle the calf around. You may have to perform artificial respiration.

Once it's breathing, step back into the shadows again. Momma should continue to lick the calf to stimulate it and get its blood pumping and its lungs working. It isn't necessary or even desirable for the mother to eat the placenta when it comes out. The only reason some cows are still programmed to do it is to keep predators from smelling it, but it can cause stomach upset. Once it's on the ground, take it away for her and dispose of it so she doesn't have to deal with it. It may take as long at 12 hours for her to pass the placenta. Don't pull on anything hanging from her back end. Suckling by the calf will stimulate her uterus to begin contracting. The contractions will help shrink her uterus back to its normal size, and in the process, facilitate expulsion of the placenta. If the placenta doesn't come out and you're 100% sure it didn't and your cow isn't acting right, consult your vet as soon as possible. It's rare, but there may be a second calf that didn't come out, or some other complication.

Make sure your cow has some hay and clean water while she gets to know her calf. Now you need to step in and treat the umbilical stump with iodine. If the calf was dropped into manure, you need to get it disinfected right away. While the calf is lying down, I've found the easiest way to disinfect the cord is to squirt a puddle of iodine into the palm of one hand and gently dump it on and around the cord or use a small jar full of iodine and dip the navel stump until it's completely immersed and saturated. Swabbing doesn't do the trick. It needs to be fully drenched in iodine. To be on the safe side, you can dip the navel several more times during the first two days, using fresh iodine each time. The stump is still capable of transmitting bacteria while moist. As soon as the stump dries up, you're in the clear. Use my tip on p. 320 for how to use and dispense iodine for first-aid use.

What do you do if your cow isn't licking her calf? Again, you're it. Using a wet towel (a pair of wet exfoliating spa gloves works even better), gently rub and massage the calf, including around its anus. Why?

Rubbing its anus stimulates a wavelike internal muscular movement in the bowel called peristalsis—a muscular contraction of the intestine. It's important for your calf to expel its pre-birth meconium (bright yellow poo that's as sticky as tar) from inside its bowels.

Colostrum

That brings us to the conundrum of colostrum. Colostrum isn't, as I once thought, just a healthy drink your calf should get in order for it to grow up to be a healthier adult. Actually, it can be a matter of life and death in the first few hours of a calf's life.

Just what is colostrum exactly and why all the fuss? The natural procedure of getting colostrum from cow to calf is actually a very cool process, but you have to be on top of it from the get-go. How, you ask? You've just watched a baby calf come into the world. You've assisted with its breathing if necessary, disinfected its umbilical cord stump, and made sure all seems well with momma and baby. You've settled into a corner of the barn or off a bit from where they are in the pasture to watch them unobtrusively to see if the calf suckles within an hour or so. If it doesn't or isn't even trying, unfortunately, you're going to have to step in as its surrogate mother. (I might add, don't be alarmed if your cow isn't getting the hang of the mothering thing right off the bat. When I had that happen to one of my most beloved cows with her first calf, she eventually came around to being a good mother. I think she was in shock or something. Who knows why that happens, but it can and does.)

From the moment a calf is born, the clock starts ticking, and along with it, the calf's ability to process colostrum in its intestinal tract. At 24 hours, if the calf didn't get an adequate amount of colostrum or none at all, it's in trouble, and the only way to sometimes save your calf is through a blood transfusion or a plasma transfusion. Who knew, right?

If you're nervous about a home birth, check with your vet to see if you can do what I did. I essentially checked one of my miniature Jerseys, Etta Jane, into a bovine birthing center (my name for it, not theirs). She had lots of eager attendants vying to attend to her every need, including taking her for short walks. (She *had* them at moo—lots of ooohs and aaahs.) And I was, of course, allowed to visit. Where was she? She was at the Washington State University Veterinary Teaching Hospital. She's very small, and it was her first calf ... and I'm a worrywart. The bill for this? I was charged $18.90/night. The extras? $2.09 for her calf's shot of BoSe (p. 291), plus another $5.80 to give the shot; $2.50 for a new record exam; and $20 for the neonatal exam when the baby came. I decided that since veterinary help for me is a 45-minute drive from my farm, this would be easier on them than a late-night call, plus they have a surgery room. Also, at the time, I didn't own a trailer if I needed to get Etta Jane to them in an emergency. The birth was perfectly normal, so the next time she calves, I'll keep her home, but with my vet on alert.

The doctors and students were so amazing and took such good care of Etta Jane and little Eliza Belle. Here's a commemorative photo I took when Eliza Belle was just 12 hours old. From left to right: Dr. Lisa Pearson, Erika Larsonberg (2nd year veterinary student), and Dr. Alexis Campbell.

Eliza Belle may just be the smallest calf ever born at the WSU Veterinary Teaching Hospital, weighing in at only 30 pounds.

287

In humans, antibodies pass through the placenta, providing protection to the baby. Not so in cows. Colostrum is their source for immunoglobulins (antibodies); it contains compounds that facilitate gut development. But the cow's placenta does not allow the transfer of immunoglobulins to the calf before birth, so calves are born without adequate antibodies—kind of like children who have to live in a bubble in order to survive because they lack basic immune functions. These essential molecules found in colostrum are allowed to pass through the calf's gut from the intestine into the bloodstream for only the first 24 hours, after which time the gut "closes." Nasty things like *Salmonella* and *E. coli* often invade the gut soon afterward, making it difficult for the calf to survive.

Even so, your calf can still develop "scours" (diarrhea). Call your vet armed with as much detail as you can muster—when it started, what color is it, etc. Scours can be serious but not as serious as if a calf doesn't get colostrum within its first few hours of life. Don't wait to get advice and help if your calf develops scours. For the record, I've never had a case of scours. I'm going to sound like a broken record, but again, proper nutrition is the guard dog you want for protecting your loved ones.

Most of us have read a Western classic (or two) that tells the story of a rancher who braves a blizzard in order to get colostrum for his calf from a neighbor because of an unexpected birth in which the mother didn't survive. How they did this before freezers were invented, I have no idea. Perhaps the neighbor also experienced a birth at the same time and his cow didn't die.

Regardless, I make sure I have a supply of colostrum in my freezer by taking some of the more-than-abundant amount my biggest Jersey yields in the 24 hours after giving birth. (Colostrum is so potent and yellow, her colostrum permanently dyed the clear hose to my milking machine.) Colostrum will keep for one year and then must be renewed. When thawing, do not heat above 120°F. But remember, pay strict attention to cleanliness. Secondary infections can occur when dirty hands handle colostrum and if a cow's teats haven't been stripped and disinfected first.

My situation with a cow that didn't take to her calf was fated from the beginning. She was a 2-year-old cow I'd brought home from another state. She'd never calved before. Once here, I put her in with my bull. Now I know the reason I never witnessed them "getting busy," but sometimes a bull and a cow will get together in the dead of the night. Besides, my bull is the quiet type and rather stealthy when it comes to wooing mooing "women." I waited about 30 days and pulled a blood sample to test for pregnancy. Affirmative! Everything was perfect, or so I thought, until three months later, just before Thanksgiving, with temperatures hovering around 15°F, when one of our employees said to my husband, "What's that out there by the shed?" It was a shivering baby calf abandoned by its mother, the cow I'd brought home recently. I wasn't at all prepared.

Perfect Udder is a nifty system designed for handling colostrum from harvest to feeding without the fear of recontamination, Animart.com.

But I am now. If I don't have colostrum in my freezer, I have powdered stuff handy—not as supremely good as the real thing but close enough. And if I haven't needed it before its expiration date, I replace it, just in case, Animart. com.

I also have a speeder feeder bottle ready. With my small hands, I can feed a calf single-handed, because it has a built-in handle, Animart.com.

I also have on hand something called a Calf Feeder Bag, an easy-to-use colostrum delivery system that puts the colostrum directly into the calf's esophagus, Animart. com.

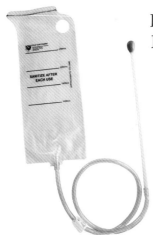

If baby doesn't suckle within the first hour, I get right on it, surrogate mother to the rescue! I might wait another 15 minutes if they seem to be making good progress. But once that critical window of time has passed, it can't be absorbed by their bodies and turns into a large yucky mass in their intestines that goes rancid and can cause all sorts of complications. My rule of thumb? Colostrum down the hatch before two hours after birth because, as the clock ticks, the window for absorption diminishes from 100% on down. Obviously, if you get right on it, 90–100% absorption is better than several hours down the road, when it's diminished to 50 or 30%.

You can try helping a baby that isn't latching on to suckle on the teats, but in my experience, even when I managed to get a teat into its mouth while holding the calf upright, mom would shift and out would come the teat. It makes sense to simply put your cow into a milking stanchion and milk out the colostrum (honoring all the rules of cleanliness before milking, p. 211) and then feed it to the calf, but with a first-time mother like I had on my hands, she'd never even been in a stanchion. Mother and baby were simply NOT interested in each other. Momma was barely used to wearing a halter. This was something I would have worked on and remedied long before her time came (that I thought was months away). In other words, her back leg was kicking like a piston.

There are several things you can try if this happens. First, put a flank rope around her (she can still fuss and shift, but she can't get a full kick in, p. 221), then a hobble. In a pinch, an extra hand to hold her tail straight up can sometimes keep a cow from kicking with such might. But remember, the 18 to 24-hour clock is ticking. You need to get colostrum into your calf. If you decide to mix up some powdered colostrum or you're able to milk some from your cow, back the calf into a corner and straddle it with your legs. Get the calf's head tucked into the shadow of your torso so that you're mimicking the privacy and sense of shelter it would have if it was sucking on a real teat.

You can't have the calf lying down on the ground while you try to put a nippled bottle in its mouth. It needs to be standing with its head pointing up, just like it would be under its mother, so that its throat is fully open and ready to receive the liquid.

Let it fuss over the nipple and keep trying. Just when you think it's hopeless, the calf will latch onto the nipple with mighty force. If it's too weak to stand up, use the Calf Feeder Bag on p. 289. Make sure that within, say, the next few hours, the calf drinks anywhere from a quart to a half-gallon to a gallon of colostrum, depending on its genetics (the size of the parents), or roughly 5–6% of its body weight. I have smaller cows in general, so a quart is what I shoot for. To be more exact, take your bathroom scale to the barn, step onto it, weigh yourself, pick up the calf, and subtract the two. If a calf weighs 36 pounds, 5% would be 1.8 lbs. Remember the rule: A pint's a pound the world around.

Do not give the calf colostrum as you near the 18–24 hour mark. Ideally, you've given it all the colostrum it needs within 4–6 hours after birth. In the meantime, you'll need to give some relief to your momma cow, and hopefully, you've coaxed some colostrum from her so her udder doesn't look like it's going to burst. Milk her as much as you can (paying strict attention to cleanliness) so that when 24 hours rolls around, she's producing milk instead of colostrum.

Milk Fever

Now you need to turn your attention to the mother and the potential for something called milk fever. Again, proper nutrition prior to calving will prevent most problems, including milk fever. It's most common in the first few days of lactation, when demand for calcium for the production of milk exceeds what the body has in reserve. Low calcium levels interfere with muscle function, causing weakness, loss of appetite, and eventually the failure of the most important muscle: the heart. It's not really a "fever" because her body temperature can still register normal. Soon after she gives birth, there's an easy preventive measure you can take by inserting into her mouth something called a bolus (Animart.com) that will supply her with enough sustained-release calcium to help prevent milk fever. But keep in mind that if you have a cow that cannot rise following calving, you need to call your vet.

Post-birth Vitamins & Minerals

In my geographical area, we have a selenium deficiency that results in white muscle disease in calves. As an aid in the prevention of it, we give calves an injection of selenium and vitamin E in the skin of their necks within a couple of days after they're born. If you've paid close attention to your cow's nutritional needs leading up to the birth, it might not be necessary, but my vet recommends it because if there's a deficiency, the shot can make a huge difference in the calf's future health. Mineral and vitamin deficiencies vary geographically—that's why it's important to work with your local veterinarian. Your area might have too much selenium and too little of something else. For details on how to give a shot, please refer to my Vet Care chapter. Your vet will need to write you out a prescription for what you'll need (it should be enough for several calves), as well as provide you with syringes and needles. I keep mine in my fridge. Make note of the expiration date; it should last a couple of years. Also refer to my Vet Care chapter for information about calf vaccinations.

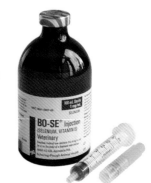

In One Ear and Out the Udder

For as many times as I've heard that I'm supposed to select a cow based on its udder, I haven't always done it. Why? Sometimes I'm shooting for a certain size of animal or coloration and then sometimes you'll get a calf born to parents with udderly good genetics regarding udder presentation and teat size and the calf will have one wayward teat that heads off in another direction. Those kinds of problems are manageable if milk is what you're after. If you're trying to raise show cows, then no. Don't get me wrong, I love what's considered a good udder and four perfect teats. But just like us humans, the mammary glands of cows differ. As long as they're fully functional, who cares what they look like? This isn't Hollywood.

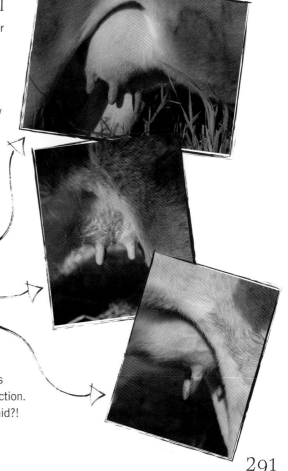

Here's the udder of one of my full-size Jerseys. Nice!

Here's the dainty little udder of one of my mini-cows. Good form. Love the curly locks of hair on the udder.

And here's the udder of another one of my cows.

See how her back teats are hidden behind her legs? It's almost like her front teats are where her back teats should be. Also, her udder is small, although that doesn't necessarily equate with less milk production. Did she nurse her calf well? Yes. Did she give me milk? Yes. 'Nuff said?!

She's in Heat!!!

A young cow (heifer) comes into heat for the first time around 10 months of age but I've seen it happen as early as five months of age. From then on, she'll continue to come into estrus every three weeks (17–24 days). Her heat period will last 24–36 hours. How do you know she's in heat? My cows start acting agitated, almost feisty. One of my girls starts moaning. And I have one who's been known to jump fences in search of relief. If there isn't a bull around, they'll mount each other. Watch out, that "each other" might be you! I've learned the hard way the importance of keeping a calendar dedicated entirely to my cows' cycles.

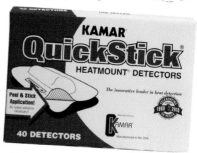

• Peel-and-stick mount detectors can tell you if your cow's been "foolin' around" (something she only does if she's in heat), Enasco.com.

Because their heats are so regular, you'll know when to expect them. I'm almost always able to confirm by looking for a clear discharge from her vulva that is slippery to the touch, rather than sticky. Slippery helps the sperm swim and facilitates penetration. A good time to check for this is when you bring her in for milking. A few hours after the physical signs of a heat begin, she'll go into what is called "standing heat" that lasts about 12 hours. This is when she'll "stand" for a bull and mounting takes place, p. 307. It's also the best time for AI (artificial insemination). Read more about AI in my Vet Care chapter.

At What Age Should My Cow Be Bred?

Opinions vary, but I have my girls get pregnant when they're 1 1/2 years old. That way, they'll be more than 2 years old when they have their first calf. Some people advocate waiting until a cow is 2 years old before breeding. Because I make sure I give them the very best feed, vitamins, and minerals possible, I've never noticed any downside to getting them pregnant at that age.

Getting a Calf Used to a Halter

The key here is to start 'em young. Once they're older, it'll take more effort and time to train them. Start by handling your calf daily and a lot. By the time it's 2 weeks old, it should not be afraid to walk up to you to be petted. That's when you start the process by dropping a rope around its neck to get it used to the feel of it. Next, a halter sized to fit. I've customized the smallest size of rope halter you can buy with just a few stitches of thread. As you lead the calf forward (don't pull), gently push on its behind with the other hand so it gets the hang of "walking" beside you, albeit not so elegantly in the beginning. It'll be a kind of a sideways hop while it struggles against the halter and the whole idea in general. Stick with it. Really, the key to halter training is lots of handling. There isn't any magic trick, just trust and familiarity.

Weaning

Opinions on weaning are as varied as cows. Ranging from 0–9 months of age, what age you choose to wean a calf will depend on your situation and setup as well as available feed, the health of the calf and cow, and how well the calf has adapted to "solid foods" while still getting routine servings of milk. Because I don't feed my calves costly milk replacer (often containing antibiotics), I can let my calves nurse longer, anywhere from 4–6 months. Nor do I milk my cows and then bottle-feed the milk to a calf that is isolated from its mother. I think the personal contact between the two triggers the cow to produce specific antibodies that are continually passed to the calf, kind of like a personalized daily vaccination. Keep in mind that most of our notions about weaning come from a dairy industry that needs *all* of momma's milk instead of just some of it, driven by consumers' demand for cheap food.

The time of year you wean also matters. When our weather turned minus 10°F early one December, a 4-month-old calf, that had become more interested in hay and alfalfa pellets than milk, regressed. Her mother, who was not even one month into her next pregnancy, seemed happy enough to let her calf nurse again regularly. And I didn't absolutely need the milk momma was giving me, so I quit milking her altogether until late March when baby and mother had a bit of green pasture again. Momma was a miniature Jersey, so the amount of milk she was giving me, after baby took what it wanted, was only about one to two quarts per day anyway.

When cattle weren't as captive as they are now, weaning was a more gradual process that happened over time. Sometimes momma didn't dry up or discourage her calf from nursing until she was ready to give birth to her next calf. In my experience as a human nursing mother, I can honestly say, I benefited from nursing as much as my babies did. There isn't any other bond quite like it and it was a wonderful bubble world to inhabit.

Calves don't develop a functional rumen until about four months of age (in other words, they don't have enough "bugs" in their gut to digest forage), even though they start nibbling on hay, following the example of momma, when they're only a few weeks old. The bulk of their nutritional needs is met through milk. If you're going to wean a calf, you need to make sure it's getting an adequate supply of feed as well as proper nutrition. Sometimes, larger cows will push a calf around. It's vitally important that you separate a calf from adult cows during feeding to ensure that it's getting what it needs before you wean it.

293

You can't just toss hay out for your herd and hope the little ones are getting their fair share, unless the timing is such that you have your cows on an expanse of pasture.

Weaning can be stressful, not necessarily because of the change in their food supply, but because their main source of comfort and security in the world has been taken away.

Something called "fenceline weaning" can help somewhat but not much in my experience. Rather than completely separating momma and baby, they're allowed to see and touch each other through a wire fence, but still, both of them pace and bawl for days. It's heartbreaking. And the stress of it puts both at risk for illness.

With one calf in particular, we survived the first day, but the second morning, my calf's eyes were glued shut with pus and it had developed a cough and a good case of the sniffles during the night. (In a larger operation, calves about to be weaned are given preventative vaccinations for weaning-related diseases 2–3 weeks ahead of time, essentially bovine "flu" shots.) I started putting Vitamin C powder (p. 215) in momma's feed and put them back together and all was well again. Three weeks later, I began the process again but this time I used what's called a "quiet wean," QuietWean.com. It's a contraption that fits easily into a calf's nose that prevents the calf from nursing but the calf can still drink water and eat forage.

Most important, the calf can still nuzzle, be licked by, and sleep with momma. After separating the calf long enough for it to eat some hay and alfalfa pellets by itself twice per day, I inserted the quiet wean and then put her back with her mother. I took it off entirely at night. I eventually left it on full-time for four days straight until baby had adapted to life without nursing and the two could be permanently separated without trauma. During that time, I took more and more of momma's milk.

If you have to wean early, make sure you're super-attentive to your calf as I've described above but make sure you're also attentive to momma. Depending on when you wean, her udder might be getting too full and you'll need to be vigilant about giving her relief by milking her (while testing for mastitis, p. 215). Take it slow with a commitment to being flexible, based on the reality of the situation, not what you've been told you should do. Every situation and every momma and baby pair are uniquely different. Remember, the calves (and their mommas) in your charge are *your* babies, too. It's okay for you to use your intuition and go with your gut. In the era I was born, the 50s, conventional wisdom was largely against nursing. Fortunately for me, my mother stood her ground and nursed all of her children but one. In the hospital, my brother was taken from her at birth and she was given a shot to "dry her up." She always regretted it and thought he had more health issues than the rest of us because of it.

Keep in mind that cows have been domesticated for thousands of years but it's only recently that we stopped sharing momma's milk with her calf by inventing things like milk replacer and vaccinations for weaning-related diseases.

Without these, the death rate for newborn calves would have negated the benefits of separation. If you've ever seen a momma cow come close to killing herself to be with her calf, you'll know why I've become an advocate for letting nature take its course when it comes to weaning.

The cycle of life really is the most heart–throb aspect of bringing a cow into your life. If you've ever enjoyed the antics of a frolicking kitten or puppy, think ten-fold and watch a calf at play. You'll have a hard time getting anything else done. In the process, you'll be providing the future owner of that calf a pretty remarkable, healthy, well-adjusted addition to their family—making the world a "butter" place, one backyard milk cow at a time.

The Importance of Cow Licks

I'm sure you're familiar with the term "cowlick"—a section of hair that grows in a spiral pattern, sticking out from the rest of your 'do. (Most right-handed people with cowlicks have clockwise swirls and most lefties have counter-clockwise swirls.) One of my childhood friends had a cowlick in her bangs, making it so a section of her hair was always reaching skyward. Her mother told her she'd been kissed by a cow. Are cows born with cowlicks like humans are, or are they the result of a momma cow licking its calf? I'm pretty sure it's the former.

That brings me to the importance of cow licking. Cow licking is the equivalent of touch in a human—you know, hugs, handshaking, cuddles, kissing. Did you know that you can be physically addicted to the pheromones emitted from your loved ones? There's about a 10-day withdrawal period. That would help explain why, when your child goes off to college, you're beside yourself for that first week, and then slowly you begin to adapt.

The complexities of how my community of cows lick each other could employ a cow psychologist full-time. It's that involved. And all of it changes when I add a new cow to the mix. It's like the constant evolution of politics at the office, including what happens at the watering hole. Here's an example: I bought an 18–month–old cow who'd never been bred before. She'd been taken from her mother two days after

birth and raised in an orphanage of sorts, no mothering. When I first got her, I put her in with a docile steer her size to serve as a companion (steers make good companions), but still she didn't seem happy or content. She mooed with a strange sadness at odd times of the day.

I finally put her in with several of my seasoned mothers and one of them adopted her, fiercely so. The others ignored her and actually bullied her a tad. Her adopted mother licked her entire body night and day for months. I was worried momma would wear out her tongue, there was so much rehab taking place. Did my little cow become increasingly content? She did! I tried for a while to keep a cow-lick diary on all my cows (Jane Goodall style), but the daily changes and complexities were too much for me to keep track of. Bulls do it too. Most of my bulls that are together do the usual slap-on-the-back, nudge-and-push routine to show their affection, especially bulls that are with their sons. But I had two adult bulls, unrelated, who were totally gone on each other. No guy-ish back slapping with those two. They licked each other constantly and slept together night and day without one or the other being dominant, that I could tell.

When a woman who owned a small dairy contacted me with horror stories of the bulls she'd brought temporarily to her farmstead to service her girls (and not having great luck with artificial insemination), I agreed to sell her one of my guys because I knew he would be a good, gentle fit for her cows, but when the time came, I was hesitant because of the relationship he had with his partner. When I finally delivered him to her home, the one left here was sad for an entire month, even though he had two of his sons with him. That was one of those times I really questioned my ability to be able to continue to take on the role of "playing God" with the cattle in my charge. However, I can provide a good home to only so many.

Cattle form elaborate bonds, expressed almost entirely, to the human eye, through licking. I consider it an honor when a calf I'm trying to befriend starts licking my hands, legs, and arms. It feels like I've finally been welcomed into its life, initiated into the herd, so to speak. Like all animals, cattle key into what your feelings are. If you're tense, unsure, angry, or resentful, they'll react to those kinds of feelings in strange ways. Don't beat up on yourself too much, though, when a stranger to your cows arrives. You know how it is when you invite someone to dinner and your children act up, right? Whenever things are getting a little tense, I offer a cow my hand, palm up, for her to lick and sniff; cows have a keen sense of smell and can smell things up to six miles away. I ask anyone meeting my cows for the first time to do the same. It's a polite bow of sorts, and it usually calms down the cow. Even though cows are affected by your vibe, they have their own lives, moods, and upsets. That's what makes it fun and intriguing to work with them on a daily basis.

Pregnancy Test

Prior to the recent invention of a simple blood test (taken 30 days after you think your cow was serviced) that determines whether or not your cow is pregnant, veterinarians and cow owners used to put on a plastic glove up to their shoulders to try to "feel" for the possibility of a fetus by inserting an arm deep into a cow's rectum. Ugh, ugh, double ugh. Plus, when attempted by the unskilled, the procedure wasn't without risk.

I'm more than happy to toss out the photo we took of that procedure and instead tell you that right here in my little home town of Moscow, Idaho, a satellite business (BioPRYN Pregnancy Test by BioTracking.com) exists that is capable of taking in blood samples from around the world, and within 24–48 hours, tell you whether or not your cow tested positive for pregnancy. And because I'm so close, I can pull a sample before 11 a.m., drive it to town, and before 5 p.m. the next day, I receive an e-mail saying "yay" or "nay," all for the price of $2.50! (If I plop down $3.50, I get same-day results.)

If I treat myself to a latte during my trip to town, I spend more on it than on buying the one thing that makes my job managing cows a whole lot easier—knowing who is and who isn't pregnant.

I have to admit, it took me a minute to get used to the blood draw part of it—the latte, not so much. Here's why. Online videos, even the instructions provided by BioTracking, have you drawing the blood directly into the vacutainer that you'll ship to them for testing—in. one. step. with. one. hand. while … the other hand holds the tail up. Either my hands aren't big enough or I'm clumsy or I simply dislike the way its design ensures that it falls out and drops on the ground at just the moment I hit a vein (I'm sure it's the latter). I had to come up with another way to pull a blood sample and it's as easy as eating pie, as simple as falling off a chair, as stress-free as sipping sap, as learnable as child's play, as carefree as a picnic, as satisfying as eating an entire bag of potato chips, as smooth as pricking a cow's tail.

1. Lock your girl into a stanchion or a squeeze chute, p. 351.

2. Talk someone into holding her tail straight out behind her for you (apparently the BioTracking people don't think we have friends willing to hold a cow's poop-y tail).

3. Disinfect the underside of her tail with iodine.

4. Put on a pair of nitrile gloves.

5. Insert an 18 gauge x 1" needle attached to a 6 cc syringe (available wherever vet supplies are sold) until it feels like you're hitting what might be her tailbone, back off a fraction, and then using your other "free" hand, draw the syringe back until it's half full of blood; pull it out.

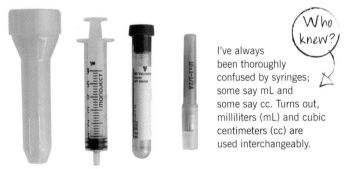

Who knew?

I've always been thoroughly confused by syringes; some say mL and some say cc. Turns out, milliliters (mL) and cubic centimeters (cc) are used interchangeably.

6. Now, grab the rubber-topped vacutainer that's in your pocket (3–10 mL red top tube, available wherever vet supplies are sold or from BioTracking) and immediately syringe the blood into the vacutainer, filling it ONLY half full. (Note: don't push too hard or too fast. Hold the vacutainer tight so it doesn't pop out of your hands under the pressure.) Dispose of syringe responsibly.

7. Label the vacutainer; fill out the paperwork provided by BioTracking giving them a credit card number or a check for $2.50. No need to keep the sample on ice. Pad it and pack it and send it via UPS, FedEx, or USPS.

8. Buy a latte.

Note: Even though I know yay or nay early on, I still get my girls to a vet later on for a pregnancy wellness exam, just like a woman would after a drug-store pregnancy test.

Gestation Table
(based on 283 days)

Date of Service	Calf Due	Date of Service	Calf Due	Date of Service	Calf Due	Date of Service	Calf Due	Date of Service	Calf Due	Date of Service	Calf Due
Jan 1	Oct 10	Mar 1	Dec 8	May 1	Feb 7	Jul 1	Apr 9	Sep 1	Jun 10	Nov 1	Aug 10
Jan 2	Oct 11	Mar 2	Dec 9	May 2	Feb 8	Jul 2	Apr 10	Sep 2	Jun 11	Nov 2	Aug 11
Jan 3	Oct 12	Mar 3	Dec 10	May 3	Feb 9	Jul 3	Apr 11	Sep 3	Jun 12	Nov 3	Aug 12
Jan 4	Oct 13	Mar 4	Dec 11	May 4	Feb 10	Jul 4	Apr 12	Sep 4	Jun 13	Nov 4	Aug 13
Jan 5	Oct 14	Mar 5	Dec 12	May 5	Feb 11	Jul 5	Apr 13	Sep 5	Jun 14	Nov 5	Aug 14
Jan 6	Oct 15	Mar 6	Dec 13	May 6	Feb 12	Jul 6	Apr 14	Sep 6	Jun 15	Nov 6	Aug 15
Jan 7	Oct 16	Mar 7	Dec 14	May 7	Feb 13	Jul 7	Apr 15	Sep 7	Jun 16	Nov 7	Aug 16
Jan 8	Oct 17	Mar 8	Dec 15	May 8	Feb 14	Jul 8	Apr 16	Sep 8	Jun 17	Nov 8	Aug 17
Jan 9	Oct 18	Mar 9	Dec 16	May 9	Feb 15	Jul 9	Apr 17	Sep 9	Jun 18	Nov 9	Aug 18
Jan 10	Oct 19	Mar 10	Dec 17	May 10	Feb 16	Jul 10	Apr 18	Sep 10	Jun 19	Nov 10	Aug 19
Jan 11	Oct 20	Mar 11	Dec 18	May 11	Feb 17	Jul 11	Apr 19	Sep 11	Jun 20	Nov 11	Aug 20
Jan 12	Oct 21	Mar 12	Dec 19	May 12	Feb 18	Jul 12	Apr 20	Sep 12	Jun 21	Nov 12	Aug 21
Jan 13	Oct 22	Mar 13	Dec 20	May 13	Feb 19	Jul 13	Apr 21	Sep 13	Jun 22	Nov 13	Aug 22
Jan 14	Oct 23	Mar 14	Dec 21	May 14	Feb 20	Jul 14	Apr 22	Sep 14	Jun 23	Nov 14	Aug 23
Jan 15	Oct 24	Mar 15	Dec 22	May 15	Feb 21	Jul 15	Apr 23	Sep 15	Jun 24	Nov 15	Aug 24
Jan 16	Oct 25	Mar 16	Dec 23	May 16	Feb 22	Jul 16	Apr 24	Sep 16	Jun 25	Nov 16	Aug 25
Jan 17	Oct 26	Mar 17	Dec 24	May 17	Feb 23	Jul 17	Apr 25	Sep 17	Jun 26	Nov 17	Aug 26
Jan 18	Oct 27	Mar 18	Dec 25	May 18	Feb 24	Jul 18	Apr 26	Sep 18	Jun 27	Nov 18	Aug 27
Jan 19	Oct 28	Mar 19	Dec 26	May 19	Feb 25	Jul 19	Apr 27	Sep 19	Jun 28	Nov 19	Aug 28
Jan 20	Oct 29	Mar 20	Dec 27	May 20	Feb 26	Jul 20	Apr 28	Sep 20	Jun 29	Nov 20	Aug 29
Jan 21	Oct 30	Mar 21	Dec 28	May 21	Feb 27	Jul 21	Apr 29	Sep 21	Jun 30	Nov 21	Aug 30
Jan 22	Oct 31	Mar 22	Dec 29	May 22	Feb 28	Jul 22	Apr 30	Sep 22	Jul 1	Nov 22	Aug 31
Jan 23	Nov 1	Mar 23	Dec 30	May 23	Mar 1	Jul 23	May 1	Sep 23	Jul 2	Nov 23	Sep 1
Jan 24	Nov 2	Mar 24	Dec 31	May 24	Mar 2	Jul 24	May 2	Sep 24	Jul 3	Nov 24	Sep 2
Jan 25	Nov 3	Mar 25	Jan 1	May 25	Mar 3	Jul 25	May 3	Sep 25	Jul 4	Nov 25	Sep 3
Jan 26	Nov 4	Mar 26	Jan 2	May 26	Mar 4	Jul 26	May 4	Sep 26	Jul 5	Nov 26	Sep 4
Jan 27	Nov 5	Mar 27	Jan 3	May 27	Mar 5	Jul 27	May 5	Sep 27	Jul 6	Nov 27	Sep 5
Jan 28	Nov 6	Mar 28	Jan 4	May 28	Mar 6	Jul 28	May 6	Sep 28	Jul 7	Nov 28	Sep 6
Jan 29	Nov 7	Mar 29	Jan 5	May 29	Mar 7	Jul 29	May 7	Sep 29	Jul 8	Nov 29	Sep 7
Jan 30	Nov 8	Mar 30	Jan 6	May 30	Mar 8	Jul 30	May 8	Sep 30	Jul 9	Nov 30	Sep 8
Jan 31	Nov 9	Mar 31	Jan 7	May 31	Mar 9	Jul 31	May 9				
Feb 1	Nov 10	Apr 1	Jan 8	Jun 1	Mar 10	Aug 1	May 10	Oct 1	Jul 10	Dec 1	Sep 9
Feb 2	Nov 11	Apr 2	Jan 9	Jun 2	Mar 11	Aug 2	May 11	Oct 2	Jul 11	Dec 2	Sep 10
Feb 3	Nov 12	Apr 3	Jan 10	Jun 3	Mar 12	Aug 3	May 12	Oct 3	Jul 12	Dec 3	Sep 11
Feb 4	Nov 13	Apr 4	Jan 11	Jun 4	Mar 13	Aug 4	May 13	Oct 4	Jul 13	Dec 4	Sep 12
Feb 5	Nov 14	Apr 5	Jan 12	Jun 5	Mar 14	Aug 5	May 14	Oct 5	Jul 14	Dec 5	Sep 13
Feb 6	Nov 15	Apr 6	Jan 13	Jun 6	Mar 15	Aug 6	May 15	Oct 6	Jul 15	Dec 6	Sep 14
Feb 7	Nov 16	Apr 7	Jan 14	Jun 7	Mar 16	Aug 7	May 16	Oct 7	Jul 16	Dec 7	Sep 15
Feb 8	Nov 17	Apr 8	Jan 15	Jun 8	Mar 17	Aug 8	May 17	Oct 8	Jul 17	Dec 8	Sep 16
Feb 9	Nov 18	Apr 9	Jan 16	Jun 9	Mar 18	Aug 9	May 18	Oct 9	Jul 18	Dec 9	Sep 17
Feb 10	Nov 19	Apr 10	Jan 17	Jun 10	Mar 19	Aug 10	May 19	Oct 10	Jul 19	Dec 10	Sep 18
Feb 11	Nov 20	Apr 11	Jan 18	Jun 11	Mar 20	Aug 11	May 20	Oct 11	Jul 20	Dec 11	Sep 19
Feb 12	Nov 21	Apr 12	Jan 19	Jun 12	Mar 21	Aug 12	May 21	Oct 12	Jul 21	Dec 12	Sep 20
Feb 13	Nov 22	Apr 13	Jan 20	Jun 13	Mar 22	Aug 13	May 22	Oct 13	Jul 22	Dec 13	Sep 21
Feb 14	Nov 23	Apr 14	Jan 21	Jun 14	Mar 23	Aug 14	May 23	Oct 14	Jul 23	Dec 14	Sep 22
Feb 15	Nov 24	Apr 15	Jan 22	Jun 15	Mar 24	Aug 15	May 24	Oct 15	Jul 24	Dec 15	Sep 23
Feb 16	Nov 25	Apr 16	Jan 23	Jun 16	Mar 25	Aug 16	May 25	Oct 16	Jul 25	Dec 16	Sep 24
Feb 17	Nov 26	Apr 17	Jan 24	Jun 17	Mar 26	Aug 17	May 26	Oct 17	Jul 26	Dec 17	Sep 25
Feb 18	Nov 27	Apr 18	Jan 25	Jun 18	Mar 27	Aug 18	May 27	Oct 18	Jul 27	Dec 18	Sep 26
Feb 19	Nov 28	Apr 19	Jan 26	Jun 19	Mar 28	Aug 19	May 28	Oct 19	Jul 28	Dec 19	Sep 27
Feb 20	Nov 29	Apr 20	Jan 27	Jun 20	Mar 29	Aug 20	May 29	Oct 20	Jul 29	Dec 20	Sep 28
Feb 21	Nov 30	Apr 21	Jan 28	Jun 21	Mar 30	Aug 21	May 30	Oct 21	Jul 30	Dec 21	Sep 29
Feb 22	Dec 1	Apr 22	Jan 29	Jun 22	Mar 31	Aug 22	May 31	Oct 22	Jul 31	Dec 22	Sep 30
Feb 23	Dec 2	Apr 23	Jan 30	Jun 23	Apr 1	Aug 23	Jun 1	Oct 23	Aug 1	Dec 23	Oct 1
Feb 24	Dec 3	Apr 24	Jan 31	Jun 24	Apr 2	Aug 24	Jun 2	Oct 24	Aug 2	Dec 24	Oct 2
Feb 25	Dec 4	Apr 25	Feb 1	Jun 25	Apr 3	Aug 25	Jun 3	Oct 25	Aug 3	Dec 25	Oct 3
Feb 26	Dec 5	Apr 26	Feb 2	Jun 26	Apr 4	Aug 26	Jun 4	Oct 26	Aug 4	Dec 26	Oct 4
Feb 27	Dec 6	Apr 27	Feb 3	Jun 27	Apr 5	Aug 27	Jun 5	Oct 27	Aug 5	Dec 27	Oct 5
Feb 28	Dec 7	Apr 28	Feb 4	Jun 28	Apr 6	Aug 28	Jun 6	Oct 28	Aug 6	Dec 28	Oct 6
		Apr 29	Feb 5	Jun 29	Apr 7	Aug 29	Jun 7	Oct 29	Aug 7	Dec 29	Oct 7
		Apr 30	Feb 6	Jun 30	Apr 8	Aug 30	Jun 8	Oct 30	Aug 8	Dec 30	Oct 8
						Aug 31	Jun 9	Oct 31	Aug 9	Dec 31	Oct 9

Let's Talk Bull

" An animal's
eyes have the
power to speak a
great language. "
– Martin Buber

In This Chapter

• Artificial Insemination .... p. 303

• Semen Collection .... p. 306

• Breeding .... p. 306

• Trich Test .... p. 307
  (managing Trichomoniasis)

• Bull Rings .... p. 308

• Steers .... p. 308

301

If you keep a dairy bull for breeding purposes, you need a setup with sufficient confinement and restraint. When I need to transport a bull to the vet or move a bull to another pasture, he's loaded onto my trailer using a series of stout corral panels and gates that form a chute. My bulls aren't "halter broke" because that isn't how I handle them. I would never lead a bull, even if I were using a bull ring (p. 309) attached to a long metal pole. All it takes is one hit from behind and you're on your way to the hospital. Bulls are involved in a considerable number of farm accidents, especially bulls that have gotten old and cranky or bulls that were handled too much by humans when they were calves. (If you're going to turn them into steers, then it's fine to handle them when they're young.) Accidents can also happen when the owner lets his or her guard down. That said, any large animal needs to be respected for its possible mood swings. If a momma cow feels like she needs to protect her young, she, too, can put her head down and harshly nudge you. I read about a man who approached a bull, one that had never before shown signs of aggression, to read its ear tag. When he reached for the ear, the bull lowered its head, turned it abruptly upward, and sliced the man's leg and femoral artery with its horn. (A bull has incredible force behind its movements.) The man survived, but those kinds of stories are the reason I prefer working with animals that don't have horns. I breed for cattle born without them, and if they're born with them, I have them removed, p. 319.
If I were going to read the ear tag of a bull, I would channel him (no, I'm not Shirley MacLaine), using a series of panels, into a squeeze chute, making sure the squeeze chute is secured to the ground adequately. Mine attaches to metal posts embedded in concrete.

meet Bo Jangles at 1 year of age

Temple Grandin, professor of animal behavior at Colorado State University, who I heard give a talk, tells us that the best way to raise a bull is to make sure we humans aren't part of its social circle. In other words, don't handle it too much as a calf if it isn't with other cows, because when it gets older, it will have a need to dominate. If a bull is raised with other cows or ideally, raised with a companion steer, he'll be keyed in to animals rather than people when he feels the need to dominate or establish who is boss.

I also think that because bulls can be dangerous, they are routinely mistreated, which in turn, heightens the likelihood of an accident. A mistreated animal doesn't easily forget. Therein lies the problem. A bull might think that when I contained him, tightened straps around him, and turned him on his side to trim his hooves, I was mistreating him (you can see the fear in his eyes and confirm it in his pulse).

To lessen what he considers mistreatment, I never use electric prods to manage my bulls; I use my brains instead. For example, if I have to work on his housing or check out his water, I move him first. I have a system where I stand by a gate (ready exit), and offer him or them (I have more than one bull) buckets of grain by shaking one (they know that sound from a mile away). As they come toward me, I put the buckets down and step outside the gate, locking it behind me.

meet samson
at 2 years
of age

While they're eating (a considerable distance from another locking gate that is behind them), I lock them into their new paddock so I can attend to my chores. With my setup, I'm able to take my bulls to the vet without help from anyone. In addition, I also have dividers in my trailer that separate them. It's all about metal—putting metal in between you and them.

My husband isn't as wary and careful when he handles them. He likes to reach out to scratch their heads when he feeds them and he walks among them, but always with an exit plan. We've both learned that if you keep your eyes on a bull, you can sense a rise in tension coming on. Usually, a bull will turn his head sideways first and give you that hairy-eyeball look—time to say "g'day mate" and leave him alone.

Artificial Insemination

By now you're probably asking, why does she have a bull (for me, it's bulls, plural) anyway? Good question. That leads us to artificial insemination (AI) versus live cover—a flesh-and-blood bull to mount your cow. (You already know about the birds and the bees.)

Technically, I'm a breeder. (I have a hard time with the terminology of the cattle industry—you can imagine why.) I like to mix and match "cows" for certain traits, but more important, I'm intent on helping people find a cow that's a good match. For that reason, I need semen. Artificial insemination has been hit or miss for me.

Artificial insemination can be attempted by two different methods. The first, and ideal in my mind, is to have a trained family member or nearby neighbor ready with the tools needed to artificially inseminate your girls because it's an on-call situation for the most part. "She's in heat! Can you come?" Once a cow shows signs of heat, you have the rest of that day to get some semen in her.

The other method for AI is "fixed-time AI"—a protocol that, in my case, involved several visits from a technician over the course of 10 days to administer a series of different hormones to my cow to *bring* her into a *planned* heat so that she got semen *exactly* when she needed it. There are many synchronization programs for fixed-time AI, and different technicians use different protocols. Most vets and AI technicians prefer fixed-time AI because the most common dairy cow, Holstein, doesn't show heat very strongly and it's too often missed.

Here's a series of photographs showing the four different visits to get my girl, Etta Jane, pregnant with her second calf. At the time, she was four months shy of 2 years of age. I had purchased semen from a specific bull in order to bring certain traits into my herd.

Day 1: Always first, a wellness check—temperature and heart rate. Then a hormone injection and a hormone suppository into her vagina that stayed there for a week.

Day 8: Once the suppository was removed (being careful to use gloves, lest hormones affect the handler), she received an intramuscular hormone injection.

Day 10 (two visits): Once at 8 a.m. and again at 4 p.m., she got a dose of frozen semen (a dose is called a "straw"—she got one straw in the morning and another straw in the afternoon—20–40 million count per straw). She also received another hormone injection.

Thirty days later, I took a blood sample (p. 298) to have it checked to see if she was pregnant. She wasn't.

I've had one failure and one success using AI, but 50% success rate for AI is not abnormal, given the fact that the semen has been frozen. I've had above-average, actually 100%, success using live cover (bulls). Twenty-four days later, when Etta Jane went into heat again (always very obvious with my Jerseys), I put her in with one of my bulls and he was successful the first try.

Day 1

304

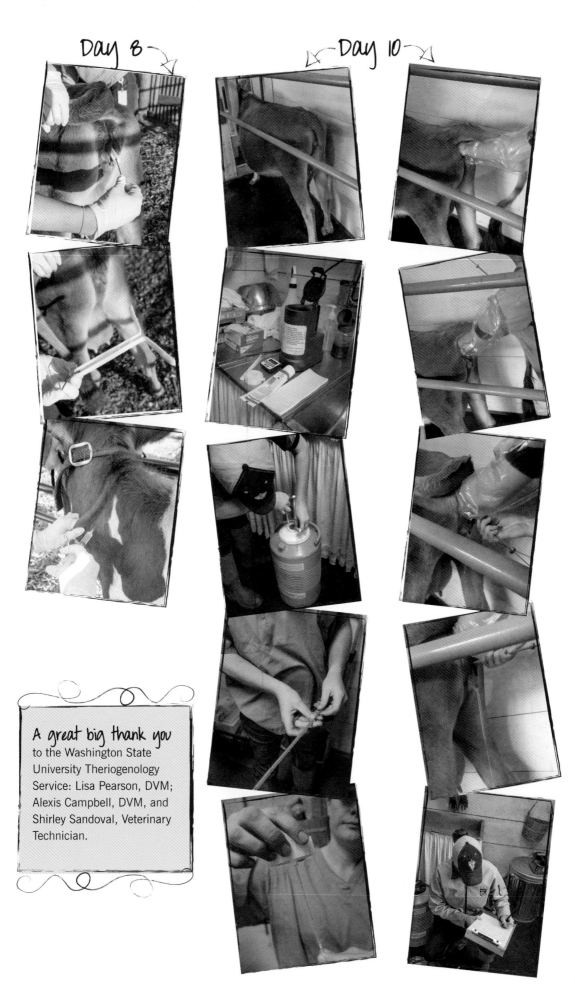

Day 8

Day 10

A great big thank you to the Washington State University Theriogenology Service: Lisa Pearson, DVM; Alexis Campbell, DVM, and Shirley Sandoval, Veterinary Technician.

Semen Collection

First, a wellness check is done (heart rate and temp).

As a breeder, I'll continue to try AI. As my bulls age, I have some of their semen tucked away in a "freezer" at the WSU Veterinary Teaching Hospital. It's a service they provide for personal use. (That terminology thing again.) In other words, I can't go into the business of selling semen, at least not the semen they store for me.

Then, an inspection and measurement of the scrotum.

My long-term goal? I'd like to get the training to do AI myself for the purpose of being on-call to help out backyard cow owners near me. Also, AI allows you to mix and match genetic traits. Even though I could do something called "line breeding" (putting mothers with their sons), I prefer a bit of genetic distance.

While the bull is being stimulated through his rectum, someone collects his semen. (Sometimes an electrical probe is used for stimulation; I prefer to have my bulls stimulated manually.) A sample of the semen is checked for motility (how well the sperm swim), among other things that indicate its viability. After that, it's taken to be frozen and stored. After it's been frozen, some of it is pulled back out to be checked for post-thaw motility (how well the sperm survived freezing).

Breeding

Bottom line? I'll always have at least one bull, or bulls. For one thing, I'm a good bull breeder (that language thing again). I can raise some serious bull when I want to for those who are looking to buy a bull. And I can bring a cow here to be bred (provided she's had all her health checks). But to be perfectly honest, I love the cycle of it, the wonder of "boy meets girl." I love the anticipation that comes with waiting nine months to see what your cupid's arrow created. On the other hand, I seem to score heavily on the bull side of things. Fewer girls than boys have been born under my tutelage; I want milk cows! Knowing that I can pay extra for semen that's been sexed is appealing to me. If I have too many more boys, I'll be a serious contender for sexed semen through AI.

Here's an example of the mix and match thing I like to do. This is my prize milk cow, Maizy. She has a good udder and great teats and her milk produces a bounty of cream. She's a fantastic mother and gets pregnant easily. She's also super-smart; not necessarily a good thing, because over time she's figured out how to open most of my gate latches.

I paired Maizy with Bo Jangles, a younger bull who is genetically smaller. His mother had a good udder and teats also, but was smaller than Maizy. His black coloration doesn't necessarily mean his offspring will be that color. When a Jersey bull has a patch of brown on its back, that means it's merely his testosterone darkening him around the face, chest, and lower torso. In this photo, you can see that he's quite a bit smaller, not a problem when it comes time for them to "get busy." The other way around, however, can be problematic (matching up a smaller cow with a bigger bull) because the cow could have a problem giving birth to a large calf. A bull's penis is long, rigid, and pointy. It reminds me of a narrow, but exceedingly long, pointed carrot. A bull is capable of mounting and penetrating in about the same moment. It happens quickly. The cow will "stand" for him only if she's in heat. I've seen an even smaller bull do his thing and then fall off to the side in the next moment. Done! Pregnant. They mess around like that on and off all day until she goes out of heat and is no longer a willing participant. He loses interest also.

Trich Test

I'm required by the State of Idaho to get a trichomoniasis test done on my bulls once every year. The law also calls for all tested bulls to be identified with its trich-program ear tag. (There are other tests, but since I also conduct them on my cows, you'll find information about those in my Vet Care chapter.)

Trich is a sexually transmitted disease (cattle STD) that causes cows to abort. As the disease spreads, more and more states are passing laws requiring producers to test their bulls. My state was the first to implement a trich testing and identification program.

What is trich? It's a parasitic protozoan (*Tritrichomonas foetus*) that resides in the tissues lining the penis, prepuce, and sheath and when spread to a cow through intercourse, interferes with a cow's ability to stay pregnant, resulting in an aborted fetus. There is no treatment, so infected bulls must be slaughtered. Fewer than 1% of cows remain carriers (most cows will clear the infection on their own), so they're usually retested before being culled. Artificial insemination is one way to avoid trich. Can you imagine having trich spread throughout your herd? If producers stay with the testing and other states get on board, the disease can't continue to spread. It's my job and obligation as a producer to help stop it in its tracks. Because bulls are the long-term carriers of this disease, they are the animals that are tested. The disease is spread when neighbors trade bulls back and forth or when bulls are bought and sold and shipped from state to state.

Here's how it came down for me. I was looking at a bull I wanted to purchase from a state that didn't yet require the test. Nonetheless, I required that the animal be taken to the vet for a trich test. The test came back negative. As it turns out, the test had been performed only two days before Idaho's annual deadline for the next year's round of tests, so I had to take the bull (now my bull) to my vet for another test. Not a problem. I was happy to oblige. There's good reason and I'm pleased my state is on top of it. I encourage everyone to have their bulls tested. We can do this!!!! Talk to your vet and get signed up if you own a bull. Also, don't put your cow with a bull that hasn't been recently tested. And find out their history of herd testing. Since it's a venereal disease, a cow could infect a bull.

It's a simple test to perform. A tiny tube (essentially a very long, skinny straw) is inserted into the sheath surrounding the penis and moved back and forth in order to collect a sampling of what's up there. The sample is put into a vial and tested. The bull gets an ear tag, indicating he has tested negative for trich.

Bull Rings

I'm not sure what possessed me to have one of my little guys outfitted with a bull ring. Maybe it's because it was a bull that I hope to sell some day and I thought the new owner might find it useful. Leading a bull around by its nose (ring) is a common practice among cattle producers. Bovine tattoo/body piercing parlor parlance, I guess. But unlike the common bovine practice of castrating and dehorning, etc. without anesthesia, I always have my vet deaden the area first using an ointment and then administer a numbing injection in the area we're going to be working on. The first problem we bumped up against was that the only size of bull ring sold is 2 1/2" wide, probably too big for a miniature bull, but I figured he'd grow into it. He healed quickly and wore it well, but eventually I realized it would be dangerous for him to try to drink water from one of my new Bar-Bar-A waterers (p. 260) because the ring could get caught on the paddle. I ended up taking his nose ring out after a month. But if you're interested in this procedure, I did snap a series of photos. Handsome hairdo, right? Looks like he applies mousse every morning.

Steers

A steer is a bull that has had his testicles removed (neutered, in the pet world). Again, I always have this procedure done after he's been numbed and I do it when he's young, about 2–3 months of age, while he's still nursing and enjoying the comfort of his mother. I like the idea of a steer, not only because it's more manageable than a bull, but a steer makes a good companion animal for a cow. Cows seem to do better with a companion animal, even if it's from another species. But if it's a steer, he can eventually be harvested for meat. How do I choose which ones become steers? Genetics. I'm breeding for certain traits in a bull, so the bulls that don't fit those traits become long-term, rotating, companion steers for my cows, bulls, or newly-weaned calves.

Let's Talk Vet Care

Thank You ...

Where would I be without the fabulous veterinarian help I've received over the years from the Washington State University Veterinary Teaching Hospital in Pullman, Washington? Thank you to Steven Parrish, DVM/Professor; Ahmed Tibary, DVM/Professor; Sallie Bayly, Veterinary Technician; Melissa Ackerman, DVM; Nathaniel LaHue, DVM; George Barrington, DVM/ Professor; Shirley Sandoval, Veterinary Technician; Lisa Pearson, DVM/Fellow; and Alexis Campbell, DVM. Also, I'd like to thank the doctors and staff at the Lewiston Veterinary Clinic in Lewiston, Idaho. Let's hear it for the guardians of our animals' health. Hats off to vets!

In This Chapter

• Hoof Trimming............................p. 314

• Vaccinations ....p. 317

• Ear Tags.....................................p. 319

• Dehorning ....p. 319

• Castration ....p. 320

• Vet-care Kit ....p. 320

• Life & Death...............................p. 320

311

Good feed, clean drinking water, and a loving environment are usually enough to keep your cow healthy. But when it isn't, you should have a relationship with a vet established ahead of time, just in case.

Illness aside, a vet can also help with routine things like required testing for diseases like TB and Bang's, vaccinations, hoof trimming, dehorning, and castration.

Living in close proximity to the Washington State University Veterinary Teaching Hospital has made taking care of my herd of cattle an absolute joy. The teachers and students always take the time to explain to me what's going on. And when I asked for permission early on to document their procedures with my camera, they responded, "Of course; after all, we're teachers."

Prior to my discovery of the veterinary help available at WSU, I'd had good luck working with doctors in nearby private clinics who work on large animals, specifically cattle. Many are "small animal clinics" (only dogs and cats for the most part), and sometimes a clinic will work with horses, but not cattle. Here's what I've discovered in working with veterinarians. They go into their line of work because they like animals and care about their well–being. It's a simple as that. Obviously, it isn't for the money. My bills have always been perfectly reasonable, definitely on the low-end, p. 287. When you have an animal that's suffering in the middle of the night or on a weekend, having someone you can call is a godsend. If you rely on them for routine help, they'll be familiar with your operation and animals when you do have an emergency. (How great is it when you take your child to your local quick-care clinic or the emergency room and the doctor on call is your family doctor?)

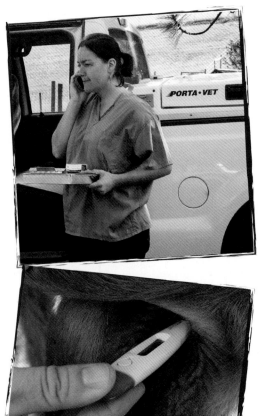

Before you call, take the temperature of your animal using a digital thermometer (rectal insertion) if you can. Anything below normal, 101.5°F, or above 103°F can be helpful information. Also, run and grab your records on the animal in question. Your vet will need to be reminded of your animal's age and medical history if you can't remember. It's easy to forget details when you're worried and anxious.

What constitutes an after–hours emergency? I've used my vet's emergency service twice, once for bloat in an adult cow (Maizy got into an orchard and ate green apples) and once for a newborn calf that had bloody diarrhea. Both times, they saved the day and I learned valuable lessons in the process. But the rest of my visits have been scheduled and routine.

If you have an animal that is bleeding heavily, or has a persistent cough or bloody feces/urine or smelly diarrhea, or has refused food and water for 12 hours, or is down and won't get up, or is struggling in childbirth, call immediately.

Also, make sure your vet knows of upcoming deliveries so that it's on her mind that you might be calling should momma and baby run into complications during birth.

This is why a relationship ahead of time is crucial. And don't hesitate to bring up the subject of money. You should know beforehand what a C-section costs versus losing a calf and starting over.

In some of the online cattle chatrooms I've visited over the years, **there's definitely a wealth of information being shared, but I've noticed a troubling tendency toward a kind of machismo tough–it–out–go–it–alone attitude** when it comes to cattle. I followed a thread once regarding the ongoing saga of someone's *really* sick cow and all the different things they were trying, when really, they needed the help of a trained doctor three days earlier. Maybe it stems from watching too many Western movies—you know, the scene where a guy knocks back a slug of whiskey because he has to knock out his infected tooth using the butt of his pistol?

My cows are family to me. When I was raising my children, prevention was my health mantra, but I never hesitated to get help when I was in doubt. **Veterinarians have invested years getting to where they are.** I'm a novice. **I'll never have the time to learn what they've learned.** That said, I've always let my vets know that I err on the side of caution and natural remedies. When I told a vet I'd given my calf a drench of aloe vera and arnica, he asked, "What's arnica?" But that doesn't mean I haven't welcomed their trained medical input and experiential learning in my decision-making when it comes to the ongoing conundrum of good health. **Fortunately, we live in an era where we can pull from the best of both worlds: old world wisdom and modern–day know–how.** It's an image that works for me: pitchfork in one hand, computer in the other.

That doesn't mean I'm not completely smitten with the idea that over time I'll master more and more of my animals' care. I've become good at giving them subcutaneous shots (still working on the finesse of intramuscular shots) and I've become good at drawing blood from a tail for pregnancy testing, p. 298. **I've figured out what I do and don't want my cattle vaccinated and tested for** (p. 318), and I know how to take down a cow with ropes if I need to (p. 316). And I want to be prepared for bloat by knowing how to run a tube down the throat of an animal for expulsion of the gases that are causing it to feel bad. But castration and dehorning? I think not. Well, maybe … down the road a long mile.

And where did I learn what I do know? My team of vets. (And study and research when I've had the time.) My long–term plans are to do the hoof trimming myself. Right? I have this idea that if I bring my cattle into the squeeze chute once per month and rasp their feet, I won't need to take them in twice a year for a hoof trim. We'll see. And if that doesn't work, check out this contraption.

I don't know about you, but **every time I see this photo, it cracks me up. Cow spa.** That's exactly how I look when I'm getting a pedicure. Check out ComfortHoofCare.com. (As an aside, I'd make sure a pretty red "spa chair" like this one is securely fastened to the ground. With concrete.)

Hoof Trimming

In my area, I have the option of using the services of a talented guy named Darron Hamilton, who drives around to farms in Washington and Idaho, pulling behind him his homemade cattle hoof-trimmer contraption. He did a fabulous job, but it proved problematic for me to get my adult bulls talked into checking out his digs (although a few more movable panels would solve that problem). You can contact Darron via e-mail (hamiltonunlinc@hotmail.com) or phone (509-952-9010).

When I take my bulls to WSU for hoof trimming, it's opportune that the teaching hospital is a gated community, complete with a series of bars my guys are more than happy to pop their heads into to see what's comin' down. They're easily "captivated."

While my animals are under their spell, they can also receive their annual tests for certain diseases, get their booster shots, have their ear tags checked, get semen collected, and receive a breeding soundness exam (an actual document that comes in handy when you're trying to sell a bull). You gotta love it when a vet cares enough to cover the face of a bull with a towel (keeping him from being so afraid) or puts a pillow under a guy's head during a particularly invasive procedure. Oh yeah, and talk baby talk to a Very. Large. Bull.

Darron Hamilton

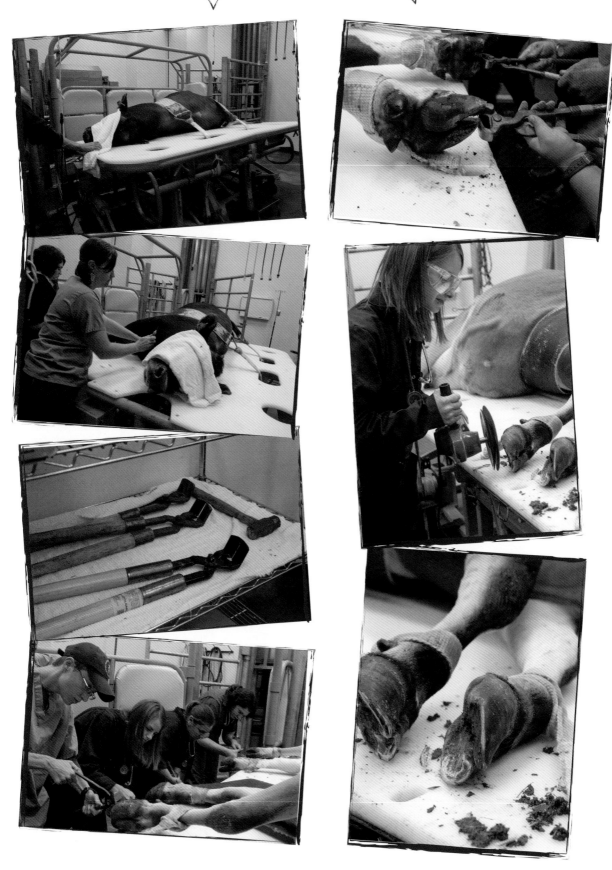

There were a few of my cows that were too small for the WSU hoof–trimming table, so we took them outside their facility for a "shake down/take down." Impressive, to say the least. Good ropes to use are either a 1 1/2" 3-strand **cotton rope** with a 10,000 lb tensile strength or a 2" **manila rope** with a 27,000 lb breaking strength, KnotandRope.com.

Tie the cow's head down low, close to the ground. Wrap her with a rope as you see here, and then stand back a safe distance with the rope tied in a loop and pull back while leaning away. If it's a large animal, like a bull, you should ask a friend (or several) to help you pull. (Grab that friend who was on the winning team in childhood tug o' wars.)

Down she goes. Keep things taut by tying the rope to a post if need be. Tie the legs (she can still move those), and get 'er done. When it's time for her to stand up, untie her legs, give some slack to the rope that pulled her back, and up she comes.

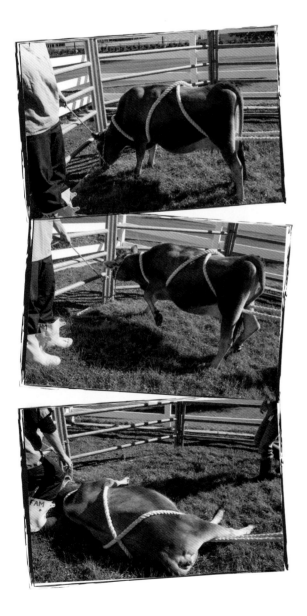

Vaccinations

This whole concept gave me pause because when it came to my children's vaccinations, my family doctor encouraged a selective approach rather than a smorgasbord approach. These days, children (on standard protocol) get 49 doses of 14 vaccines before the age of 6.

The annual vaccinations I give my cattle are listed further on. But don't take my word for it. ValleyVet.com has vets available for your questions and a wealth of information on their website. And if you click on the "manufacturer/label information tab" under a particular vaccine, you can reach one of the vets the manufacturer has on call (in addition to clicking on some good, clear descriptions of what the disease is). Keep in mind that different geographical areas have different diseases that are problematic. Also keep in mind that if your operation is small, perhaps as small as one single milk cow, many of the diseases that can be vaccinated for are often a result of modern-day big/bigger/biggest operations. Not all animals receive the care you give yours, but instead are subject to routine antibiotics, growth hormones, GMO feed, toxic fly sprays, anti-parasite chemicals, and lack of pasture and fresh air. The result? Unhappy and sad (mad?) cows that are prone to disease.

The vets on call through ValleyVet.com who I talked to were incredibly helpful and patient with me. Over the years, I've Googled plenty of cattle diseases, often ending up on the websites of agricultural universities, but the information I have access to from Valley Vet's vets and the manufacturers' vets, like the Colorado Serum Company, is more condensed and less confusing to me. I took care of 14 Dexter cows one winter for a neighbor. I could see after they were delivered that several of them had facial warts. There are helpful vaccines for a host of maladies, including warts. Once you decide what you want to guard against, you can buy your vaccinations online.

Or you can work with your local vet and get your cattle on a regular schedule for vaccinations. I do all my routine vet work every fall. All in one fell fall swoop, we do vaccinations, hoof trimming, and testing for diseases. If I'm collecting semen from a bull for storage, I do that as well, p. 306. However, I do that first thing in the morning before my guys become stressed—a pillow helps only so much.

My annual vaccination schedule every fall:

(Note: As knowledge, technology, and diseases change, so do vaccinations. Again, ValleyVet.com for staying up on the latest.)

• **Ultra Choice 8** for all healthy cattle, including pregnant cows and heifers, and calves of any age. No milk withdrawal. 21-day slaughter withdrawal. 2 mL, SQ neck (subcutaneous—under the skin injection). Vials come in 10 dose or 50 dose. Record ear tag #. REPEAT in four weeks if it's a first-time vaccination for a cow, bull, or calf. Thereafter, an annual booster is adequate. Contains protection against: *Clostridium chauvoei* (commonly called blackleg, a soil-born, non-contagious, highly fatal disease, mainly seen in cattle from 6 months to 2 years of age); *Cl. septicum* (malignant edema); *Cl. novyi* (black disease); *Cl. sordellii* (gas gangrene); *Cl. perfringens* Types C & D (often associated with endotoxemia and enteritis); plus *Cl. haemolyticum* (bacillary hemoglobinuria/red water—not to be confused with leptospirosis). Application: 6 cc syringe and 16-gauge x 1" needle, aluminum hub (calves: a 14-gauge x 1" needle, aluminum hub).

Note: The reason you give the same amount of vaccine to any size cow is because it isn't like an antibiotic. That amount is required in any size animal to trigger an immune response.

Note: Afterward, some of my animals had lumps on their necks where the vaccine had been injected. I think it might have to do with the delayed dispersal component of the vaccine. The lumps eventually came down in size, but for one of my bulls, it took a couple of months.

• **CattleMaster GOLD FP5 L5** (FP stands for fetal protection) for all healthy cattle, including pregnant cows and heifers and calves of any age. No milk withdrawal. 21-day slaughter withdrawal. 5 mL, SQ neck (subcutaneous—under the skin injection). Vials come in 5 dose, 10 dose, or 25 dose. Record ear tag #. REPEAT in four weeks if its a first-time vaccination for a cow, bull, or calf (label says 3 weeks, but 4 weeks is fine so you're doing it at the same time as Ultra Choice 8.) Thereafter, an annual booster is adequate. Contains protection against: IBR (infectious bovine rhinotracheitis [AKA red nose], viral, causes abortions); BVD (bovine viral diarrhea, causes abortions, can be spread to humans) Types I and II; PI3 (parainfluenza virus 3); and BRSV (bovine respiratory syncytial virus, affects all ages of cattle, but is more severe in young calves); and 5 strains of leptospirosis (called Lepto, AKA Red Water—dark red, foamy urine caused by a bacteria found in the environment; cattle die within 12 hours; can be spread to humans). Application: 6 cc syringe and 16-gauge x 1" needle, aluminum hub (calves: a 14-gauge x 1" needle, aluminum hub).

Also, when my calves reach four months of age, I take them to my veterinarian for a Bang's (brucellosis) vaccination. It must be done before they are 12 months old. After 12 months, they can't be vaccinated, only tested.

• Subcutaneous (SQ) shots are given under the skin rather than in a muscle. Pull out a fold of skin from the neck, where the skin is loose, and slip the needle in under the skin you've pulled out, aiming the needle parallel to the animal so it doesn't go in the muscle or come out the other side of your "skin pull."

My testing–for–disease schedule:

I test all my animals annually, starting at 1 year of age, for TB (cows only), Bang's, Q fever, BVD (bovine viral diarrhea), BLV (bovine leukosis virus), Johne's, and trich (bulls only, p. 307). Testing is done by my veterinarian and they send verification paperwork to the state regarding trich (as required by Idaho law), TB, and Bang's (as required by federal law). And any new animals entering my herd must test negative within 30 days prior to coming onto my property. Any animal you buy must have accompanying paperwork from a veterinarian verifying that the animals being transported tested negative for TB and Bang's, and in my state, trich.

Not only am I required to have a veterinary check to ensure that an animal I am considering buying is free of TB, Bang's, and trich, I require, in addition to my legal requirements, a current negative test for Q fever, BVD, BLV, and Johne's.

Did you know? TB, Q fever, Johne's, BLV, and trich **cannot be vaccinated against** and are only kept at bay through vigilance and adherence to laws designed to isolate and eradicate them. All of them can be tested for by a veterinarian. TB and Q fever can be spread to humans through handling animals and drinking unpasteurized milk.

Did you know? Bang's, BVD, and Lepto (red water) can be vaccinated against, Bang's before 12 months of age. All can be spread to humans through handling animals and drinking unpasteurized milk. Bang's and BVD can be tested for by a veterinarian.

Ear Tags

What do they mean? An **orange metal tag** (vet supplied/issued by the USDA) has a paper trail associated with it. The tag is put in a female's right ear when given a Bang's vaccination. Also at that time, her right ear is tattooed in case the orange metal tag ever falls out. (In a female, this tag can then be used as an ID tag for her other required tests/tracking.) Bulls *tested* for Bang's (they aren't vaccinated) can be tracked using an ID tag. A **silver metal tag** is simply an **identification** tag (vet supplied/issued by the USDA) used for tests like Bang's (bulls) and TB (cows, if they've lost their orange tag). Even though metal tags can come out (the reason chips are becoming more popular), it is considered a permanent tag given to a particular animal and also has a paper trail associated with it. If you're considering shipping an animal to another state, it must be issued a health certificate first by an accredited vet (meaning the vet has approval to perform required tests

and issue health certificates) and tracked based on its ear tag. If you wish to brand an animal with a number and/or letter, you can tattoo its left ear yourself using a kit (StoneMfg.net), but I prefer to use an animal's existing metal tag.

Plastic trich tags (bulls) are state-specific, good for only one year (Sept 1-Aug 31), and the numbers change every year so the tag is replaced annually. When you see an animal with several plastic ear tags, it's something the owner has done for identification within their herd. Here's the glamour part of it: My girls (1 year or older) have an orange metal tag in their right ear. My bulls (that are old enough to be sexual) have both a large plastic trich tag in their right ear and a silver metal ID tag in their left ear.

Dehorning

Because I have a mix of animals that are born with or without horns, it takes a few weeks for me to be sure I'm actually seeing and feeling horn buds in order for them to be removed safely. As I do more and more DNA testing, I'll know before a calf is born whether or not it will have horns. By pulling a few hairs from beneath the tail of a cow or bull and sending them along with a check for $25 to the Veterinary Genetics Laboratory at the University of California Davis, you can find out whether or not your animal carries a gene for horns, hence, if its offspring will have horns. Go to VGL.UCDavis.net to print out a form and learn more details. Because I'm selecting for the polled gene in future calves, I hope to phase out the need to dehorn my cattle.

Not only can horns on adult cattle hurt people, cattle can hurt each other, as well as get their horns stuck in wire fencing. Plus, I'm uncomfortable around cattle with horns. I don't like the way a moving horn can be the same height as a child's eye.

When dehorning a young calf, the horn area is numbed, and then a red–hot iron (shaped like a ring) that fits around the bud is pressed against the head of the calf. About 10 seconds after pressing firmly, there has been adequate heat applied to kill the corium (germinal cells that become the horn). It's more problematic to dehorn adult cattle. It's best to dehorn calves before or after fly season and before winter.

319

Castration

I make sure my young bulls (that are about to be turned into steers) have been numbed before proceeding. It's best done at a young age, while they're still nursing but before or after fly season and before winter.

Vet-care Kit

For doing my own vet care, I keep a fishing vest loaded with the things I'll need.

- digital thermometer with disposable sleeves
- needles, syringes, and vacutainers, p. 298 and p. 318
  Sizes: 3 cc and 6 cc syringes (the part that holds the liquid) and sizes 14 x 1", 16 x 1", and 18 x 1" needles with an aluminum hub
- scratch pad and pen
- scissors
- stout pair of pliers
- iodine kept in a teat-dip cup with the outer ring removed, turning it into a squirt bottle
  (kept inside a plastic bag so it doesn't leak on things)
- latex gloves
- flashlight
- headlamp
- cell phone (always a good idea when you're out alone with your animals)
- probiotics
- vitamin and mineral supplements
- small plastic bag for odds and ends refuse

A quick dose of vitamins and minerals can't hurt, but a little goes a long way. Follow the instructions on the package to the T; don't overdose!

Whenever things just don't seem right, I like to try a dose of probiotics to see if that helps.

Life & Death

When it comes to cattle, not only are you in charge of their lives, you're also in charge of their deaths.

On a winter night, I awoke around 11 p.m. to the sound of cattle bawling, one in particular that gave me pause—my bull, Milky Way. He's rarely verbal. When I got to where my cattle bed down at night, my 6-year-old Emma (3 months pregnant) was close to expired. She was lying away from her shelter with her head contorted almost straight back. (At first glance I thought she'd broken her neck somehow.) There was froth around her mouth. Her eyes were fixed and her breathing was coming in short bursts. She was on her side. I could see she'd been struggling prior to when I found her. But she was so bloated by the time I arrived, her legs were barely touching the ground. I went through several scenarios of what it would take to try to save her and knew it was impossible.

Perhaps if I'd found her a couple of hours earlier, I could have called my vet, or if she was still standing but wobbly, I could have loaded her into my trailer and taken her to my vet. But Emma's situation had become severe; she was slowly suffocating to death (stomach bloat puts pressure on the lungs). The rest of my cattle were clearly distraught over what she'd been going through.

If you find yourself in this situation, you have several options—all of them dependent on prior planning. A vet can put an animal down in one of two ways. If they use a euthanasia solution, the carcass is considered toxic waste and can't be buried on your property. The regulations regarding this are complicated—the reason why it must be discussed with your vet ahead of time. The second method allows you to bury the animal on your property. Your vet will use a captive bolt gun that knocks the animal unconscious. Afterward, they inject a concentrated potassium chloride solution into a vein to stop the heart. If you don't have a vet who can come to your aid quickly, a sheriff or police officer might be willing to shoot a large animal for you. I grew up familiar with firearms, so my choice is to do it myself—less time that a hopelessly injured or desperately sick animal needs to suffer.

You want to use a gun that doesn't pose a danger to you.
A .22-caliber rifle (loaded with .22-long-rifle cartridges) is my firearm of choice. You want to shoot one bullet directly into the brain without it exiting. Where do you shoot? Stand next to the animal and hold the point of the gun 1" out from the place where you're going to shoot.

If you were to draw an imaginary X across a cow's face, going from the top of where the ear attaches to the head and across to the center of each opposing eye, the lines would intersect in the spot for a frontal shot that would enter the brain directly.

If you need to take a side shot, take aim no more than 2" forward toward the face from the center of the hole in the ear. The charge from a .22 cartridge isn't enough of a blast to do anything other than put one tiny hole in the skull.

Emma died instantly. My husband brought the tractor and I attached a chain to her two back legs. He pulled her down the road to a clearing. Early the next morning, using the backhoe attachment, he dug a deep hole with a slope on it so we didn't have to drop her in, but instead, could gently pull her into the place where she'd be buried. Throughout, I got lots of hugs from my husband.

Do I know what happened to Emma? I assume it was bloat, but why? None of my other cows showed any sign of trouble with the hay I'd fed them that night. She seemed fine when I last saw her, and hay rarely causes an animal to bloat. In speaking with my vet the next day, he pointed out that the bloat might have been secondary, happening after she'd gone down with whatever made her so violently ill.

Emma was a sight-unseen adoptee (from someone local who could no longer provide care) when she was 4 years old and pregnant with her first calf—my bull, Bo Jangles. Soon after he was born, I asked the vet about Emma's heavy, labored breathing, thinking she had a nasty respiratory infection. After an examination, he said, "The good news? It doesn't sound like it's in her lungs, nor does it sound like she has a current infection in her bronchial tubes; it's more in her throat and trachea, possibly from an injury or a prior infection resulting in scar tissue. She sounds worse than she is." Emma gave us one more calf, a bull, before she died. Sometimes a cow that has suffered a respiratory infection has a damaged vagus nerve that makes her more prone to unexplained bloat. We'll never know.

If you don't have a tractor or a truck to use for disposal, locate someone who does and would be willing to help.
Again, plan beforehand for a large animal's death and burial.

Let's Talk Cowpanions

" Cows are amongst the gentlest of breathing creatures; none show more passionate tenderness to their young when deprived of them; and, in short, I am **not ashamed** to profess a deep love for these quiet creatures. "

– Thomas de Quincey

In This Chapter

• Milk Cow Companionship.............p. 324

Milk Cow Companionship

What is it about pets? Why, collectively, are we so gaga over Fifi and Fido? My grandmother was absolutely bonkers over her canary (and years later, me too, over my canary, Daffodil, who filled my world with beautiful blue eggs). I think I know why. Perhaps.

I can say without hesitation, I love humanity. But do I love people? Hold on, now. That's a different question. People can be so ... complicated. Animals? Not so much. Certainly, my cows and yes, even my bulls, have incredibly diverse personalities that I can describe in detail. I have watched as my husband has quietly taken it upon himself to give a dose of love to my bulls several times each day. Sure, he jokes about it being a guy thing as he scratches their heads, but it's obvious he's feeling that *thing* that happens.

It seems our reaction to animals is the kind of reaction we have for a child who can't yet speak. Our hearts melt. We want to protect them, advocate for them, make the world a better place for them. We feel called upon in an unspoken way. Unspoken—we like that. It's uncomplicated. *It brings out the humanity in us.*

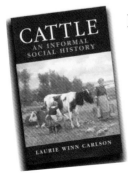

It's easy enough to picture a woman with a companion dog or cat, but a cow? An 1850 agricultural census found that 75% of U.S. farms had at least one milk cow. According to Laurie Winn Carlson in her book *Cattle: An Informal Social History*, milking those cows, making butter, and then distributing the extra was largely the domain of women—a cottage industry that was an important source of income for farm families. By 1910, women on the plains of Montana were using butter money to buy windmills. Into the 20th century, women sometimes owned 10 cows. Without refrigeration or reliable transportation, women traded their fresh butter to local country stores for things like flour and gasoline. Laurie's book points out that for most of our recent history, a milk cow represented economic freedom for a woman.

Central to human existence since time began, cattle have played a vital role in our history not only as a source of food, but also as a means of labor, an economic resource, an inspiration for art, and even as a religious icon. Prehistoric people painted them on cave walls; explorers, merchants, and landowners traded them as currency; many cultures worshipped the cow as a sacred and divine deity. In *Beef: The Untold Story of How Milk, Meat, and Muscle Shaped the World*, Andrew Rimas and Evan D. G. Fraser tell the story of cattle in its entirety. *Beef* tells a tale that spans the globe—from ancient Mediterranean bullfighting rings to the pastoral grazing grounds of 18th-century England; from the quiet farms of Japan's Kobe beef to remote villages in East Africa, home of the Masai, a society to which a cow means everything. It's truly an excellent and lively read—well done, Andrew and Evan!

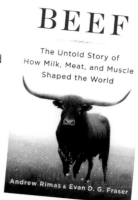

But a companion cow in the 21st century can be about even more. Consider this. There are some 30 million acres of lawn in the U.S. Ohio farmer Gene Logsdon points out in his book, *All Flesh Is Grass*, that if homeowners added white clover to their lawns, their "grass farms" could produce eight tons of dry forage per acre per year. That's what good farmland produces, meaning some 240 million tons of what could be good hay (in the form of grass clippings) is going to landfills. It's a tall order, I know. But if you wanted to sign up right away (keeping a lawn means you've already proven you're a little bit farmer), you could start with a backyard cow.

Joan Jensen's book, *With These Hands: Women Working on the Land*, confirms the important relationship between women and cows with excerpts like this one from Judy Van der Veer's memoir of life in the 1930s: "I've 'most got Wilbur talked into the notion of lettin' me buy a cow … I've sewed for the neighbors till I 'most put my eyes out; I've made underwear for myself and the kids from feed sacks, and if that heifer looks at all good to me, I'm a-gonna buy her."

If I haven't yet convinced you that animals hold the key to your humanity, here are a few visual aids that might do the trick.

Conventional wisdom holds that, of course, a cow can't cry, let alone shed tears. And certainly, an elephant can't. Saddle up a cow instead of a horse? Hold onto your heartstrings, because the next few tales will give 'em a tug.

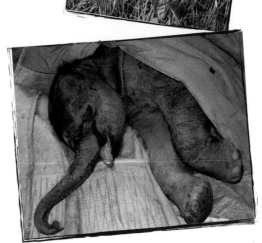

A newborn elephant was rejected by his mother at the Shendiaoshan Wild Animal Nature Reserve in eastern China. The little guy was rescued and wrapped in a blanket, but he cried inconsolably for hours. Elephants are known to express emotion, but capturing one crying on camera is rare. "The calf was very upset, and he was crying for five hours before he could be consoled," the keeper said. Finally, he perked up and bonded with the keeper who saved him, drinking milk from a bottle and batting his trunk playfully with zoo staff.

Being in the presence of my cow when I'm milking her enlarges me. The bigness of the care that I give her, the concern, the touching, the feeding—it pours into me like broth.

"They'll still be able to see each other ... so it shouldn't be too traumatic," said a farmhand who suggested we wean a calf by putting momma and baby on opposite sides of a wire fence. (I've since come up with another method for weaning a calf, p. 294.) We survived a couple days of bawling, and eventually I moved her calf to the other side of the farm. Because her calf was a male and I couldn't possibly accommodate any more bulls, I needed to get him dehorned and castrated ("neutered" in the pet world), but only by a vet willing to numb both areas first. (In the cattle world, these procedures are usually done without numbing.) When I brought him home afterward, I made the mistake of walking him within sight of his mother. This time, her bawling and perimeter pacing was even more intense than when he was weaned. She obviously knew he had suffered injuries and wanted to comfort him. (He, on the other hand, didn't seem at all bothered.) Sometime around midnight, I heard the wire fence creaking and then the sound of a thick wooden fence post breaking. I ran down with a flashlight to see her eyes ablaze with cowpassion, her nose and head covered in caked dirt from trying to dig her way under the fence. She's a big cow, so I was a little nervous about approaching her when she was so fiercely determined. As I walked toward her, I started talking, explaining everything in detail while reassuring her that he was okay. She walked up to me, stopped, put her head down, and buried it in my chest. She proceeded to cry a stream of tears and her nose ran like a river. I held her head, occasionally wiping her eyes and nose, and let there be silence while she poured her heart out to me. When I finally left, she went over to her shelter and slept. She was back to normal the next day. But I was forever changed.

Cows conduct graveside services when ... Debbie, a cow who had been rescued by the Poplar Spring Animal Sanctuary, fell down ill. As recounted in Amy Hatkoff's book, *The Inner World of Farm Animals*, the other cows at the sanctuary formed a circle around her and mooed and bellowed until a staff member arrived. Sadly, the vet determined that Debbie's arthritis was crippling and that it would be best to put her to sleep.

"We dug a grave for Debbie, and when she was lying there, all the cows came and gathered around her and just cried and mooed," recalled Terry Cummings, the sanctuary's director. "They were so distressed. And when we put her in the grave, they lay down on it. Then the whole group went off together somewhere on our 400 acres and didn't come back for grains for two days. I never expected a reaction like this. I had no idea they were so aware of each other and so bonded."

The cow jumped over the ... makeshift hurdle of beer crates and logs. When Regina Mayer's parents, of Germany, refused to buy her a horse, the 15-year-old taught one of their cows how to trot, canter, and eventually jump. Regina started training her cow, Luna, by taking her for walks in the woods. Two years later, Luna soars like a regular show jumper.

"The best thing I ever did for my child was give her a cow to take care of," said a 4-H mother when asked about her daughter's dairy cow entry at our local county fair. "Better than a horse, a cow serves a higher purpose. It's a pet that helps put food on the table—a great life lesson for my daughter. In addition, animal chores build character."

One last thing ... a cow needs companionship. If you can't give your cow an animal companion, you're it. You'll need to touch and talk to your cow every day. Too much loneliness will ruin a good cow. Make sure she's getting the love she needs and deserves. When you aren't milking her daily because she's in the later stages of her pregnancy (slowly decreasing the amount of milk you take), don't hesitate to walk your cow like you would a dog—she'll love it! Human contact can be a source of immense pleasure for a cow. (Don't forget to pack an extra-large, biodegradable, doggie-poo bag if you're in suburbia, p. 293.)

" In ways that **matter**, we are all the **same**.
I have yet to find an **emotion** that is normally attributed
to **humans** that is not displayed by **animals**.
Just because they don't **speak** our words doesn't
mean they are not **communicating**.
They are **constantly** communicating.
Once you click in, you can **see** it.
If we **let go** of the unconscious **limits** we normally
impose on **animals** and simply **look** at them,
listen to them, and **pay** attention, they have a whole
lot to **say**, and they say it **clearly**. "

– Kathy Stevens, founder, Catskill Animal Sanctuary,
from *The Inner World of Farm Animals* by Amy Hatkoff

329

Let's Talk Business

" To be successful,
you have to
have your heart in
your business, and
your business
in your heart. "

– Thomas Watson, Sr.

In This Chapter

• Legalities of Selling Raw Milk ....p. 333

• Entre*manure*ship .... p. 337

• Changing Zoning Codes to
Allow for Backyard Cows.............p. 338

• Selling Milk ....p. 342

331

When I was a wee one, I remember my father showing me photos of him when he was a child. In one photo, taken in 1923, he's a young lad (5 years old, to be exact) and he's milking the family cow, named "Red," while his cousins Walter and Harold stand watch—and then in another photo, the boys are on a horse.

In that moment, I was star-struck, not with the idea of a horse (usually the case with young girls), but with Red. I thought, "A child my age can milk a cow?" I dearly loved my chickens and rabbits, but a cow? By then, it was obvious to everyone in my family that I was keyed into farm animals.

As parents often will, my father knew something about his daughter that even he didn't know he knew. "Did you love her?" I asked him. "Did she have babies?"

I continued to pepper him with questions—after all, in that moment, my destiny was actuating its unfolding. Finally, I asked, "Can I have a cow?"

He replied, "Someday. In the meantime, you should continue to help your Aunt Louise [my father's sister] take care of hers." Louise, and her husband, Stewart (Lou and Stew), owned a small dairy 45 minutes from our home. Their daughter, Christine, my same age, was my reason for weekend visits throughout the summer. I loved Christine. But there was something else, something … inexplicable.

There are plenty of scenes from my childhood I can no longer recreate, but to this day, I could draw you an exact blueprint of their milking parlor, their house, the yard, muddy boots lined up on the porch, the front gate. And I can describe to you in detail the bottles of milk I carried to and from the barn, the walk to the barn, the silo, the kitchen, the meals, the dishes, the mound of coal out back waiting to heat the house, the piano. Every night, when Stew came in after taking care of their 40 cows, Lou had a bath waiting for him in the clawfoot tub. Then she'd go back to getting dinner ready.

Christine and I washed the dishes after the evening meal (Lou's kitchen sink is a picture-perfect photo in my mind), and then back down to the barn we'd go for some evening play. Particular rooms in their large house and our secret hideaway down by the creek still show up in my dreams.

To this day, I favor, no *love*, the smell of cow's breath. Tell me it doesn't smell like molasses to you, a mixture of new-mown grass and sweetness. I can't get enough. I often shut my eyes and move in close, breathing away all the stuff in my life—worries, everything.

"Someday," my father promised.

Legalities of Selling Raw Milk

Retail sales of raw milk are legal in only a few states: Idaho (my state), Washington, California, Arizona, New Mexico, Maine, Connecticut, Pennsylvania, and South Carolina. In a handful of other states, licensed on-farm sales are legal. But some states have laws against selling raw milk. Federal law prohibits the interstate sale of raw milk.

Just what does selling raw milk mean? Usually, it means you have a few cows and you'd like to sell the extra milk your family doesn't need—and do so legally. Idaho's program says we can't have more than three lactating cows. In other words, small-scale, nothing fancy—milk that isn't officially pasteurized. But three cows can give a fair amount of milk, so that means you'd supply your friends and neighbors and possibly a store or two. Even though I heat–treat the milk I sell, it's still considered raw unpasteurized, p. 18. Should I ever decide to officially pasteurize the milk I sell, I'd be looking at an investment of tens of thousands of dollars. In order to justify that, I'd want to be milking more than three cows at a time! In some states, large, raw-milk dairies are allowed as opposed to large, pasteurized-milk dairies. It all depends on the state you live in. I live in Idaho, so I abide by Idaho law.

In "cow share" programs, consumers who wish to have access to raw milk enter into a "share" agreement with a farmer. They purchase a share of a milk cow, then pay the farmer a fee for boarding and milking it. Then when they want raw milk, they simply make a trip to the farm and pick up a gallon. This way, it's legal for them to *legally* obtain milk from a cow they *legally* own. But with a cow share program, you can't sell milk to anyone. No sales of milk whatsoever.

Idaho has both a cow share program (no sales of milk) and a raw milk program that allows us to sell milk, p. 336.

In some states, like Wisconsin, cow share programs are also illegal. In these states, farmers are setting up "farm share" corporations in which consumers hold non-voting shares, permitting them to get raw milk from the farm because they share ownership in the farm.

Before you get started on any paperwork, the first thing you need to do is get your water tested (if you pull from a well) for bacteria. Keep those tests on file, should you ever need a record of your water quality. I started testing my well water annually when I opened up my B&B in 2006. I also test for the kinds of farm chemicals that are used in my area. My well is 400' deep and goes through granite, so my tests have always come back free of contaminants. Fortunately for me, I have a well-known water-quality lab in my town, AnatekLabs.com. But because testing for bacteria requires getting a sample to them within 30 hours, you'll need to find a lab in your locale. The best way to find one is to contact your local health department. My health department has always been super helpful whenever I call them with questions. We have a food-packaging facility at my farm as well as a commercial kitchen, so at this point, we're on a first-name basis.

If you'd like to set up a cow share or farm share program, your best bet might be to join the Farm-to-Consumer Legal Defense Fund (FarmToConsumer.org). For an annual membership fee of $125, you'll get:

Free legal consultations with Pete Kennedy, expert raw milk lawyer and author of RealMilk.com. He'll provide legal contracts and answer questions like:

• What's the best kind of operation for my state?
• Are cow shares legal in my state?
• What kind of contracts do I need?
• What are my risks/benefits?
• Do I need to create an LLC?
• Reviews of cow share contracts for existing operations.
• A free copy of the *Raw Milk Production Handbook* by Tim Wightman.

If wading through bureaucratic red tape gets your dander up, I have some advice: Avoid thinking "us" and "them." Sure, you'll bump into some cranky employees along the way, but the very person who "gets" what you're about and wants to help does, in fact, exist. I promise. And they're in the perfect place to advocate for you. But put yourself in their shoes. Can you imagine wanting to take a chance and help someone who has a prickly "I hate bureaucrats" demeanor? To a possible ally, a quiet soldier, it's a big red flag.

Creating social change is almost always slower than any of us would like. I can promise you that, also. (I have quite a few stories I could tell.) But I learned a valuable lesson in 1990. The process of organic certification was just getting started. California had a good strong program, so a group of Idaho farmers, including me, got together to come up with a government-sanctioned program like California's. We wanted to get in on the action and compete on a national level by offering our foods for sale with the word "organic" on the label. Naming our group "Idaho's Organic Advisory Board," we hooked up with a state employee named Jim Boatman who worked in the Idaho State Bureau of Weights and Measures. With Jim's help, along with Lane Jolliffe (Jim's boss) and others in the department, we fashioned Idaho's law on paper, mimicking California's. I was organic grower #8. At that time, I was the only farmer on the board—or in Idaho, for that matter—who was "manufacturing" an organic food. In addition to growing fresh produce, I was also grinding local organic garbanzo beans and turning them into a value-added dry mix, falafel. I was initially Paradise Farm (sole proprietorship) and then Paradise Farm Organics (corporation), DBA as MaryJanesFarm.

Two days before we thought our proposed new law allowing the word "organic" on processed foods would sail through committee, Jim called me. "We're running into problems. There's a group of politicians who don't want to allow you to put the word "organic" on your labels. Can you get here in time?"

I hopped on a plane, flew to Boise (a six-hour drive otherwise), and guess what? We got a thumbs-down. (Even though I'd slept on pink foam curlers the night before.) After my presentation to a room full of legislators, I was in the hallway trying to explain to one of them why anyone who supports agriculture needed to also support new and emerging agricultural markets. "We're in this together," I was saying when a towering figure walked over to say to me, "You people get more money for your food and it isn't any different than ours and that's why we're not going to let you label it differently."

As a group, we licked our wounds, put on smiles, and hatched a plan (Jim providing the blueprint) for an end-run around those in our way. (Let me say this: I think the real culprit in all of this is our collective, perceived right to cheap food. According to the U.S. Department of Agriculture, nearly 25% of our household income was spent on food in the 1930s. Today, we spend 15%. We can choose to spend more on food now, or pony up later at the doctor's office. There. Got that off my chest.) Within the year, Idaho had a statute regarding processed organic foods. And if you haven't noticed lately, look where the organic movement is today. It takes a village. My advice: Put together a team, lock elbows, and hang in there. Find that person on the inside. Ours was a guy named Jim. (And I still have my pink curlers I can lend you if you don't have any.)

Aren't I lucky to live in a state with a raw milk program that includes a legally sanctioned cow share program also? I'm not just *benefiting* from someone's hard work. That doesn't begin to convey how it feels to me when my local state veterinary inspector, Scott Barnes, shows up once per month to test a sample of my raw milk and conveys to me in no uncertain terms that he WANTS me to succeed. If you think drinking raw milk is nutritious, knock back a dose of the pride we all feel to be one of only nine states that allow it. Following is a copy of our regulations for selling milk from a small herd and also for creating a cow share program (called herd share in Idaho). They're simple; they're to the point. Put on a smile and land a copy of them here and there, everywhere in your state, if sales of raw milk are still illegal. Let's increase that number from 9 states to 50.

Small Herd Exemption (IDAPA 02.04.13 Rules Governing Raw Milk)
Available at www.agri.idaho.gov.

Those with a small herd (no more than 3 lactating cows, 7 lactating goats, or 7 lactating sheep) wanting to legally sell or provide raw milk for human consumption for other than immediate household or non-paying guests may do so if the following criteria are met:

1. Facility and responsible party are issued a Small Herd Permit from the Idaho State Department of Agriculture (ISDA).
    a. Completely fill out registration form. (see registration form)
    b. Provide copy of Tuberculosis testing results on all animals used in the small herd raw milk program.
    c. ISDA will conduct a Brucellosis Ring Test (BRT) at least semi annually on Raw Milk samples collected from the monthly milk quality collection for cow milk.
    d. BRT tests on goat and sheep milk are not official, therefore goats and sheep must be blood tested annually by a licensed Veterinarian for Brucellosis and documentation of testing results provided to ISDA.
    e. Provide individual animal identification for animals participating in the program, such as ear tags, or tattoos.
    f. All female bovine dairy animals must be brucellosis vaccinated between four (4) months and twelve (12) months of age.
    g. If your bovine is over (12) twelve months of age and is not vaccinated for Brucellosis, your veterinarian must draw a blood sample. If test results are negative, the animal can be adult vaccinated through a permit issued by the state veterinarian, if the animal originated in Idaho.

Milk/Drug Testing Criteria:

1. ISDA will test raw milk a minimum of four (4) times (in separate months) in any consecutive six (6) month period for SPC, SCC, Coliform, Drugs, and Temperature.
2. Each batch of milk shall be tested and test negative for drugs using ISDA approved drug testing protocols.
    a. Each commingled batch of milk intended for human consumption must be tested negative for drugs. (Delvo, Snap, or Charm type tests).
    b. In lieu of certified analysts, the person conducting the test must be able to demonstrate acceptable ability to conduct the tests.
    c. If other than B-Lactam drugs are administered to animals Delvo or equivalent test needs to be used.
    d. Any batch of milk that tests positive for drugs must not be used for human consumption (other than members of immediate household).
3. See Table below:

	Standard Plate Count	Coliform	Somatic Cell	Drugs	Temp
cows	15,000 mg/l	25	500,000	neg	40°
goats	15,000 mg/l	25	750,000	neg	40°
sheep	15,000 mg/l	25	750,000	neg	40°

4. Whenever three (3) out of the last five (5) tests exceed SPC, SCC, Coliform, or Temperature the milk cannot be used for human consumption outside the immediate household.

Other Requirements:
1. Raw milk or raw milk products cannot be sold to restaurants or other establishments where a consumer may not know the milk is from a raw milk source.
2. Must have ISDA label approval if sales take place at locations other than the point of production.

Herd Share Program for Acquiring Raw Milk (Title 37 Chapter 11)
Available at www.agri.idaho.gov.

Herd share "owner" is a person who has a contractual agreement for the ownership or care of cows, goats, or sheep that produce milk for human consumption and receive raw milk or raw milk products for such care or ownership. Applicable for raw milk from 1 to 7 lactating cows, 1 to 15 lactating goats or lactating sheep intended for human consumption.

1a through 1g same as at left.
h. Submit a copy of the contractual arrangement between the herd share owners and the farmer.

Milk/Drug Testing Criteria same as at left.

Other Requirements:
1. Raw milk or raw milk products cannot be sold.
2. A person who is not a herd share owner can not receive raw milk or raw milk products from a herd share owner.
3. Provide share owners milk quality and cow testing results.
4. Raw milk and raw milk products must be obtained at the point of production.

Here's an example of the results I get back when my milk is tested.
(All milk naturally contains some somatic cells, which enable cows to fight infections and ensure good health.)

DAIRY QUALITY ASSURANCE LABORATORY
2230 Old Penitentiary Road
Boise, Idaho 83712
208.332.8584, FAX 208.334.4619

Product Source:
MARYJANES FARM

Accession: 6768

Collected: Date: 4/15/2013 Time: 1:30 PM Temp: 35.00 F by SB
Received: Date: 4/17/2013 Time: 10:00 AM Temp: 1.10 C by KR
Tested: Date: 4/17/2013 Time: 10:30 AM Temp: 1.00 C by KR

Product	PAC /ml or gr	Coli /ml or gr	IST	SCC /ml
Raw Finished Milk	< 2500 E	< 1 E	0.0000 NF DR	120000

NOTES:

Karen Riggs
Karen Riggs
State Laboratory Evaluation Officer

EntreMANUREship

Want to know more about the legal issues of starting a farm business? Here's how you can dream your future farm alive while staying at home in your PJs.

FarmCommons.org is a nonprofit organization founded by Rachel Armstrong of Wisconsin. From working on farms, to managing a community garden, to starting a catering company that used local foods, to running a nonprofit local foods consulting program, Rachel has been involved with food and farms for years. Local food system development is her lifelong passion and career. Now, as an attorney, she is devoted to helping farmers resolve the business legal issues that hinder local, organic, and direct sales farmers from achieving their goals.

Her "Farm Business Webinars" are offered through a platform that doesn't require any additional software or downloads. Those without a reliable Internet connection can listen to the presentation over the phone.

Here are some examples of webinars offered by Farm Commons:

- Overview of Farm Legal Issues
- Community Supported Agriculture Legal Issues
- Hosting On-farm Events
- Workers and Employees
- Selling Products to Larger Buyers
- Starting a Farm
- Adding Value to Farm Products
- Food Safety Liability and Regulations

Changing Zoning Codes to Allow for Backyard Cows

Zoning codes can be difficult to understand, and the logistics of changing them can seem like a bit of overload. But the people who have the power to change your city's zoning code are usually your city council members—you know, people you might know or people you know might know. Think six degrees! But as has been proven over and over again, zoning codes in many cities and towns across America that prohibit chickens and goats have been challenged and successfully changed. Changing zoning codes to allow for large animals, like goats and cows, can and does happen. But sometimes it takes longer than you'd like.

Here's an example: I started a dues-paying Farmgirl Sisterhood organization that has 6,000-plus members. We earn merit badges (think Girl Scouts for grown-ups). Along the way, we share our triumphs and heartbreaks, FarmgirlSisterhood.org. Every year, we choose a Sister of the Year. Our awardee for 2013, Karen Price (Sister #411), set out to change the zoning code in her hometown of Fenton, Michigan, to allow for backyard chickens. After spending a great deal of time talking with people and providing accurate information, she showed up for the city council meeting wearing a dress made from fabric covered in chickens. If that wasn't enough, she walked around the room handing out plastic Easter eggs with treats inside, asking, "Have you hugged a chicken today?" She remained upbeat and pleasant throughout the entire process, never combative. How could they possibly say no? They didn't.

10 Steps for Changing Your Zoning Code

(1) Study up: Zoning laws can contain more twists and turns than a corn maze, so it's critical that you get informed and move methodically. Before you storm City Hall with a list of demands, get your hands on a written copy of the ordinance(s) that affects your property. This can include both city and county regulations, and state laws may even affect local ordinances. Start by contacting your local planning agency, and follow the chain of command to the top so that you have a solid understanding of the law, existing exceptions and waivers, and the obstacles you'll need to tackle.

(2) Make friends: Get friendly with your local municipality staff. You'll inevitably need their help in the course of challenging zoning laws, so it's a good idea to launch these relationships with a light heart and laughter. It's like your grandmother always said, "You catch more flies with honey than you do with vinegar."

③ Call on neighbors: The zoning law that governs your property—and the changes you'd like to make—affects your neighbors. So now is a great time to start knocking on doors and making your case to the people who will either be your strongest supporters or your most adamant adversaries. Equip yourself with a concise set of objectives, on paper, that you can fall back on if you feel flustered. Present your case with a smile. Even if someone disagrees with you, keep the conversation civil. In time, your opponents may just jump on the bandwagon.

④ Develop answers: Once you start talking about your ideas publicly, you'll get a sense of the kind of opposition you'll encounter. Put some thought into clear, memorable, and succinct answers to common arguments. Write them down and share them liberally with your supporters so that you form a cohesive alliance with ready responses. For help developing answers to common questions, go to EatWhereULive.com and search for "Myths vs. Facts."

⑤ Get the word out: Now that you've started creating a clear vision of the changes you'd like to see, you need to create a mechanism for attracting, capturing, informing, and mobilizing supporters. A Facebook page can be a great way to do this. You can also write a catchy e-mail that explains what you're trying to do and send it to people you know in your area, asking them to help you spread the word. Consider creating a simple Web page or blog to serve as a reference point for anyone who's interested in learning more about your cause.

⑥ Educate your community: Begin talking with community groups about your ideas and the proposed ordinance. Sustainable living organizations are good to focus on first because they'll be easy to talk to and will ultimately form the base of your supporters. Eventually, you want to focus your energy on your city's registered neighborhood organizations, groups, or associations. They have a strong position of influence in local elections, which means their opinion matters a great deal to your city council.

⑦ Lobby your council members: Request separate meetings with your city council members to discuss your ideas for changing an ordinance or creating a new one. If they act like they're going to need extra convincing ("I need to see what my constituents think."), you can rally your supporters to call and send e-mails. Try to identify a "champion" on your council who seems supportive of the changes you're seeking and ask if he or she would be willing to sponsor an ordinance or give you some advice.

⑧ Form a task force: The actual writing of a proposed ordinance probably won't be done by just one person. Work with the council member who is sponsoring the ordinance to gather a group of qualified individuals to help research the issue and draft an ordinance for your city. The task force may include council members, community leaders, and people from your city's zoning department. Other agencies may also be included (such as folks from your animal-control agency) when writing a food-producing-animals ordinance.

⑨ Gather endorsements: Once the task force has drafted a proposed ordinance, find community organizations willing to formally stand behind it. Groups focused on environmental issues, poverty, food justice/access, and healthy food/living are all good possibilities. Also consider asking neighborhood mothers' groups to voice their support, as well as any groups willing to formally stand behind the ordinance.

⑩ Rally your troops and pack the meeting hall: The last step in the process is for the proposed ordinance to formally come before your city council or county commissioners. In some cases, by the time it gets to this point, most of the council members will have a pretty good idea of how they're going to vote. That doesn't matter. It's still important for community members to speak on the record at the meeting. That way, an appeal down the road carries more punch, and more history. Do what it takes to fill the room with supporters, even if they say nothing. It's always helpful when supporters address critical points and objections in a friendly manner. The issues will be heard, and the proposal will be put to a vote. With any luck, your hard work will pay off with a win!

Here's how the previous 10 steps for making change played out for me. In order for me to build a new business facility at my farm, I needed to get a conditional-use permit from my county. Initially, I packaged food in a dedicated, health-department-approved room in my 1905 farmhouse. I had one to two employees. Not a problem. That was legal. When my house burned down in 1996, I moved my business into the old Grange building in town. Meanwhile, back at the farm, we began the long process of rebuilding (we were doing it ourselves, along with the help of volunteers), but it was turning into more of a business facility than a home because my business in town was growing and employing more and more people. But I longed to be back at the farm for my work-a-day world.

In order to have a commercial building in the county (zoned for agriculture and residential only), I needed to get permission. There had been a few upbeat articles in my local newspaper about my endeavors, so I thought my permit would be a slam-dunk when I brought it before the Planning and Zoning Commission. It wasn't. I was turned down. And not for any reason in particular, just "No."

I appealed the decision, so it was scheduled to go before the next level, my county commissioners.

This was my last chance. I needed a "Yes" this time.

I tackled Steps One and Two and then turned my efforts to Step Three—the most important one, in my mind. I needed to get the permission of my neighbors because what I was proposing would put more traffic on the road—employees driving to work, semi-trucks, and a UPS truck coming and going every day. I also wanted to open a B&B—more cars. "Neighbors" where I live are never preceded by the words "next-door." We're fairly spread out. I contacted those within a 2–3 mile radius, not with the intent of talking them into anything—I wanted to find out how they really felt. I didn't get mere shoulder shrugs, they were fully and enthusiastically on board. It was an empowering experience, and if nothing else, they made me feel like I'd already succeeded. Then I checked in with our county road commissioners. They sent a statement to the county commissioners saying the amount of road traffic my business would generate would not degrade the roads in any way.

Next up? I went to the press and started a campaign to have people write letters to the editor. I created a flyer that I left in businesses around town. I sat down with a lawyer to help me wade through all the what-ifs and to prepare me for what lay ahead. I met with one of our county commissioners in person.

And then I did away with Step 10. I didn't pack the meeting hall. Instead, I asked some 80 people (including my neighbors) to write letters to the commissioners well in advance of the meeting. I handed out stamped, addressed envelopes. My thinking? If I wanted my commissioners to be in my camp, why would I put them through a meeting that might last until midnight because of the sheer volume of people showing up, hoping the commissioners would be inclined to vote in my favor, when at that point, they've heard it all and are probably annoyed and tired? My family and I, and a handful of employees, went to the meeting, our hopes and dreams in hand, fingers crossed. I also made sure someone from our local newspaper would be there. My conditional-use permit was approved unanimously. That was cool. But the really cool thing was this: One of the commissioners, a man with a farming background, took the time to make a statement. Essentially, he said, his vote wasn't merely a yes vote, it was an enthusiastic yes vote. He went on to say that my kind of enterprise is exactly what's needed in rural America and he would like nothing more than to see me succeed.

There you have it. Put yourself in the shoes of those who have your future in their hands (neighbors included) and then lead with your heart but go with your gut. Oh, and offer them milk from your future backyard cow. Or do what my father did (p. 272) and offer them manure for their flower beds. That'll moo-ve most anyone. And as is the case in many locales, if you already have an ordinance that allows for milk goats, making room for a milk cow should require just a tiny text tweak. Let's turn all the lawns grown in America into food for our tables. My dream is to see small backyard "farms" dotting the landscape again.

" Where there is a *home*, there must be a *cow*."

– R.M. Gow, 1936

Selling Milk

My system for selling milk and milk products isn't rocket science, but it took me a while to get it figured out, so I think it's worth sharing. Keep in mind that if you can get approval from your state to sell raw milk like I did, you'll have instant customers who will value it immensely, and handsomely! My home delivery customers pay $6 for a half-gallon of my cream-line milk. Feta cheese lovers pay $8/8 ozs and $8/lb for butter. I chose those two value-added items because feta requires skim milk, and then I have cream left over for butter. Both are super-easy to make.

With most of my families, I deliver 2 gallons of milk every week. That's $96 per month. Let's say you milk a cow that gives you 20 gallons/week milking once a day (twice a day would add 1/3 or more volume to that figure). That's close to $12,000/year. If you have only one cow, she won't always be producing milk, year after year, because she'll need 60+ days off every time you cycle her to put her energies into her unborn calf. Also, toward the end of her "milk duty" stint, the amount of milk she gives will start to diminish. But if you bring on a second cow and manage their cycles to overlap, you're looking at $20,000/year in milk sales alone. If you want to increase your profits by doing something value-added, like cheese and butter, you'd have yourself a going concern. (If you sell your milk and cheeses to a store, you won't make as much money—the reason I ended up going solely with direct sales after trying retail sales.)

Keep in mind that if your main purpose is to supply your family with quality milk, you might as well sell some of it too, since you're going to the effort of milking every day anyway. It would offset your expenses. If your state doesn't have a raw milk program like my state (Idaho) does, you could look into selling "cow shares," p. 334.

343

Milk deliveries for me got off to a rocky start. I designated a rendezvous place in town, but people would forget to come or show up late. I wasn't happy. When I finally decided to deliver milk to their doorsteps like I used to with my CSA (veggies), they'd sometimes forget to set a cooler out on the porch if they weren't going to be home. That's when I decided to invest in coolers that hold a gallon of milk (two 1/2-gallon canning jars) with room for ice packs and orders of cheese and butter as well, so that I could just drop the coolers off on customers' porches. (If you use coolers that are bigger, it won't feel so effortless.) Once everyone got the routine down (Tuesday evenings sometime after 5 p.m.), there are always, without fail, coolers, bottles, and ice packs from the previous week waiting for me on their porches. I include a record of delivery every time, and then once per month, my son-in-law charges their credit cards accordingly. Just like those UPS logistics TV ads, I'm happy, they're happy. Everyone is happy, happy.

Supplies

I like putting my milk in 1/2-gallon canning jars. Rather than the metal lids that come with them, I prefer using Ball wide-mouth, plastic storage caps. The coolers I use are Coleman's 16-quart Excursion model. Each cooler holds two 1/2-gallon canning jars, two 3 3/8" x 6 1/2" x 1 1/2" FreezPaks, and one 5 1/2" x 7 1/8" x 1 3/8" FreezPak. In a pinch, when I didn't have enough of those handy little ice packs, I used Snap-tite freezer containers (both the 2-cup and 4 1/2-cup containers), but they did leak water once the ice in them thawed. I gift new customers a Melamine 7 1/2" mini soup ladle ("cream separator"), p. 34.

The labels on top of my feta cheese and milk are removable (but only if you take them off before you get them wet): Avery laser/inkjet 3 removable white labels, 6 labels to a sheet, #3000 CR-BK. The clear plastic container has a "tamper-evident lid" that locks as soon as the lid is attached to the container (FreundContainer.com, item #2332T11). The butter label is Avery #8252. The tiny white sheet labels, Avery #5160, go on the bottom of every bottle with my UPC code and batch number from when I process the milk at my farm. The folded label hanging by a piece of twine on the front of each bottle of milk has my UPC code and a story about my cows with photos. (A basic hole punch for the twine is too big, so I use a specialty 1/8" punch.) And finally, I put a tamper-proof shrink band around each bottle of milk by shrinking it into place using a heat gun, both available at AssociatedBag.com, Items #524-3-24 and #10-13.

P.S. Don't you love the vintage, wooden, milk-bottle carrier the flowers are in? It holds one 1/2-gallon canning jar. It looks easy enough to make a replica. Nice for gifting a bottle of milk or as a way of telling someone you're gifting them a month's supply of local, raw milk.

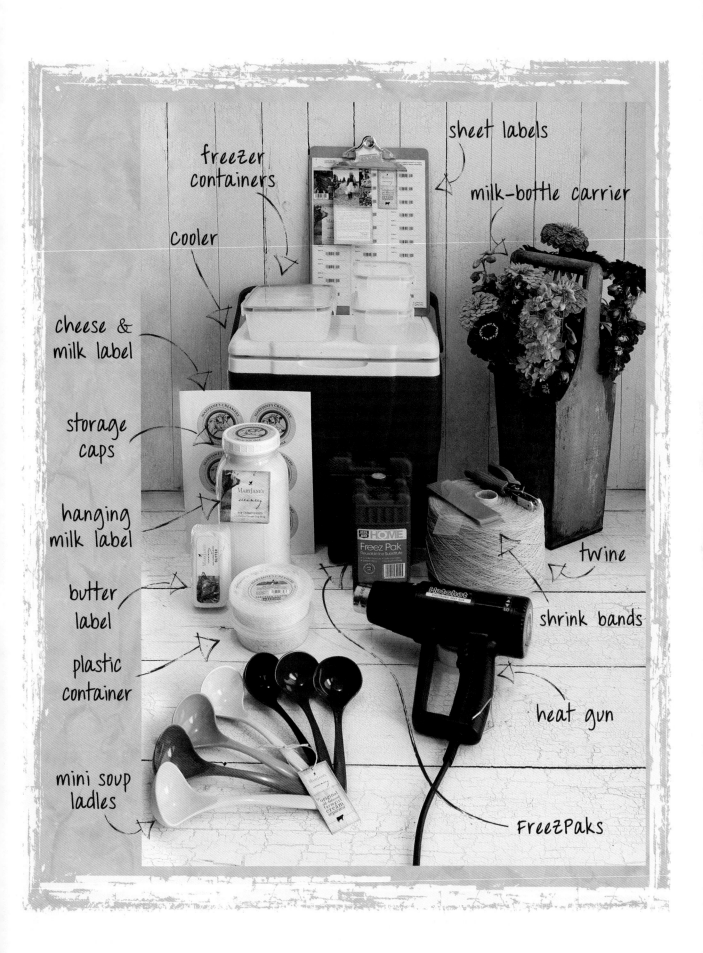

freezer
containers

sheet labels

milk-bottle carrier

Cooler

cheese &
milk label

storage
caps

hanging
milk label

butter
label

plastic
container

mini soup
ladles

twine

shrink bands

heat gun

FreezPaks

Let's Talk
Farm Equipment

" Our perfect
companions never
have fewer
than four feet."
– Colette

In This Chapter

• Not Your Daddy's Tractor ....p. 348

• Cattle Trailers ....p. 352

Not your daddy's Tractor

More and more women are buying and driving tractors; after all, **female farmers are the fastest-growing group buying and operating small farms.** For the past 25 years, the number of farms run by women has increased 86%; there are now approximately a quarter-million women-owned farms in the U.S.

Even if you're a farmer wannabe, tell me you haven't eyed that green-yellow John Deere, that orange Kubota, that red Case, or that vintage red-gray Massey Ferguson. How about that handsome *old* New Holland that makes your heart sing the wannabe blues? Unfortunately, there's more to owning a tractor than meets the eye. There are model numbers to know, attachments to buy, and particulars to figure out—such as, "Do I want a manual or hydrostatic transmission?" The trained eye, garnered from women who drive tractors, wants YOU to benefit from OUR mistakes.

The most common mistake a woman makes when buying her first tractor is this: she buys one that is too small—not enough horsepower, not enough oomph. (When you have your front-end loader full of heavy, wet manure, you don't want your tractor feeling tipsy; you want counterweight.) I suspect we think small is appropriate. But more so, I suspect, most tractor salesmen are just that (men), so we end up getting sold on small. Well, it can be a small, but costly, mistake. That said, one of my friends, whose husband surprised her with a new tractor for her 40th birthday, says she's ready for a bigger tractor after five years, but is of the opinion that starting out with a small tractor (hers is a John Deere 2305, 24 horsepower) helped build her confidence. She recommends starting small and then trading up.

The second mistake? We buy what someone else outgrew or a tractor that had a fix-or-repair-daily sign on it that was ditched just as you drove up. If you picture yourself attending vintage tractor shows, then by all means, buy that adorable old tractor. Just make sure you buy a trailer for hauling it from point A to point B (yes, even on your farm) and be prepared to update your grease-monkey certification. When was the last time you bought a '63 Rambler with 200,000 miles, thinking it would be state-of-the-art safe AND get you to work on time AND rarely break down?

The third mistake? We don't ask for a model that has a roof. Even if you wear a hat and sunglasses and lather on the sunscreen, a roof is more than just a nicety. It'll prolong the life of your skin and help you maintain your cool.

I own a 2009 Kubota model L4240 HST with a mid-mount PTO. (See what I mean about homework?) And no, this isn't a Kubota ad. They don't know me from Adam (or Eve). But the dealer was offering interest-free loans on new tractors when I bought mine a few years ago.

It all started at the county fair. I was working a booth across from a tractor dealer's booth, and those bright-orange "I Love Lucy" tractors just begged me to saunter on over the minute someone showed up to give me a break. When I finally bounced over, full of giddy enthusiasm, the first salesman I talked to dismissed me outright. Ouch. But two things I don't lack is an understanding of *that* and how to plow right past it.

What *was* getting my goat that day was thinking about how many times a year I rent equipment to move or lift things, dig trenches, mow the orchard, plow snow, fix sewer lines, and replace culverts. And every year when spring approached, I cringed at the thought of how many days it was going to take to rototill our gardens behind a walking, fume-y rototiller. On top of all that, I was well aware of the fencing projects we continued to put off because of how long it takes to hand-dig fence-post holes.

I don't recommend a particular brand, but this I will say: do your homework, particular to your needs. If, for example, you're going to use your tractor mainly for row-cropping and not as a general-purpose tractor like I do, you'll need to buy accordingly. To get started on all the confusing terminology, try Massey Ferguson's website, TractorAdvisor.com. Ask, ask, and then ask some more.

Reading up on tractors BEFORE you show up on your dealer's doorstep is essential. (The more common brands have websites, but more importantly, the Internet is full of customer reviews—type in "review" after the name of the tractor you're wondering about.) Homework first will make you more confident. And definitely do some test driving.

" THE FRIENDLY COW, ALL RED AND WHITE, I LOVE WITH ALL MY HEART...99
– Robert Louis Stevenson

After you've been shown how to use it, ask if you can explore the tractor on your own. (I'm always more comfortable making my mistakes in private.)

Model L4240 HST on my Kubota means mine is an automatic (hydrostatic transmission) with the power of 42 horses. I wanted a mid-mount PTO (Power Take Off—the means by which a tractor can power something other than itself) so that my snowblower would hook on in front rather than behind—easier on the neck and those unfortunate souls who might be driving towards me when I'm turned in my seat looking backwards.

Here is what my Lucy has accomplished since I bought her: She's moved 60,000 pounds of gravel; chipped truckloads of brush trimmings from fallen trees into mulch for human and livestock pathways (eliminating boot-sucking mud); moved massive amounts of dirt for a new barn; put in dozens of fence posts; cleaned ditches; dug trenches for new water and sewer lines; removed tree stumps; graded our gravel road countless times; rototilled several acres of ground in one day instead of weeks; lifted heavy objects without fail;

kept not only our three driveways clear of snow for several winters, but also those of our neighbors; mowed our orchards and pastures; and moved tons and tons of our most precious commodity, manure.

The attachments I purchased that allow Lucy to do the above are: front-end loader, back blade, front-mount snowblower, backhoe, mower, woodchipper, posthole digger, and rototiller.

Do I have any regrets? Only one. I regret that for us less-than-big-body types, the Kubota (and it seems like this is the case with most other brands) has a safety switch in its seat that shuts the tractor off when it senses lift-off, or in my case, petite. But what a pain in the behind it is. One of my girlfriends said, "My John Deere has the exact same seat feature, and it's definitely a drag when I so much as lift just slightly to look over my shoulder." Ergonomics is another important reason to take a test drive first. She added, "When I have my mower hooked up, I can't quite reach the button that lifts the grass bucket, so I have to lift up, and that shuts the motor off."

Female tractor drivers, unite! Tell tractor manufacturers what I've told them: This ain't your daddy's tractor no more.

I owned a milk cow for many years before I was able to buy equipment like a squeeze chute, tractor, and cattle trailer. An old woodshed (sans door) served as a combination cow shelter/milking parlor, where I milked my girl by hand every day, year-round, in any kind of weather. During those sessions, I pondered the universe, but I also dreamed of upgrades. When my cow needed something like a hoof trim, my vet would show up, trailer in tow, to transport her to the clinic for whatever was needed. A squeeze chute is a handy thing when it comes to on-site vet care. Mine is a Big Valley MX-V (BehlenCountry.com) that I special-ordered through my local feed store. It's anchored in place with metal posts embedded in concrete.

WOMAN-SIZE TRACTOR
MORE POWER FOR BIG JOBS

I love Lucy!

351

Cattle Trailers

High on my convenient-but-not-necessary list is a trailer. Before I owned one, I either borrowed one from a friend or had my vet show up with hers in order to transport my cows to her clinic for care.

Before you buy a trailer, do your homework and read online reviews. Don't make your decision quickly. Take your time. I was able to purchase a new trailer that's manufactured in my home state of Idaho. I found several trailers online that fit my criteria, but when I inquired, the manufacturers told me they serviced only local clientele and didn't ship trailers out-of-state. I find this heartening. Wouldn't it be cool if cars were built this way?

I looked at used trailers for several months—close to a year, actually. During that time, I borrowed a friend's trailer. When I checked with my local credit union regarding a loan to buy one, I found out I could get much better terms if I purchased a new trailer, using the amount of money I'd saved for buying a used trailer as a down payment on a new one. I was okay with that. I liked the idea of bringing home something brand-spanking-new that I could then care for properly to avoid what I was seeing on used trailers—hopeless rust.

I found a new trailer (a Charmac I was eyeing, CharmacTrailers.com) that someone had special ordered but then reneged on, bringing the cost down for me. It was perfect except for two things I knew I wanted. "Not a problem," said my local manufacturer. "We'll bring 'er back into the shop and get 'er done." Gotta love that!

What did I have them install?

I knew I wanted what's called a "stud divider" on the hinged, inside dividers to extend them all the way to the floor. I didn't want the kind of extended divider that leaves a gap of several inches, lest an animal fall down and then snap its leg because a hoof had slipped beneath the divider.

Having transported animals before, I also knew I didn't want a small calf underfoot a bigger cow that was struggling to stay upright.

352

With an extended divider, when I have to take a momma and her calf to the vet, I can separate them completely with a divider that extends to the floor. The calf can't get beneath the divider to her mother, and more important, she can't get under her mother's feet. Dividers are also good because they keep a cow exactly where you want it. When I loaded two mature bulls side by side who'd never even met before, they couldn't cause a ruckus getting "acquainted."

Never keep a cow tied to the inside of a trailer once you're in motion. Falling while its head is tied could cause serious injury. If you've ever traveled standing upright in the back of a pick-up, you can imagine what it's like for a cow. As the driver, you'll need to keep that in mind—no quick stops or starts. On long trips, a cow will eventually lie down so that it's not constantly struggling to stay upright.

The other feature I also wanted was a fold-down loading ramp in back. I suppose you could train a cow to climb a flight of stairs if you wanted to, but with a ramp, it's one thing I don't have to do—train a cow to step (no, hop; no, jump) into a trailer. It's a million times easier to coax a cow to walk than to hop. And should a cow panic while getting in and out of a trailer with a ramp, she's not likely to sustain an injury to her leg.

Another feature I looked for in a trailer was a plank floor (usually 2x6s) covered by black stall mats that are permanently attached, as well as black stall mats forming a wainscoting around the trailer—not just for cushioning the cows, but because of their non-slip qualities. (This is a common feature in new trailers, not so much in older trailers.) I don't put straw or sawdust on the floor of my trailer unless I'm going to be on the road for more than an hour. It's less cleanup when I get home. It doesn't matter how cold it is or how busy I am, I always unload my cows and then spray the trailer clean using a high-powered nozzle attached to a garden hose in conjunction with the use of a broom-handled scrub brush. Once the manure has dried on, it's a lot more work getting things clean again. The plank flooring allows the water I used for cleaning to drain away, and without the use of straw for absorbing the treasures they leave behind, I don't end up with a mountain of debris afterward that I have to haul away.

Most fully-enclosed trailers are actually horse trailers ("stock" trailers are for cattle and rarely have glass that opens and closes in the top windows), so mine also came with a tack room up front. I keep halters, ropes, etc. in it, but not saddles. It's actually a room big enough for me to sleep in if I were on a long trip. "For that matter," my husband said, "We could rent it out for, say, $20 a night. Guests could fall asleep listening to the wonderful, therapeutic sounds of a cow eating."

And obviously, you need a truck or a mighty big SUV to pull it. Make sure you match the weight of the trailer, fully loaded, to the pulling capacity of your vehicle.

Let's Learn Cow Speak

meet sweetheart
at 2+ years
of age and
son, sir charles,
at 2 months
of age

Perhaps due to the strong influence of ancestral cows who have always been more than willing to pose for cameras, "say cheese" has become ingrained in the lexicon of human culture. Always say "cheese" son. It makes humans smile.

In This Chapter

• Unmasking Insider Nuance .... p. 356

Unmasking Insider Nuance

When I first set out to "git myself some bull," I dang-near felt like an idiot around cattle folk. On the phone with a woman from Arkansas to discuss a bull she had for sale, our conversation went something like this: "He's bloomed and po-ed (rhymes with "knowed")." "Excuse me," I said. She said it louder, "He's po-ed." I replied, "Could you repeat that?" Even louder she said, "He's po-ed and bloomin'!!!!!" "Oh," I said, giving up, because I was too intimidated to admit that I was out shopping for a bull (for a cow I already owned) but couldn't talk the walk. What I'd asked her was, "Does he have horns?" What she could have said was, "He was born without horns." As it turns out, the term "polled" (po-ed) can mean different things to different people, depending on where you live. Usually it refers to an animal born without horns, but it can also refer to an animal that was dehorned at an early age. And blooming? That's a term used to describe the look of a healthy animal, referring specifically to an animal with a shiny coat.

Here are a few terms that might come in handy, but my best advice is, speak up!!! Say right out loud what it is you don't understand. And with a twinkle in your eye, ask, "What is the transmissible genetic merit of the bovine of which we speak?"

Heifer is supposed to mean a young female less than a year old but beyond the calf stage (hasn't had a calf yet). But its meaning has morphed—the reason I avoid the term. There's bred heifer (pregnant with her first calf), first-calf heifer or first-calver heifer (has had one calf and is 2–3 years old), heiferette (older than 2 years without calf), and spring heifer, summer yearling heifer, spring heifer calf, winter heifer ... the list goes on. HeiferInternational.org is a well-known organization founded by a Midwest farmer when he had a thought regarding world hunger: What if they had not a cup, but a cow? Today, you can give the gift of a cow to an impoverished family to help them achieve self-reliance. Or would that be a heifer?

Cow is an adult female, bull is an adult male, steer is a bull that has had his testes removed (he's good for beef or as a companion animal) and stag, AKA a gomer or teaser bull, is a full-grown bull that has had a vasectomy and a penile translocation. A what?! Because he's used to detect cows in heat, he still needs testosterone (hence a vasectomy instead of castration); penile translocation means his penis gets rerouted to come out closer to his hip. Craaazy. Collectively, they're cattle. A dairy steer comes from a breed of cattle best known for dairy rather than beef. If someone asks, "Is this an animal you're going to beef?" they're asking if it's meant for the freezer. Speaking of steers, the topic of home butchering is a whole 'nuther book. In other words, it's an endeavor and then some. Keep in mind that cattle are large and squares of freezer paper are small. If you're new to home butchering, you might consider the services of a nearby meat locker while you warm up to the idea of processing an animal by yourself. We have a local locker that bills itself as our town's "family butcher." I've used their services before, as well as another local service that tans the hides (cowhide rug p. 360) of my butchered animals.

If I'm going to butcher an animal, I want to use as much of it as I can. I also ask for the bones so I can use them to make broth. So when you say you're going to "steer a bull," it has nothing to do with driving (although we've all heard of "cattle drives"), and it has nothing to do with steering a bull away from a china closet, nor does it have to do with the advent of power steering—steerable. It has everything to do with meat (although I also use steers as companion animals when I have a cow that is isolated for one reason or another.) If he's still a bull, he goes into the buller pen (place where bulls are kept). But a buller is a cow or steer that mounts others (close relative to bully). They all eat from a bunk (feeding trough) that's usually slicked up when finished (bunk licked up slick). Slick also refers to the slippery mucus of estrus (nature's vaginal lubricant). Are your cattle freestall? (Cattle free to enter and leave a shelter for bedding down as opposed to being confined.) How about bedded pack? (Open housing in a barn next to a feeding area.)

Closed herd means no outside breeding stock are introduced. Linebreeding (a form of inbreeding) allows the breeder to concentrate on certain genetic traits. Crossbreeding is the mating of different breeds, and conformation is the end result—the "look" or appearance of the animal—things like a straight back, toed in (pigeon toed) or toed out or calf-kneed, sometimes referred to as back-at-the-knees (knees pointing inward toward the rear).

When someone says, "Every now and then she throws a white-faced calf" (or a black calf, etc.), that means a cow gave birth to an animal that doesn't look at all like her or the bull that serviced her (the old skeleton-in-the-closet problem). And a scur doesn't help conformation ratings any (a remnant piece of horn remaining after an adult animal was dehorned, resulting in a piece of bone that isn't attached to its skull but is held on by skin). Broken mouth is a cow that is starting to lose her teeth. Smooth mouth means she's in the market for dentures. Greasy heel describes a crack in the back of a cow's hoof due to overly wet conditions.

358

Twice as much isn't necessarily twice as good when it comes to twins. Ninety percent of females are infertile when born twin to a male (male twins can also be subfertile). Infertile twin females are called "freemartins"—a combo of the word "ferry" or "farrow" (which means barren) and martin (which is a generic term for cattle). A cryptorchid is a male with one or both testes undescended.

A springer cow is a cow about to give birth or is close to parturition (the act of giving birth). Fresh cow or freshened cow is a cow that has recently given birth to a calf and is producing fresh milk. If she's milking off her back, she isn't in good health (or isn't getting proper nutrition) and producing milk is wearing her down and she's losing weight. Easy keeper is a term used to describe a cow that gains and maintains weight easily. An easy keeper is cheaper to feed than a cow that *isn't* an easy keeper. I have a cow that isn't. I don't mind it though, because I never have to cow-culate how much feed I'm allowing her to eat. Dry cow is a cow that isn't lactating. Mastitis is also called garget.

A2 milk and A1 milk are genetic variants of the beta-casein protein found in milk. A2 milk is a trademark owned by the A2 Corporation in New Zealand, based on the findings of a scientist and promoted by author Keith Woodford, who links A1 milk to serious illnesses such as diabetes and heart disease. A genetic test developed by the corporation determines an animal's status, and then the corporation may or may not issue a license to a milk producer whose cows produce A2 milk, which they claim is superior to A1 milk, the most common form of milk sold today.

Presently, A2 milk is sold mainly in Australia, New Zealand, and the United Kingdom, but the corporation wants to promote the brand in China based on an increased after-tax net profit that resulted because of Woodford's book. The A2 Corporation has raised a vast amount of money from investors. "The question remains as to whether the additional $20 million of cash that they now have in their war chest will be enough for such an initiative," Woodford said in December of 2013. "Establishing a brand in China is going to be expensive." With the debate raging and millions of dollars at stake on both sides, the debate promises to continue until the A–whatever cows come home.

One gallon of milk weighs somewhere around 8 pounds, depending on the amount of butterfat in it. Would that be A1 or A2? If A2, you can't market it as A2 milk (any more than you can sell Nike milk) because remember, A2 milk is trademarked. (How much does a license agreement with them cost?) The A2 Corporation even owns the rights to the DNA test that told you whether or not your cow produces A1 or A2 milk (check the fine print). Weighty issue!

A liner slip or a squawk refers to the claw of a milking machine slipping off. The streak canal is the canal at the tip of a teat, also called the teat meatus.

A get are calves sired by the same bull; get–of–sire is a show division in which all the animals are sired by the same bull. A short yearling is a calf between 12 and 18 months of age. A long yearling is between 19 and 24 months, and a yearling is between 12 and 24 months. And when someone says "pass the slickem, please," you pass the butter and get the conversation going by asking, "You got your get yet?"

Meet Wheeletta Wholesteel (left, also p. 398), resident cow at the Dahmen Barn in Uniontown, Washington, located only a half hour from my farm. Known to locals as the "big white barn behind the famous iron-wheel fence" (p. 236), the barn is home to dozens of artists, in addition to serving as a community event center. (If you have a barn in your area that deserves preservation, check out the inspiring story of the Dahmen Barn on their website, ArtisanBarn.org.) Wheeletta was created by John Bergen, Jr., a retired welder living in Pierce, Idaho.

" You know, sometimes
the world seems like
a pretty mean place.
That's why animals are
so soft and huggy. "
– Bill Watterson

In This Chapter

• Milk Cow Décor ....p. 362

• Milk Paint ....p. 370

• Milkmaid Fashion........................p. 374

• Baling Twine Re-use....................p. 384

MILK COW DÉCOR

When the last remaining small-scale dairy in the area where I live announced it was closing its doors in 2007, I paid them a visit. An older couple, the Strattons had dairy-ed their entire lives, but all the new federal regulations for things like water quality and equipment had them flummoxed. They were going to sell their equipment to a scrap yard, auction off their small herd of cows, and retire— sleep in for once in their lives. The first thing I noticed when I was invited into their living room was Joyce Stratton's collection of all things cow—shelves and shelves of knickknacks, paintings, drawings, and photos. "Our customers have given me all this over the years. You see, I'll always have cows."

I ended up buying their milking equipment, not because I had an obvious use for it (I only had one cow at the time), but because I couldn't bear to have them see their life's work go to a scrap yard. The first items I brought home with me were two stainless-steel sinks and several of their milk cans, now in use at my farm. Wooden crates, bottles, and other odds and ends became décor, and the rest—a 300-gallon holding tank, pasteurizer, bottle-filling machines, compressors, and conveyers—stayed at their dairy collecting dust while I paid the taxes on them. A former apprentice of mine, a young woman from New York who worked at my farm one summer, had a dream—she didn't want to be a farmer herself, she wanted to marry one! Eventually, she found her guy, a handsome, hard-working young man who had grown up on a dairy farm and wanted to continue in that line of work. They married, started a family, and the Strattons' equipment found a new home.

Stratton's Dairy. 1959

" A dream you dream alone is only a dream. A dream you dream together is reality. "
– John Lennon

Following Joyce Stratton's example, you can surround yourself with cows too. Here's an inexpensive way to bring cow-themed oil paintings into your home (painting at left). Go to Wikimedia.org, then Wikimedia Commons, a free media repository, and search for "cow paintings." There are many. I typed in "butter churns." Up popped this classic Ralph Hedley piece, "The Butter Churn," 1897. Pre-1923 images are in the public domain and copyright-free. I made note that it was 7" x 9 1/2" at 300 dpi (dots per inch), and easily downloaded it. I wasn't sure how well it would enlarge, but as it turns out, oil paintings around that size look like an original when enlarged, transferred onto canvas, and glued to foam board, ArcherStudio.com. For presentation, I cut an old door in half. The bottom became a table; the windowed top became the frame.

Here are some décor ideas to get you started. When antiquing, watch for vintage "cow creamers" or shop for them on eBay.

Have you heard about the cow parade? No, it's not something that happens every day when it's time for my girls to come in from the field and line up for milking. CowParade was the world's largest public art event aimed at supporting art and generating funds for charity. Thousands of life-size cows are on display in cities around the world, in office buildings, museums, and city streets from New York and Chicago (where the idea began—the brainchild of Lois Weisberg) to São Paulo and Johannesburg to London, Paris, Copenhagen, Milan, Moscow, and Tokyo. Designed and created by local artists in their respective cities between 1999 and 2007, more than 25 million dollars was raised for charity. Smaller commemorative statues are available at CowParade.com, Amazon.com, and eBay.com.

Udderly Sun Flowers, CowParade.com
City: West Hartford, CT
Artist: Jodi Mendlinger, 2003
4 1/2" tall x 6" long

CowParade Postcard Book, CowParade.com

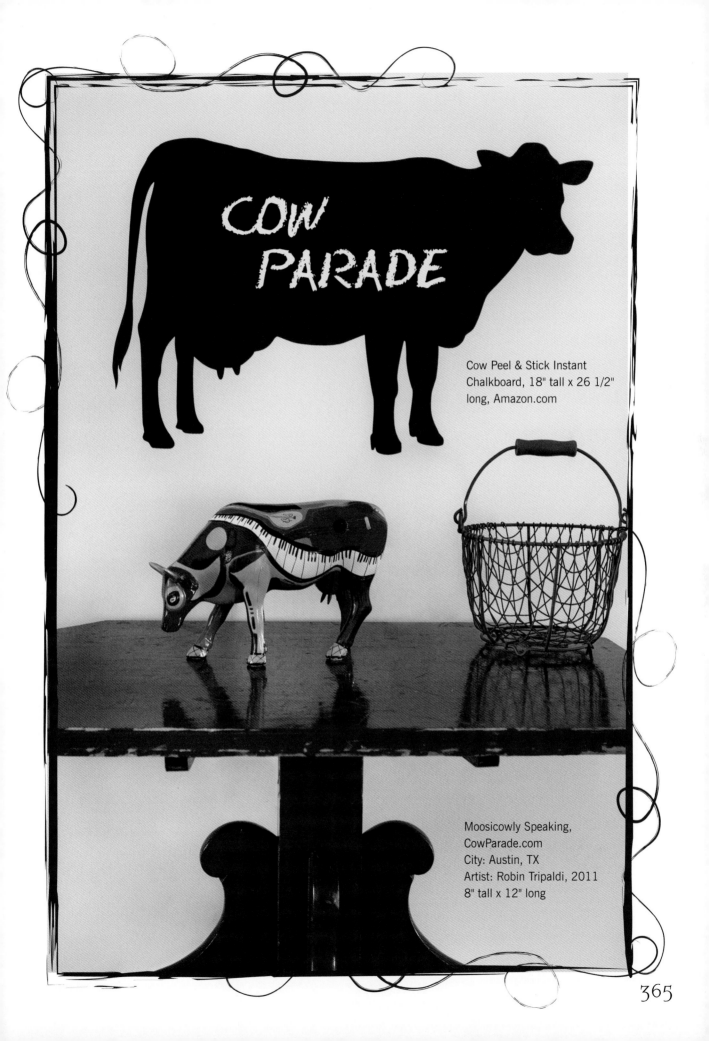

COW PARADE

Cow Peel & Stick Instant Chalkboard, 18" tall x 26 1/2" long, Amazon.com

Moosicowly Speaking, CowParade.com
City: Austin, TX
Artist: Robin Tripaldi, 2011
8" tall x 12" long

For a free bumper sticker,
go to HeritageJersey.org.

COW *(Lovin')* GAL

heritagejersey.org

Shasta
TRAILERS

DAIRY FRESH
MILK 15¢
GRADE 'A'

Natures most nearly perfect food

We offer this set of four barnyard coasters
for sale in my retail store in Coeur d'Alene,
Idaho. Visit Facebook and search for
MaryJanesFarm Store to ask if they're still
available. I can't guarantee I'll have any left by
the time you get there, but I'm sure we'll have
other cow décor. Cows are making a comeback!
Move over, March of the Penguins.

Beautiful Cows note cards,
IvyPress.co.uk

Diane Whitehead's cow paintings can be viewed and purchased at her fine art website, FineArtAmerica.com/art/paintings/diane+whitehead/all.

Pastoral Cow Scenes, Wood & Sons "Woodland" China Series, circa 1910, Burslem, England

You don't need expensive photo transfer paper to make "memory pillows." Find instructions for fabric transfers using freezer paper in the magazine section of my website, MaryJanesFarm.org/Recipes-Patterns-Instructions.

We offer these blackboard cows in my retail store in Coeur d'Alene, Idaho. Visit Facebook and search for MaryJanesFarm Store to find out if they're still available.

Metallicow, CowParade.com
City: Houston, TX
Artist: Heather N. Griffin, 2002
4.5" tall x 7" long

ADRIA

MIA

STELLA

Milk Chocolate

Milk
Paint

Milk has been used as a base for paint for thousands of years. Some of the oldest documented colored surfaces, including cave paintings and Egyptian artifacts, were painted with a milk mixture and have survived intact throughout the years with rich, vibrant colors.

Before the availability of commercially prepared paint in the late 1800s, paint was made at home based on recipes handed down from generation to generation. Milk paint, a simple mixture of milk and lime (pulverized limestone), was widely used to paint furniture, houses, and barns. Casein, a protein found in milk, dries to an extremely hard finish. The finished surface is so durable that even harsh chemical paint strippers do nothing to remove it. Earth-based pigments can be added to tint the paint, producing intense, velvety colors.

Milk paint is completely non-toxic, biodegradable, and without nasty fumes. It adheres easily to wood, and can be used over a latex-painted surface with the addition of a bonding product like Ultra Bond. The mixture is thinner than standard paints, and when used on clean, unfinished surfaces, is self-priming. The wood will partially absorb the first layer of milk paint, but additional layers go on much like latex-base paints. Milk paint does not stick well to metal surfaces, plastics, or oil-based paints.

Whitewash, a cousin to milk paint (Remember Tom Sawyer whitewashing Aunt Polly's fence?), is made from water, lime, and chalk. It's not as durable as milk paint, but it has long been used in dairy barns to coat surfaces that are difficult to wash, providing mild antibacterial properties.

You can make milk paint at home using the following recipe, or buy powdered milk paint and color tints from RealMilkPaint.com.

Homemade 1870s Milk Paint Formula
(courtesy of The Real Milk Paint Co., RealMilkPaint.com)

- 1 qt skim milk, at room temperature
- 1 oz hydrated lime by weight, available at building centers (Don't use quicklime, as it will react with the water and heat up. Hydrated lime has been soaked in water, then dried.)
- Optional: 1 to 2 1/2 lbs of whiting chalk may also be added as a filler (available at EarthPigments.com).

1. Stir in enough skim milk to hydrated lime to make a cream. Stir in remaining skim milk; mix well.
2. To tint, add powdered pigment (available at RealMilkPaint.com) to desired color and consistency (pigment powder must be lime-proof). Stir well for a few minutes before using.

For best results, continue to stir paint throughout use. Apply with a cheap, natural-bristle brush. Allow to dry before applying next coat, and dry thoroughly 3–4 hours before use. For extra protection, give paint a coat of oil finish or sealer. Colors may change; test in an inconspicuous area. Mixed paint may be kept for several days in the refrigerator, until the milk sours.

Muuu Traviesa, CowParade.com
City: Mexico City, Mexico
Artist: Leslie Zaide Zaidenweber, 2006
5 1/2" tall x 6" long

The Moo Potter, CowParade.com
City: Kansas City, MO
Artist: Meredith McCord, 2001
4 1/2" tall x 6" long

MILKMAID FASHION

> **" Fashion** is not something that exists in dresses only. **Fashion** is in the **sky**, in the **street**; fashion has to do with **ideas**, the way we **live**, what is **happening. "**
>
> – Coco Chanel

When cows are what's happening, there's definitely some style protocol also happening at my farm. (That or kick-butt red lipstick.)

Whether it's summer or winter, you're probably tempted to think that work and weather trump fashion. Not so. A cute pair of bloomers in the summer can't curdle milk; a pair of earrings in the fall won't cause a stampede; and no doubt, my girls love it when I show up for their morning milk parade dressed like I'm in one (thanks to some of my chickens, who allow me to feel all aflutter with the fanfare, fancy, and frill of a flock in my hair). In other words, milkmaid status doesn't require frumpiness. Lace knickers? Why not?!

Baby, It's cold outside ...

For winter milking, I slip into a one–piece insulated Carhartt—perfect for tucking a skirt into if need be. No big makeover needed, just a wear-over. If a briefcase is how you do your day, then by all means, park it by the front door and slip into something comfortable (your Carhartts). Pull on a warm pair of boots (no one will know if your socks are actually "stockings") and you're good to go.

But wait! Carhartts aren't designed for people with butts (assets, you know), waists, and hips. With seam-ripper in hand, I picked apart their male-oriented bodysuit (in the rear compartment, mind you), cut away the excess, and then sewed it back together again.

Carhartt, can you hear me? I've been remaking your pants and bodysuits since the early '80s, when I worked construction year-round. Love your clothes, but even your new line of women's dungarees and coats that you launched in 2007 (even going so far as to offer matching two-tone clutches) doesn't include a female version of your signature insulated bodysuit. How about accommodating our best assets in a one-piece suit? Come on, you guys, there must be someone there who wants to get waisted with me?

When Mother Nature gets bizzy giving you a blizzard, it's time for a polar fleece balaclava (headgear that covers your entire head, exposing only the eyes, Amazon.com) and a hat. But not just any hat. You haven't lived until you've worn a Hand Candy Sweater Newsboy Hat made from sweaters, old denim, corduroy jeans, and old-man tweedy suit coats, fully lined in stretchy, soft fleece. Be green and increase your cow WOW factor. How cute are you? Each hat is a one-of-a-kind handmade original, HandCandyMittens.com.

When the worst of winter starts to ebb, I switch my one-piece insulated suit for a two-piece made by Lakin McKey Trading Co. Why? Anyone who has ever worn both styles in nasty weather can tell you that somehow, some way (it defies logic), your body leaks heat around the bottom of your coat, no matter how snug it is. With a bodysuit, you stay significantly warmer—just a law of physics, I suppose. So when the weather turns a tad milder, I switch to a two-piece suit because when I go inside to process the milk, all I have to do is take off my coat to keep from getting overheated.

With plenty of utility pockets, bodysuits make it easy to keep a pair of gloves handy. For super-cold weather, you'll want to invest in a pair of insulated, waterproof Gore-Tex gloves. Hotfingers Women's Gore-G Gloves have fleece storm cuffs with, get this, pre-curved fingers that aren't too stiff for chores like tying a knot in a lead rope or buckling a halter.

For lightweight warmth without all the bulk of insulation, I like Mountain Hardwear Women's Heavyweight Power Stretch Gloves that are really liners for mountaineering mitts. I like the cuffs as well as the gripping patches on the palms, and once soiled, they're easily tossed into a washing machine (I have a basket by my door with several pair so I'm not reusing poop-y gloves).

Both suits have a zip-to-hip feature that you'll love for taking off your boots.

What milkmaid doesn't love the perfect pair of boots? While looking for a better boot years ago (rubber work boots seem to conduct the cold in the winter and heat in the summer), I stumbled across the Suffolk Ladies Boot of England.

Maybe it was because the description had words like "robust rubber sole, leather upper, easy on/off Velcro closure that expands to accommodate long pants, and warm and toasty wool lining." I took a chance. I'm on my second pair and my daughter is lovin' her first, BackInTheSaddle.com.

They come treated with Scotchgard water repellent, but because I have a system for milking my cows that involves hosing off their feet before I take them into my milking parlor, that means I also hose off my feet (my boots), so I need them to stay waterproof over time. Once every couple of months, I clean them well, let them dry, and then spray them with a fresh coat of silicon. I like Kiwi's Heavy Duty Water Repellent, but here's a word of caution: Do your spraying outside with plenty of ventilation and then let your boots dry for 24 hours outside on your porch until the smell goes away.

Total comfort aside, rubber rain boots now come in a rainbow of happy colors, USA.Hunter-Boot.com. Waterproof and durable, rubber boots and dairymaids go together like biscuits and butter.

One of the best ways to take good care of your back is to spend 10 bucks on a bootjack (boot puller), Amazon.com.

And because everyone at my farm is in and out a lot, we have a boot scrubber by every door, Amazon.com. I like a model with a folding step plate so you don't have to screw it in place—difficult to do on a concrete porch.

I've always been a fan of the traditional bandanna (love the look), but once I stumbled upon Buff's imposter, a seamless tube of stretch fabric, I discovered a million different uses for "the most creative item since the napkin." Hairband, foulard, neckerchief, balaclava are now part of my scarf repertoire. But its most important use for me is as a dust mask. A traditional bandanna requires a re-tie every time I'm working with dusty things like sawdust or hay. The multi-tasking Buff allows me to just pull it from my neck up and over my mouth and nose in one quick step. Love it! The Original Buff Headwear can be found at BuffUSA.com.

After pampering your cows, you're due for some pampering yourself. You can try our recipes for homemade body care on p. 224 or you can put your feet up and reach for some ready-made concoctions that feed your face some live dairy culture, DairyFace.com. It's so fresh (and refreshing), it lives in your fridge.

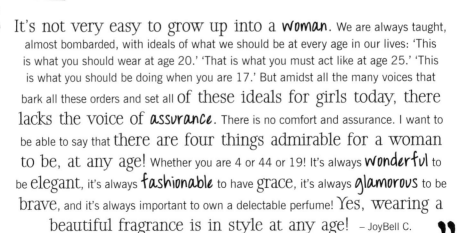

" It's not very easy to grow up into a woman. We are always taught, almost bombarded, with ideals of what we should be at every age in our lives: 'This is what you should wear at age 20.' 'That is what you must act like at age 25.' 'This is what you should be doing when you are 17.' But amidst all the many voices that bark all these orders and set all of these ideals for girls today, there lacks the voice of assurance. There is no comfort and assurance. I want to be able to say that there are four things admirable for a woman to be, at any age! Whether you are 4 or 44 or 19! It's always wonderful to be elegant, it's always fashionable to have grace, it's always glamorous to be brave, and it's always important to own a delectable perfume! Yes, wearing a beautiful fragrance is in style at any age! – JoyBell C. **"**

Ready for a scentuous encounter with solid perfume? Pungent fir, smoky sandalwood, honeyed beeswax, and lush lavender?

Welcome to Drift Perfume.

Specializing in the splendor of nature's bouquet, Drift is the creative calling of Jennifer Bové, a passionate *parfumeuse* who traces her inspiration back to the top drawer of her mother's antique dresser.

"I remember peeking into that mysterious cache of satin and lace and finding a slim compact," Jen recalls. "Inside, I discovered this incredible trio of golden-green scented waxes. They weren't the acrid, alcohol-based spritzes I think of as today's 'perfume.' These were something special—rich, resinous aromas of forests, fields, and faraway places. I was enchanted."

The allure of that scented compact, which was one of the Sweet Earth series created by Coty in the 1970s, lingered with Jen throughout her ventures into careers and motherhood, and it surfaced when she needed it most.

"I was at a point where I longed for creative expression, yet none of the obvious artistic media really moved me," Jen confesses. "Despite my love of nature's fragrances, I'd never even considered perfume. Honestly, just the thought of it gave me a migraine. Then, out of nowhere, the serendipitous memory of my mom's 'secret' scents sparked a fire in my heart."

Talking with Jen about perfume was a revelation for me. I realized that the synthetic spray perfumes I've encountered throughout my life have often left me feeling downright ill. Headaches, fatigue, the works ... you know, that headache–inducing perfumed woman sitting next to you on the airplane? But, as Jen confirmed, these symptoms were my response to chemicals like benzaldehyde, ethyl acetate, and a-terpineol that are added to perfumes in order to augment and prolong scent.

When I learned that natural fragrance oils can be suspended in a base of beeswax, I was captivated because I'd tried a dab of essential oil before, but because it's so concentrated, I would sometimes end up with a rash where I'd applied it.

According to Jen, "A semi–solid wax base allows us to bind the most exquisite natural essences into a robust perfume that contains none of the weird additives. Plus, raw beeswax smells fantastic. It's a perfume in its own right. As a result, solid perfume exudes a warm, rich fragrance that melds beautifully with the skin."

Unlike sprays, solid perfume is applied like a balm, and there's something so much more sensuous about smoothing it onto your pulse points—places that are enlivened by the passage of blood beneath the surface. Jen's fragrances seem to marry with my skin, evolving over hours to reveal intricate layers of scent.

Here's the deal: I keep a slim compact of Jen's scents right next to my computer.

Because (let me get this off my chest), I was not wired to sit for long stretches in front of a computer. But alas, can you imagine the countless hours of computer time this book required? My solution to the dilution of my very soul? DriftPerfume.com. Drift isn't for those sitting next to me, it's all mine, my personal journey AWAY. Gone.

❝ I doubt if there is any sensation arising from sight more delightful than the odors which filter through sun-warmed, wind-tossed branches, or the tide of scents which swells, subsides, rises again wave on wave, filling the wide world with invisible sweetness. A whiff of the universe makes us dream of worlds we have never seen, recalls in a flash entire epochs of our dearest experience. I never smell daisies without living over again the ecstatic mornings that my teacher and I spent wandering in the fields while I learned new words and the names of things. Smell is a potent wizard that transports us across a thousand miles and all the years we have lived. **❞**
– Helen Keller

> **"** If I want to knock a story off the front page, I just *change* my *hairstyle*. **"**
> – Hillary Rodham Clinton

It's the latest in fashion, the milkmaid look. Wedding websites give tutorials on milkmaid braids and movie stars model the look on the red carpet. You can imagine how much this trend makes my heart sing. Here's a how-to, courtesy of WeddingChicks.com.

① step one

② step two

③ step three

④ step four

⑤ step five

⑥ step six

To *celebrate* how much milkmaid braids as a trend make my *heart* sing, Meg, my daughter; Karina, book designer; and Saralou, recipe tester, showed up for work one day in milkmaid braids. Don't you think Hollywood should begin their next movie star recruitment at my farm?

Picture This ...

Sandra Bullock riding a bicycle with a chicken on her handlebars. I mean, hey, who hasn't done that?

Most of us chicken lovers can't claim super-celebrity status (outside of our own households, anyway). But fame hasn't stopped Sandra from sticking to her farmgirl roots.

She tells it like it is. According to a 2013 article in *Vogue*, chickens are IT. "Back in California, she keeps chickens named for comediennes: Carol Burnett; Wanda Sykes; and a Phyllis Diller, until she was revealed to be a rooster and rechristened Phil Diller," reveals interviewer Jason Gay.

Rest assured, her California chickens are not a flight of fancy. Sandra has a history with hens, a longstanding rapport with roosters. "When I was like 12, I had a chicken named Colonel Sanders and he was not a chicken chicken," she revealed a few years ago. "He liked people. He would stand on the top of your handlebars while you were riding your bike through the neighborhood."

Can't you just see it now? Someone fabulous like Sandra taking her backyard milk cow for walks around the neighborhood?

Sandra Bullock, from *Hope Floats*, 1998 © 20th Century Fox

Sandra Bullock, from *Infamous*, 2006 © Warner Independent

Baling Twine Re-use

If you think shopping bags create a lot of waste, **think about all the plastic twine from hay and straw bales that isn't recyclable. A solution? Upcycle your twine into durable shopping totes, bowls, chair repair, and even hair bun covers.**

In our area, twine is available in two different sizes (thicknesses). Baling twine that is used on the standard rectangular bales of hay or straw is about **3/16" thick.** Baling twine that is used for the great big, round bales of hay is about **1/8" thick.**

Crochet Abreviations

ch	chain
chs	chains
hdc	half double crochet
rnd	round
sc	single crochet
sk	skip
sl st	slip stitch
st	stitch
dc	double crochet
sp	space
sps	spaces

3/16" Baling Twine Crochet Bag

YOU'LL NEED:
crochet hook, size P
3/16"-thick scrap baling twine
matching all-purpose thread
(see crochet abbreviations at left)

Rnd 1: ch 3, sl st together.
Rnd 2: ch 1, 8 sc in center hole, sl st to 1st sc.
Rnd 3: ch 3 (counts as 1st dc), *2 dc in top of each sc*
around, sl st to 1st dc. (Total of 15 dc.) Sl st in next sp.
From this point forward, all rounds begin with ch 3
(counts as 1st dc), and end with sl st to 1st dc.
Sl st in next sp.
Rnd 4: *2 dc in each of next 2 sps, dc in next sp*
around, 2 dc in each of last 2 sps.
Rnd 5: *2 dc in next sp, dc in next sp* around.
Rnd 6: *2 dc in next sp, dc in each of next 2 sps*
around.
Rnd 7: dc in each sp around.
Rnd 8: repeat rnd 7.
Rnd 9: *2 dc in next sp, dc in each of next 3 sps*
around.
Rnd 10–16: repeat rnd 7.
Rnd 17: dc in each of next 4 sps, ch 3, skip 3 sps,
*dc in each of next 5 sps, ch 3, skip 3 sps; dc in each of
next 4 sps, ch 3, skip 3 sps,* around, dc in each of next
6 sps, ch 3, skip 3 sps.
Rnd 18: dc in each of next 3 sps, dc in each ch st and
in each st before and after the chs (5 total), *dc in each
of next 4 sps, dc in each ch st and in each st before and
after the chs; dc in each of next 3 sps, dc in each ch st
and in each st before and after the chs* around, dc in
each of next 5 sps, dc in each ch st and in each st before
and after the chs.
Rnd 19: repeat rnd 7, end off, weave loose end to the
inside of bag, tie a knot to secure, and finish weaving in
loose end.

To Make Handle:
Ch a strip 55" long (about 77 chs), dc in 3rd ch from
hook and in each ch to the end. End off, leaving a long
tail. Weave end of handle through openings in bag.
Using tail, sl st handle ends together. Tie a square knot
with ending tail and beginning tail. Weave in loose ends.
(Use a square knot for piecing twine together for handle.
Stitch loose ends with thread so knots don't interfere
with sliding action.)

Finishing:
If desired, stitch loose twine tail with thread to hold
securely.

Gauge: 5" = 7 dc

Tips:
Leave a long beginning tail of twine to crochet over
as you go, or weave in after finishing your bag. It will
increase strength and decrease the likelihood of the
bag starting to unravel.

To knot twine pieces together, just use an overhand
knot if you want the tails to stick out for decorative
purposes. Use a square knot to tie twine pieces
together if you want to sew the loose ends to the bag.

3/16" Baling Twine Crochet Bowl

YOU'LL NEED:
crochet hook, size P
3/16"-thick scrap baling twine
matching all-purpose thread
(see crochet abbreviations on p. 384)

Rnd 1: ch 3, sl st together.
Rnd 2: ch 1, 8 sc in center hole, sl st to 1st sc.
Rnd 3: ch 3 (counts as 1st dc), *2 dc in top of each sc* around, sl st to 1st dc (total of 15 dc), sl st in next sp.
From this point forward, all rounds begin with ch 3 (counts as 1st dc), and end with sl st to 1st dc, sl st in next sp.
Rnd 4: *2 dc in each of next 2 sps, dc in next sp* around, 2 dc in each of last 2 sps.
Rnd 5: *2 dc in next sp, dc in next sp* around.
Rnd 6: *2 dc in next sp, dc in each of next 2 sps* around.
Rnd 7: dc in each sp around.
Rnd 8–9: repeat rnd 7, end off, weave loose end to the inside of bowl, tie a knot to secure, and finish weaving in loose end.

Finishing:
If desired, stitch loose twine tails with thread to hold securely.

Gauge: 5" = 7 dc

(see Tips on p. 385)

1/8" Baling Twine Crochet Bag

YOU'LL NEED:
crochet hook, size L
1/8"-thick scrap baling twine
matching all-purpose thread
(see crochet abbreviations on p. 384)

Rnd 1: ch 3, sl st together.
Rnd 2: ch 1, 8 sc in center hole, sl st to 1st sc.
Rnd 3: ch 3 (counts as 1st dc), *2 dc in top of each sc* around, sl st to 1st dc, (total of 15 dc), sl st in next sp.
From this point forward, all rounds begin with ch 3 (counts as 1st dc), and end with sl st to 1st dc, sl st in next sp.
Rnd 4: *2 dc in each of next 2 sps, dc in next sp* around, 2 dc in each of last 2 sps.
Rnd 5: *2 dc in next sp, dc in next sp* around.
Rnd 6: *2 dc in next sp, dc in each of next 2 sps* around.
Rnd 7: dc in each sp around.
Rnd 8: repeat rnd 7.
Rnd 9: *2 dc in next sp, dc in each of next 3 sps* around.
Rnd 10–11: repeat Rnd 7.
Rnd 12: repeat Rnd 9.
Rnd 13–17: repeat Rnd 7.
Rnd 18: *2 dc in next sp, dc in each of next 10 sps* around, 2 dc in next sp, dc in each of next 8 sps.

Rnd 19–26: repeat Rnd 7.
Rnd 27: *dc in each of next 7 sps, ch 3, skip 3 sps* around, dc in each of last 2 sps.
Rnd 28–30: repeat Rnd 7, end off, weave loose end to the inside of bag, tie a knot to secure, and finish weaving in loose end.

To Make Handle:
Ch a strip 55" long (about 99 chs), dc in 3rd ch from hook and in each ch to the end. End off, leaving a long tail. Weave end of handle through openings in bag. Using tail, sl st handle ends together. Tie a square knot with ending tail and beginning tail. Weave in loose ends. (Use a square knot for piecing twine together for handle. Stitch loose ends with thread so knots don't interfere with sliding action.)

Finishing:
If desired, stitch loose twine tails with thread to hold securely.

Gauge: 5" = 9 dc

(see Tips on p. 385)

Natural Twine Market Bag

YOU'LL NEED:
Size I (5.50 mm) crochet hook
1 roll Wellington Cordage 43915 2500' 1-ply
   Natural Sisal Twine, Amazon.com
(see crochet abbreviations on p. 384)

Ch 2
Rnd 1: 6 sc in second ch from hook (6 sc).
Rnd 2: 2 sc in each st around (12 sc).
Rnd 3: sc in next st, 2 sc in next st, repeat around (18 sc).
Rnd 4: sc in each of next 2 sts, 2 sc in next st, repeat around (24 sc).
Rnd 5: sc in each of next 3 sts, 2 sc in next st, repeat around (30 sc).
Rnd 6: sc in each of next 4 sts, 2 sc in next st, repeat around (36 sc).
Rnd 7: sc in each of next 5 sts, 2 sc in next st, repeat around (42 sc).
Rnd 8: sc in each of next 6 sts, 2 sc in next st, repeat around (48 sc).
Rnd 9: sc in each of next 7 sts, 2 sc in next st, repeat around (54 sc).
Rnd 10: sc in each of next 8 sts, 2 sc in next st, repeat around (60 sc).
Rnd 11: sc in each of next 9 sts, 2 sc in next st, repeat around (66 sc).
Rnd 12: sc in each of next 10 sts, 2 sc in next st, repeat around (72 sc).
Rnd 13: sc around in back loop only (72 sc).
Rnds 14–18: repeat rnd 13 (72 sc).
Rnd 19: hdc in next st, ch 3, sk 1 st, repeat around, join last ch 3 with a sl st to the top of the original hdc (36 hdc/ch combos).
Rnd 20: hdc in ch 3 sp of previous row, ch 3, repeat around, connect rnd with sl st (36 combos).
Rnds 21–27: repeat rnd 20 (36 combos).
Rnd 28: 2 sc in each ch 3 space from previous rnd (72 sc).
Rnd 29: sc in each st around (72 sc).
Rnds 30–31: repeat rnd 29 (72 sc).
Rnd 32: sc in first 9 sts, ch 20, sk 18 sts, sc in next 18 sts, ch 20, sk 18 sts, sc in next 9 sts.
Rnd 33–34: sc in each st around, fasten off.

Option for handles: Wrap in strip of fabric and tie with a bow as shown above, left.

Natural Twine Bun Cover

YOU'LL NEED:
size I (5.50 mm) crochet hook
1 roll Wellington Cordage 43915 2500'
   1-ply Natural Sisal Twine, Amazon.com
hair elastic
ribbon
(see crochet abbreviations on p. 384)

Ch 2 loosely
Rnd 1: 12 dc in 2nd ch from hook, connect with a sl st to top of 1st dc (12 dc).
Rnd 2–4: ch 4 (counts as 1st dc, ch 1 in rnd), *dc in next st, ch 1*, *repeat around (12 dc).
Rnd 5: ch 3, dc in ch 1 space of previous row, ch 1, *2 dc in ch 1 sp of previous rnd, ch 1*, *repeat around (24 dc).
Rnd 6: ch 1, *sc in ch 1 sp of previous row, ch 1*, *repeat around.

FINISHING OPTIONS:
a) When completing rnd 6, crochet around a strong, thick, elastic hair band. To use: wind hair into a bun and cover.
b) Weave a ribbon through the spaces of rnd 6. To use: wind hair into a bun, place cover over, tighten with ribbon, and finish with a bow.

Twixt & "Twine"

①

YOU'LL NEED:
1 roll Wellington Cordage 43915 2500' 1-ply Natural
  Sisal Twine, Amazon.com
hammer
upholstery tacks
scissors

Hammer upholstery tacks halfway in on two parallel sides
of seat, 1/2" apart. Using twine, attach one end to any
underside corner of seat with tack. Tautly wrap twine around
nearest tack, string across to parallel tack, wrap tautly, and
repeat across. Partially hammer in tacks on remaining two
parallel sides of seat, 1/2" apart. Starting at nearest tack,
tautly wrap twine around tack, weave through cross twines
to parallel tack, wrap tautly, and repeat across. Cut twine
and secure on underside. Hammer all tacks down securely.

 ②

YOU'LL NEED:
1 roll Wellington Cordage 11345 1/4" x 100' Natural
  Fiber Twisted Sisal Strand Rope, Amazon.com
upholstery tacks
scissors

Using rope, secure one end to underside of chair with
upholstery tack. Create a weave pattern that you like,
one that is strong and suits the look you're after. Secure
end on underside with tack. Trim ends.

Heritage Jersey Organization

In a few places throughout my book, I've mentioned the Heritage Jersey Organization. What is it and why did I start it? Several years ago, when I was new to the concept of buying a "registered" Jersey, I located the one and only registry that existed for the purpose of registering "backyard" Jerseys—actually it was a registry for miniature Jerseys, and I had a mix of sizes, so I got to wondering what the back story was regarding miniature Jerseys. If you search the Internet or speak with historians seeking the history of Jerseys, you're soon confused. They originated in Africa, no Asia. Maybe they have a Scandinavian influence, or French. Some historic accounts place the Jersey in the U.S. as early as 1657. Hardy in drought and heat conditions, the Jersey cow seems to have more in common with

non-European cattle, in certain cases, but given their name, clearly we think of them as coming from the Isle of Jersey in Great Britain.

And then there are the modern-day breeders in the U.S. who claim they own the direct descendants of the original Jersey from the Isle of Jersey, and for the convenience of a storyline, they say the modern-day miniature Jersey is the original Jersey. But breed standards set up by the Royal Jersey Agricultural Society in 1834 don't confirm this. And the Jerseys first photographed in the U.S. weren't pint-sized, either. They also weren't the modern-day, full-size Jersey that you see in many large-scale dairies.

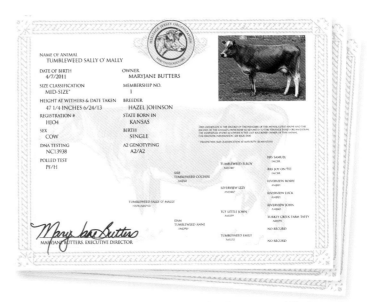

I founded the Heritage Jersey Organization in order to pay homage to the original mid-size Jersey cow. What exactly is a standard (full-size), mid-size, or miniature Jersey? Through modern-day selective breeding and crossbreeding, we've ended up with not only bigger Jerseys, but also miniature and even micro-miniature Jerseys. The miniature Jersey concept seems to have come onto the scene some 20–40 years ago, depending on who's claiming credit for finding (owning) what they call the "original" Jersey breed. It has brought us some adorable tiny animals, but it has been beset with fraud, arrests, dishonest crossbreeding and record-keeping, intentionally misleading height measurements, and the mismanagement of registries. Regardless of size and origin, I dearly love all my Jerseys—full, mid, mini, and micro—and I am fully committed long-term to the resurgence of the ideal backyard cow reminiscent of the iconic, original tether-grazed Jersey cow shown with her "cowmom" at the turn of the century.

I want to promote the original purpose of the Jersey as a mid-size family milk cow like those found on the Isle of Jersey and elsewhere in the early 1900s. Many historic photos clearly establish its size, now considered mid-size in the world of modern-day cattle. Modern Jerseys are bred for commercial production, and in many cases, produce more milk than the average family needs. There are over a dozen well-established Jersey registries for sized-up Jerseys throughout the world. Smaller "mid-size" Jerseys are often seen as undesirable to use as breeding stock because they don't produce enough milk for large-scale operations.

I decided it was time for someone to establish a registry for the original mid-size Jersey—the ideal backyard, small-scale production cow. I wanted to create an organization that would be around for the long haul—the reason for our non-profit status and board of directors. I wanted an organization that would outlive its founder! I draw my inspiration from a breed registry headquartered in my hometown. The Appaloosa Horse Club was established in 1938 by a handful of people wanting to preserve the Appaloosa's heritage and history.

Its first, single-page newsletter was created in the home of George Hatley, a local man who eventually came to be known as "Mr. Appaloosa." Mr. Hatley passed away in 2012, but today, the organization's 630,000 members span the globe.

No one wants to go to the expense of registering an animal, only to have the registry disappear. I also know that if you're considering purchasing a particular Jersey from a breeder, you'll want to check bloodlines. To that end, I wanted to create an online registry visible to the public. That way, you don't have to take someone at their word—you'll see bloodlines backed up by DNA testing. In order to create a permanent genetic marker for a Jersey (we allow the registration of all sizes of Jerseys in order to track breeding bloodlines), all you have to do is go to the HeritageJersey.org website, print up a form, "borrow" a few tail hairs from your calf/cow/bull, take a photo of the left side of your animal, and send it off for testing. Done.

Over time, we'll develop a classification program using a scale of points, setting forth categories for evaluation—things like stature, back, rump and tail, feet, legs, dairy character, chest and barrel, polled or horned, fore udder, rear udder, teats and mammary system, etc. But we're in the early stages for anything other than general breed character. As more and more people rediscover the benefits and joys of small-scale food production, the demand for what we call a "Heritage Jersey" is growing. If you're interested in milk production, some cow's teats are less than desirable, and in some cases, simply too small to milk; or the amount of milk a miniature cow produces won't be worth the daily effort; or a full-size cow will produce too much milk for a family's needs. Through proper, long-term registration (the 70+ year plan), strict DNA testing, and the highest possible standard of breeding practices, along with honesty that flows as readily as cream from a Jersey, we believe we can re-establish the unique characteristics of the time-tested, all-time favorite backyard milk cow—the Heritage Jersey.

MaryJane

For updates to the information in my book, go to the chatroom on HeritageJersey.org. If you need phone numbers for the Internet links I've given you for product resources listed throughout my book, give my son, Brian, a call (208-882-6819) and he may be able to help you.

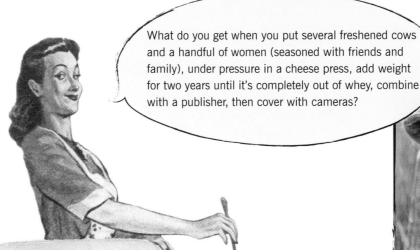

What do you get when you put several freshened cows and a handful of women (seasoned with friends and family), under pressure in a cheese press, add weight for two years until it's completely out of whey, combine with a publisher, then cover with cameras?

Acknowledgments

To help me whip up pages, Karina Overfelt churned in front of her computer, eyeballed plenty of photos, and then topped it off with a generous dusting of sketches; Ashley Ogle, my daughter-in-law, got totally cheese-y, not in front of the camera, but in our bunkhouse test kitchen molding cheese recipes and creating meals; Saralou Houlihan stirred in a dab of recipe-testing here and there while polishing off our photos with her digital prowess; daughter Megan Rae milked cows, shoveled poo, edited, posed, and posited; Bobby Austin prodded and proctored; Alicia Carlson sprinkled in plenty of food photos before moving to Seattle; college intern Katie Otanez, now in the Peace Corps in Africa, was a good egg when asked to put down her hoe and get gussied up for *glamoo* shots; grandgirls Stella Jane, Mia Marie, Adria Ruth, and Alina Kathleen (future milkmaids) provided me with the reason for the book in the first place; Suzanne Taylor, creative director at Gibbs Smith Publishing, brought a sense of humor and guidance to the mix; the visionary himself, Gibbs Smith, whose mission "to enrich and inspire humankind" has indeed; Carol Hill and Priscilla Wegars proofed; Brian Westgate drilled and hammered; son-in-law Lucas Rae kept things from boiling over (paid the bills); son Brian Ogle offered up his usual over-the-top support; and husband Nick Ogle, never one to stall, did his fair share of mucking, garnishing the end result with clean straw. My gaffer and photographic key grip, hubby, loved *all* our food creations, good and bad; stood on his head for my camera (if that's what was needed); kept my bulls from feeling neglected; milked my cows when I couldn't; tossed in dollops of moral support whenever I needed it (usually by surprising me with a bag of potato chips); and knew exactly the moment to add a pinch of playful when things were starting to sour. Best served with love and buttered buns.

MaryJane

Karina Overfelt
Book Design, Artwork, Photography

Ashley Ogle (daughter-in-law)
Recipe Development, Food Styling

Saralou Houlihan
Recipe Testing, Digital Imaging

Megan Rae (daughter)
Editing, Recipe Testing

Index

About My Index ...

I decided not to create an index by using my computer to search for, say, teats, and then give you a long list of pages where that term shows up. Why? I'm not a big fan of those kinds of indexes because you have to go back and forth dozens of times between the index and the pages of the book in order to find the one or two pages that actually provide you with solid information about the subject. No doubt, it's easier to let the computer generate an index, but my team and I decided to go through my book page by page with a highlighter in order to compile its index thoughtfully. Besides, I'm hoping you'll join me from start to finish because the content definitely connects, weaves, and layers from beginning to end. Also, I always like a blank page in a book so I can create my own index based on what's important to me.

A2 milk, 359
alfalfa pellets, 212, 259
All Flesh Is Grass, 325
Allan Savory, 274–276
Amy Hetrick, 208–209
annatto, 72
apple cider vinegar, cattle, 262
Armstrong, Rachel, 337–338
artificial insemination (AI), cattle, 303–306
baling twine bun cover, 388
baling twine chairs, 389
baling twine crochet bags, 385, 387
baling twine crochet bowl, 386
baling twine market bag, 388
bandannas, 378
Bang's (Brucellosis), cattle, 318
Barnes, Scott, 335
Beef: The Untold Story of How Milk, Meat, and Muscle Shaped the World, 325
birth and delivery, cattle, 283–290
blackleg, cattle, 318
bleach, 234
BLV, cattle, 318
Boatman, Jim, 334
boot scrubbers, 378
bootjacks, 378
boots, 377
bottling milk, 227
breeding, cattle, 306–307
brine, cheese making, 78
BRSV, cattle, 318
Brucellosis (Bang's), cattle, 318
Bullock, Sandra, 383
bull ring, 308
bulls, 300–309
butter molds, 37
butter, difference between sweet cream and cultured, 39

butter, jar method, 32
buttermilk, 16, 21–22
Butters' Buttermilk Hair Conditioner, 224
buying a cow, 197
buying a cow, checklist, 199
buying a cow, contracts, 200
buying a cow, insurance, 200
buying a cow, price, 200
buying a cow, transportation, 200
BVD, cattle, 318
calcium chloride, 18, 24
calf blanket, 93
California Mastitis Test, 214, 215
canning-jar lids, 109, 344
Carhartts, 375–377
castration, cattle, 320
cattle trailers, 352–353
Cattle: An Informal Social History, 324
CattleMaster GOLD, 318
cheese (fridge) cellar, 31
cheese coloring, 24
cheese making, 14–31, 52–57
    annatto, 72
    brine, 78
    cheese cellar, 31
    cheese coloring, 24
    cheese making equipment list, general, 26
    cheese making equipment list, special, 27
    cheese making ingredients list, 25
    cheese making, special equipment list details, 28–29
    cheese molds, 29
    cheese press, 85
    cheese weights, 84
    cheesecloth, 28
    citric acid, 24
    clean break, 63

cheese making (continued)
    cultures, mesophilic, 54
    cultures, thermophilic, 54
    curd knife, 28
    cutting the curd, 63
    dairy thermometer, glass, 28
    dairy thermometer, stainless-steel, 28
    distiller, 31
    draining tray, 29
    equipment list, general (cheese making), 26
    equipment list, special (cheese making) details,
        28–29
    equipment list, special (cheese making), 27
    gloves, 29
    hydrometer, 29
    hygrometer, 31
    ingredients list (cheese making), 25
    labels, cheese, 81, 344–345
    lipase powder, 23
    mesh, 28
    mesophilic cultures, 54
    microwavable grill, 29
    mold, cheese, 31
    non-iodized salt, 24
    pasteurizer, 30
    penicillium camemberti, 23
    penicillium roqueforti, 23
    plastic containers, cheese, 81
    plastic mesh, 28
    propionibacteria, 23
    redressing, 89
    rennet, 22–23
    ripening mat, 29
    salt, 24
    sterilizing equipment, 56
    thermophilic cultures, 54
    vinegar, 24
    waxing cheese, 69
    weights, 84
    white wrap, 28
    wrap, 28
cheese making equipment list, general, 26
cheese making equipment list, special, 27
cheese making equipment list, special, details, 28–29
cheese making ingredients list, 25
cheese molds, 29
cheese press, 85
cheese weights, 84
cheese, aging, 16
cheesecloth, 28
ChillOver Powder, 183
churning butter, 34
citric acid, 24
clean break, 63

Cleopatra's Milk Bath, 224
clopyralid in hay/straw, 265
clotted cream, 8
coliform (*E. coli*), 230
colostrum, 287–290
compost, 276
coolers, milk, 227–229, 344–345
cooling milk, 227–229
cow check list, 199
Cow Cookies, 265
cow décor, 360–373
cow licks, 295–297
cow share programs, 333–335
cowpanions, 323–329
CowParade, 364–365, 369, 372–373
cow-trough gardening, 268–271
cultures, cheese making, mesophilic, 54
cultures, cheese making, thermophilic, 54
curd knife, 28
curtail (clopyralid) in hay/straw, 265
cutting the curd, 63
Dahmen Barn, 359
dairy thermometer, glass, 28
dairy thermometer, stainless-steel, 28
DairyFace products, 378
death, cattle, 320–321
décor, cow, 360–373
dehorning, cattle, 319
delivery, cattle, 284
Diane Whitehead, 368
diatomaceous earth, cattle, 263
distilled water, cheese making, 21
distiller, cheese making, 31
draining tray, cheese making, 29
Drift perfume, 379–380
dust masks, milking, 378
ear tags, cattle, 319
emergencies, cattle, 312
equipment list, general, cheese making, 26
equipment list, special, cheese making, 27
equipment list, special, cheese making, details, 28–29
estrus, cattle, 292
farm equipment, 346–353
farm share programs, 333–335, 337
FarmCommons.org, 337–338
fashion, milkmaid, 374–389
feed bunker, cattle, 240–241
feed, cattle, 254–267
fencing, 246–253
flank rope, 221
flies, cattle, 277–278
freezing milk, 191
FreezPaks, milk, 344–345
gestation table, cattle, 299

gloves, cheese making, 29
grain, feeding, cattle, 212
gravy, about, 140
hair conditioner, Butters' Buttermilk, 224
hairstyles, milkmaid braids, 381–383
halter-training, cattle, 292
hay, 255–259
hay/straw shed, DIY, 266–267
hay/straw storage, 266–267
heat treating milk, 14–18
heat, cattle, 292
Heather Laudie, 207
heirloom plants, 147
herd share programs, 337
Heritage Jersey Organization, 56, 197, 199, 281, 367,
    390–391
Hetrick, Amy, 208–209
hitchin' post knot, 203
hitchin' rail knot, 202
hobbles, cattle, 212, 221
hoof trimming, cattle, 314–316
hornets, cattle, 279–280
hydrometer, 29
hygrometer, 31
IBR, cattle, 318
ice-cream makers, 187
ingredients list, cheese making, 25
inspiring milkmaids, 204–209
insurance, cattle, 200
iodine, 214
Jenny Padgett, 204–206
Jim Boatman, 334
Johne's, cattle, 318
Jolliffe, Lane, 334
knot, hitchin' post, 203
knot, hitchin' rail, 202
kelp, cattle, 263
Kleen-Flo pasteurizer, 17
labels, butter, 344–345
labels, cheese, 81, 344–345
ladles, milk, 344–345
Lane Jolliffe, 334
Laudie, Heather, 207
legalities of selling raw milk, 333–338,
    342–345
leptospirosis, cattle, 318
lettuce, iceberg, 127
lipase powder, 23
"Makin' Hay" exhibit, 264
manure, 272–276
MaryJanesFarm store, 367, 369
Mason jar lids, 109, 344
Mayer, Regina, 327
mesh, cheese making, 28

mesophilic cultures, 54
microwavable grill, cheese making, 29
milk bath, Cleopatra's, 224
milk fever, 290
milk mask, moisturizing, 224
milk paint, 370–371
milk, 1% low-fat, 20
milk, 2% reduced fat, 20
milk, allergies, 16
milk, cream-line, 20–21
milk, extended-shelf-life, 14–15
milk, heat-treating, 14–17
milk, high temperature, short time, 18
milk, homogenization, 15–16
milk, pasteurized, 14–18
milk, raw, 14–18
milk, skim, 20
milk, testing, 230
milk, thermized, 17–18, 24, 227
milk, ultra-high-temperature, 14–15
milk, ultra-pasteurized, 14–15
milk, whole, 20
milk/drug testing criteria, 336
milking by hand, 216
milking by machine, 218–219
milking machines, 210, 218, 225, 231
milking parlor, 238–239
milking stanchion, DIY, 244–245
milking, 210–235
milking, bottling, 227
milking, chlorine bleach, 234
milking, cooling, 227–229
milking, mini-cows, 220–225
milking, post-cleanup, 231–235
milking, pre-cleanup, 211–215
milking, sanitizing, 234–235
milking, straining, 226
milking, thermizing, 227
milkmaid braids, 381–383
milkmaid fashion, 374–389

Moisturizing Milk Mask, 224
mold, cheese, 31
Otterness, Tom, 264
overalls, 375–377
overgrazing, 274–276
PI3 (parainfluenza virus 3), cattle, 318
Padgett, Jenny, 204–206
parasites, cattle, 281
pasteurizer, 30
pasteurizing milk, 14–18
penicillium camemberti, 23
penicillium roqueforti, 23
perfume, 379–380
pest control, 277
plastic containers, cheese making, 81
plastic mesh, cheese making, 28
Poplar Spring Animal Sanctuary, 327
pregnancy tests, cattle, 297–299
propionibacteria, 23
putting down a cow, 320–321
Q fever, cattle, 318
Rachel Armstrong, 337–338
radishes, cutting in spirals, 125
Raw Milk Production Handbook, 334
raw milk, selling, 333–338, 342–345
Recipes
    Beet & Plum Salad, 123
    Blueberry French Toast Casserole, 115
    Butter, Cultured, 39
    Butter, Sweet Cream, 37
    Buttermilk Biscuits, 139
    Buttermilk Ranch Dressing, 125
    Buttermilk, Cultured, 43
    Butternut Squash Gnocchi, 121
    Butters, Flavored, 41
    Cabbage Soup with Blue Cheese, 133
    Caesar Dressing, 129
    Caramel Apple Cheesecake, 175
    Caramelized Honey Meyer Lemons, 129
    Caramels, 177
    Cauliflower Crust Pizza, 143

Chicken & Cream Mexicana, 159
Chili with Lime Cream, 169
Chorizo Burgers, 161
Coffee Creamers, 109
Condensed Milk, Sweetened, 107
Creamy Blue Cheese Dressing, 127
Creamy Garlic Breakfast Potatoes, 113
Easy Cheese-y Macaroni, 149
Eggplant Parmesan Rounds, 119
Farm Kitchen Gravy, 141
Flourless Chocolate Cake, 173
Four-Cheese Macaroni, 151
Gravy, 141
Greek Meatloaf, 135
Greek Yogurt, Cultured, 49
Grilled Cheese & Pear Sandwiches, 117
Half-and-Half, DIY, 185
Hors d'Oeuvres, 137
Ice Cream Sandwiches, Coconut Macaroons w/
    Pistachio Ice Cream, 191
Ice Cream Sandwiches, Decadent Triple Chocolate
    Cookies w/Short-order Strawberry Ice Cream,
    192
Ice Cream Sandwiches, Ginger Snaps w/Short-order
    Avocado Ice Cream, 192
Ice Cream Sandwiches, Oatmeal Cookies w/
    Peaches & Cream Ice Cream, 193
Ice Cream, Coffee Can Chocolate, 189
Ice Cream, Express, 185
Ice Cream, Peaches & Cream, 193
Ice Cream, Pistachio, 189
Ice Cream, Pumpkin, 187
Ice Cream, Salted Caramel, 187
Ice Cream, Short-order Avocado, 187
Ice Cream, Short-order Strawberry, 185
Ice Cream, Sweet 'n' Spicy Chocolate, 188
Kefir, Cultured, 51
Lasagna, 155
Macaroni & Cheese Dinner, 153
Make-ahead Spaghetti Pie, 167
Maple Cream Syrup, 115

Milk Syrups, 107
Pastor's Pie, 145
Pastor's Wife's Pie, 183
Peach Crisp, 181
Plain Yogurt, Cultured, 47
Roasted Red Pepper Tzatziki, 131
S'more Pie, 179
Salt & Pepper Salmon Chips, 137
Scalloped Potatoes, 163
Soft Cheese Tapenade, 137
Sour Cream, Cultured, 45
Stuffed Pepper Scramblers, 111
Stuffed Portobellos, 147
Sweet Corn Casserole, 165
Vegetable Galette, 171
White Chili with Chicken, 157
Recipes, Cheese
Asiago, 98
Blue Cheese, 100
Brie, 102
Brine, 79
Cheddar, 71
Colby-Jack, 75
Cottage Cheese, 62
Cream Cheese, 61
Feta, 80
Gruyère, 87
Manchego, 83
Monterey Jack, 67
Mozzarella, 64
Parmesan, 95
Soft Cheese, 58
Soft Cheese, Flavor Blends, 59
Swiss, 91
red nose, cattle, 318
red water, cattle, 318
redressing, cheese, 89
Regina Mayer, 327
rennet, 22–23, 60
ripening mat, 29
rodents, 280–281
rope twist storage, 203
salt, cattle, 262
salt, cheese making, 24
Sandra Bullock, 383
sanitizers, milking, 234–235
Savory, Allan, 274–276
Scott Barnes, 335
selling raw milk, 333–338, 342–345
semen collection, cattle, 306
shrink bands, milk, 344–345
small herd exemption, 336
sodium bicarbonate, cattle, 263
soil mix, trough, 271

somatic cell count (SCC), 230
sour cream, 16
standard plate count (SPC), 230
steers, 308
sterilizing equipment, cheese making, 56
storage caps, milk, 344–345
storage, hay/straw, 266–267
straining milk, 227
Stratton's Dairy, 363
straw, 259
straw/hay storage, 266–267
strip cup, 214
supplies for selling raw milk, 342–345
TB (Tuberculosis), cattle, 318
teat wipes, 214
teat-dip cup, 214
teat-dip, 214, 219
terminology, cattle, 356–359
testing milk, 230
The Inner World of Farm Animals, 327, 328
thermizing milk, 17–18, 24, 227
thermophilic cultures, 54
tractors, 349-351
trailers, cattle, 352–353
transportation, cattle, 200
treats, cattle, 265
trichomoniasis, cattle, 292, 307–308, 318
Tom Otterness, 264
Tuberculosis (TB), cattle, 318
tying up a cow, 202–203
Ultra Choice 8, 318
vaccinations, cattle, 317–318
ValleyVet.com, 317
vet care, 310–321
vet-care kit, 320
vinegar, cattle, 262
vinegar, cheese making, 24
vitamin C, cattle, 215, 263
vitamins and minerals, cattle, 261–262, 291
Washington State University Veterinary Teaching
    Hospital, 311, 312, 314–315, 316
water, cattle, 260–261
waxing cheese, 69
weaning calves, 293–295
weights, cheese making, 84
Whitehead, Diane, 368
white wrap, cheese making, 28
wrap, cheese making, 28
yogurt maker, Brod & Taylor, 51
yogurt maker, DIY, 49
yogurt maker, Donvier, 47
yogurt, 16, 22
zoning laws, cattle, 338–341

398

Make Note!

About the Author

Beginning each day by milking her Jersey dairy queens—Maizy, Miss Daisy, Sally O'Mally, Sweetheart, or Etta Jane, MaryJane Butters supplies milk, feta cheese, and butter to local residents in her hometown of Moscow, Idaho, where she runs her many businesses that include a successful organic farm, product lines, and *MaryJanesFarm* magazine, launched in 2001, available nationwide. This is her fifth book. Through example, she inspires women to reach for their dreams when they find out that as a landowner and businesswoman, she is entirely self-made—nary a penny from family or marriage. "When I left home at age 18, my parents gave me a box of home-canned peaches, a dozen eggs, and a sewing machine."

After graduating from high school in 1971, she was the first woman to attend the Skills Center North Trade School in Ogden, Utah, in carpentry. With a certificate of proficiency in hand, she was hired to build houses at the nearby Hill Air Force Base—the only woman on the crew. From there, she spent her summers watching for fires from a mountaintop lookout in northern Idaho; worked in the Uinta Mountains as one of the first women wilderness rangers in the U.S.; and in 1976, became the first female station guard at the Moose Creek Ranger Station in Idaho's Selway-Bitterroot Wilderness Area (the most remote Forest Service district in the continental U.S., 25 miles from the nearest road, in the dead of winter, living in a wall tent with five feet of snow up the sides). She built fences in the Tetons of Wyoming; herded cows on the Snake River below Hells Canyon; and in 1979, moved to a ranch in White Bird, Idaho, where she welcomed her first child and brought home her first milk cow.

After moving to her Moscow, Idaho, farm in 1986, she founded a regional environmental group still thriving today (PCEI.org). After four years, she resigned as its director to develop new products for locally grown organic beans that would provide a secure market for farmers transitioning to sustainable production. Along the way, she married her neighbor, Nick Ogle, whose farm borders hers on two sides. Since then, her unique agricultural enterprise has been featured in nearly every major magazine in the country, and in 2008, she was awarded the prestigious Cecil D. Andrus Leadership Award for Sustainability and Conservation. She also sponsors an organic farm apprentice program called Pay Dirt Farm School and for nine years invited people to her farm for farmstays in her wall tent B&B.

From her farm, she sells 60 different organic prepared foods and shares the message of simple organic living with readers of her magazine, website (MaryJanesFarm.org), and daily blog (RaisingJane.org). In addition, she is the creator of Project F.A.R.M. (First-class American Rural Made), an organization that employs rural women who sew totes, quilts, dolls, and more. She is also the owner of the historic Barron Flour Mill in Oakesdale, Washington, and owns a retail store in Coeur d'Alene, Idaho. "Nanny" to half-a-dozen grandchildren, MaryJane likes to brag that "going granny" has been her most important accomplishment to date. Two of her grown children and their spouses are employed full-time at her farm.

Follow MaryJane's "milk-her-once-a-day-not-twice" backyard milk cow movement at HeritageJersey.org.